Celebrity Philanthropy

Celebrity Philanthropy

Edited by Elaine Jeffreys and Paul Allatson

intellect Bristol, UK / Chicago, USA

First published in the UK in 2015 by
Intellect, The Mill, Parnall Road, Fishponds, Bristol, BS16 3JG, UK

First published in the USA in 2015 by
Intellect, The University of Chicago Press, 1427 E. 60th Street,
Chicago, IL 60637, USA

Copyright © 2015 Intellect Ltd

All rights reserved. No part of this publication may be reproduced, stored in a retrieval system, or transmitted, in any form or by any means, electronic, mechanical, photocopying, recording, or otherwise, without written permission.

A catalogue record for this book is available from the
British Library.

Series: Part of the *Studies on Popular Culture* series
Series editors: Bruce Johnson and Hannu Salmi
Series ISSN: 2041-6725
Electronic ISSN: 2042-8227

Cover designer: Holly Rose
Copy-editor: MPS Technologies
Production manager: Amy Rollason
Typesetting: Contentra Technologies

Print ISBN: 978-1-78320-482-3
ePDF ISBN: 978-1-78320-483-0
ePUB ISBN: 978-1-78320-484-7

Contents

Series Editors' Preface	vii
Notes on Contributors	ix
Acknowledgements	xiii
Chapter 1: Celebrity Philanthropy: An Introduction Elaine Jeffreys and Paul Allatson	1
Part 1: Rethinking Celebrity Philanthropy	**17**
Chapter 2: On Celebrity Philanthropy Elaine Jeffreys	19
Chapter 3: Philanthropy, Celebrity and Incoherence Jonathan Paul Marshall	41
Part 2: Branding and Development	**59**
Chapter 4: Tyra Banks' Celebrity Philanthropy: *Top Model*, TZONE and the Communication of Female Empowerment Dara Persis Murray	61
Chapter 5: Celebrating Development Through Sport: Right to Play and Basketball Without Borders Rob Millington	83
Chapter 6: World Relations and Development Issues: Framing Celebrity Philanthropy Documentaries Hilde Van den Bulck, Nathalie Claessens and Koen Panis	105
Chapter 7: Raising Africa? Celebrity and the Rhetoric of the White Saviour Katherine M. Bell	125

Part 3:	**India, China and the Americas**	**149**
Chapter 8:	Arundhati Roy versus the State of India: The Politics of Celebrity Philanthropy Devleena Ghosh	151
Chapter 9:	Celebrity Philanthropy in China and the Zhang Ziyi Scandal Elaine Jeffreys	171
Chapter 10:	Shakira, Ricky Martin and Celanthropic Latinidad in the Americas Paul Allatson	191
Chapter 11:	Afterword Paul Allatson and Elaine Jeffreys	211
Index		219

Studies on Popular Culture

Series Editors' Preface

In academic institutions, there is increasing interest in the meaning and place of 'the popular' in the definition of modernity and postmodernity. In particular, in the twenty-first century, it is through popular culture in its various forms that the tensions between the local and the global are acted out most immediately, not only through the content of popular cultural forms, but also in their means of production, distribution and reappropriation through consumption. Indeed, a study of the evolution of the term 'popular' is an essential analytical key to the understanding of the various confrontations – class, race, gender and place – that define contemporary power relations. The study of popular culture helps us to understand the contradictions in the contemporary sensibility. It gives us a more direct understanding of how we invent ourselves, how we imagine the possibilities of the world we live in, its ethical and moral dimensions and specific social practices.

The International Institute for Popular Culture (IIPC) is a multidisciplinary research unit, concerned not only with issues in contemporary popular culture but also in its history and transformations. The Institute places special emphasis on the questions of popular culture as heritage and the social role of popular culture. The Institute was developed during 2005 at the Department of Cultural History, University of Turku, Finland, and was formally inaugurated in 2006 with an international conference under the title *The History of Stardom Reconsidered*. Apart from continuing regular conference activity, the Institute maintains a refereed online publication series for monographs and conference proceedings (http://iipcblog.wordpress.com/publications/) and presents its monthly IIPC Debates featuring international speakers, available online at http://iipcblog.wordpress.com/iipc-debates/. IIPC facilitates international scholarly collaborations, offers its own doctoral programmes, and fosters engagements with private sector stakeholders in the culture industries. The series *Studies on Popular Culture* is a collaboration between IIPC and Intellect, presenting contributions to a critical understanding of popular culture and its history in all its forms. The series is particularly open to comparative and international approaches, and it places special emphasis on the transdisciplinary nature of popular culture studies. Its objective is to present leading research in the field, with a particular emphasis on work in and from what may be thought of as 'off-centre' research areas.

Celebrity Philanthropy

Bruce Johnson and Hannu Salmi, Series Editors

Contact: International Institute for Popular Culture, Department of Cultural History, University of Turku, Kaivokatu 12, F-20014 Turku, Finland
http://iipc.utu.fi

Notes on Contributors

Paul Allatson is an Associate Professor in the Faculty of Arts and Social Sciences, University of Technology Sydney. Paul has published widely in the areas of Latino and transamerican cultural studies, and cultural, post-colonial and sexuality studies more broadly. His publications include: *Key Terms in Latino/a Cultural and Literary Studies* (2007 Blackwell), *Latino Dreams: Transcultural Traffic and the U.S. National Imaginary* (2002 Rodopi), and the co-edited *Exile Cultures, Misplaced Identities* (2008 Rodopi).

Katherine M. Bell is an Assistant Professor of Communication at California State University, East Bay. She worked as a journalist for more than 20 years. Her research explores celebrity as a form of cultural authority, and of identity construction in digital life and consumer culture. Recent publications include: 'Affective expertise: The journalistic ethics of celebrity sourcing', in S.J.A. Ward (ed.) *Global Media Ethics: Problems and Perspectives* (2013 Wiley-Blackwell), pp. 214–34; and (2011) '"A delicious way to help save lives": Race, commodification and celebrity in Product (RED)', *Journal of International and Intercultural Communication* (2011, 4, 3: 163–80).

Hilde Van den Bulck is Full Professor of Communication Studies and head of the Media, Policy and Culture research group, University of Antwerp (Belgium). She has published extensively on celebrities' role in mediated social and ethical discussion. Recent publications include: journal articles in *Celebrity Studies* (2013, 4, 1: 46–57), *Critical Studies in Media Communication* (2013, 30, 1: 69–84) and *Javnost – The Public* (2012, 19, 3: 75–92); and book chapters in K. Howley (ed.) *Media Interventions* (2013 Peter Lang); and R. Clarke (ed.) *Celebrity Colonialism: Fame, Representation, and Power in Colonial and Post-Colonial Cultures* (2009 Cambridge Scholars Publishing).

Nathalie Claessens is guest professor at the Media, Policy and Culture research group, University of Antwerp (Belgium). In 2013, Nathalie completed her Ph.D. focusing on the relationship between celebrities, media and audiences. Recent publications include: journal articles in *Journalism* (2014, 15, 2: 218–36), *Celebrity Studies* (2013, 4, 1: 46–57), *Critical Studies in Media Communication* (2013, 30, 1: 69–84) and *Northern Lights* (2013, 11, 1: 35–50); and book chapters in L. Harrington, D. Bielby and A. Bardo (eds) *Aging, Media, Culture* (2014 Lexington Books); and K. Howley (ed.) *Media Interventions* (2013 Peter Lang).

Devleena Ghosh is Associate Professor and Director of the Indian Ocean and South Asian Research Network at the University of Technology Sydney. She is the author, with P.A. Gillen, of *Colonialism and Modernity: Histories and Themes* (2007 UNSW Press); editor of *Shadowlines: Women and Borders in Contemporary Asia* (2012 Cambridge Scholars Publishing); and co-editor, with H. Goodall and S. Hemelryk-Donald, of *Water, Sovereignty and Borders in Asia and Oceania* (2008 Routledge).

Elaine Jeffreys is an Australian Research Council Future Fellow (FT100100238) and Associate Professor at the Faculty of Arts and Social Sciences, University of Technology Sydney. Elaine is the author of *Sex in China*, with Haiqing Yu (2015 Polity); *Prostitution Scandals in China: Policing, Media and Society* (2012 Routledge) and *China, Sex and Prostitution* (2012 [2004] Routledge). She is the editor of *China's Governmentalities: Governing Change, Changing Government* (2011 [2009] Routledge); *Celebrity in China*, with Louise Edwards (2010 Hong Kong University Press); and *Sex and Sexuality in China* (2009 [2006] Routledge).

Jonathan Paul Marshall is a Senior Research Associate, Faculty of Arts and Social Sciences, University of Technology Sydney. Jon looks at the social usages of technology, the psychology of climate change, the sociology of geoengineering, and the social dynamics of coal usage. Recent publications include: *Crisis, Movement, Management: Globalising Dynamics*, with James Goodman (eds) (2013 Routledge), *Depth Psychology, Disorder and Climate Change* (ed.) (2008 Jung Downunder); and *Living on Cybermind: Categories, Communication and Control* (2007 Peter Lang). A forthcoming text is *Disorder and the Disinformation Society: The Social Dynamics of Information, Networks and Software*, with James Goodman, Francesca da Rimini, and Didar Zowghi (Routledge).

Rob Millington is a Ph.D. candidate in the School of Kinesiology and Health Studies at Queen's University in Kingston, Ontario, Canada. His dissertation focuses on the history of Sport for Development and Peace (SDP) at a UN-policy level and its implementation in the global South through SDP programs and sport mega-events. A recent publication is: 'Constructing and contesting the Olympics online: The Internet, Rio 2016 and the politics of Brazilian development' (with Simon Darnell), *International Review for the Sociology of Sport* (2014, 49, 2: 190–210).

Dara Persis Murray is an Assistant Professor of Media Studies in the Department of Communication and Media at Manhattanville College. Her work has appeared in the *Journal of Communication Inquiry, Feminist Media Studies, and Celebrity Studies*. She has also published chapters in *The Routledge Companion to Media and Gender* and *Cyberfeminism 2.0*, as well as pieces in the online academic collaborative *In Media Res*.

Koen Panis is a postdoctoral researcher at the Media, Policy and Culture Research Group, University of Antwerp (Belgium). His doctoral dissertation involved a quantitative analysis of public perceptions and media coverage of celebrity involvement with non-profit organizations. Recent publications include: 'In the footsteps of Bob and Angelina: Celebrities' diverse societal engagement and its ability to attract media coverage' (with Hilde Van den Bulck), *Communications: The European Journal of Communication Research* (2014, 39, 1: 23–42); and 'Celebrities' quest for a better world: Understanding Flemish public perceptions of celebrities' societal engagement' (with Hilde Van den Bulck), *Javnost – The Public* (2012, 19, 3: 75–92).

Acknowledgements

This research was supported under the Australian Research Council's Future Fellowship (FT100100238) and Discovery Projects (DP0985710) funding schemes.

The editors and publishers would like to thank UTSePress, Sydney, Australia, for permission to reproduce parts of Katherine M. Bell (2013) 'Raising Africa?: Celebrity and the rhetoric of the white saviour', *PORTAL Journal of Multidisciplinary International Studies*, ISSN: 1449-2490, 10, 1: 1–24, DOI: http://dx.doi.org/10.5130/portal.v10i1.3185, http://epress.lib.uts.edu.au/journals/index.php/portal/article/; and Elaine Jeffreys (2011), 'Zhang Ziyi and China's celebrity-philanthropy scandals', *PORTAL Journal of Multidisciplinary International Studies*, ISSN: 1449-2490, 8, 1: 1–21, DOI: http://dx.doi.org/10.5130/portal.v8i1.1627, http://epress.lib.uts.edu.au/ojs/index.php/portal/article/view/1627/2292.

Finally, for overseeing this book into print, we would like to gratefully acknowledge the generous support of the International Institute of Popular Culture at the University of Turku, Finland, and in particular, Bruce Johnson and Hannu Salmi, the editors of the *Studies on Popular Culture* series.

Chapter 1

Celebrity Philanthropy: An Introduction

Elaine Jeffreys and Paul Allatson

Cultural Studies has not devoted much notice to one of the keynote developments in modern culture over the last 30 years: namely, the rise of various charity projects fronted and, in the public mind, defined by celebrities.

(Rojek 2014: 127)

In the very noisy and complicated world that we have, people that reach large numbers of people, like Madonna does, have an extraordinarily important role to play [in promoting philanthropy]. When they're devoting their time, their money, their name, a lot of effort, a lot of organization skill to all of this, it makes a huge difference.

(Jeffrey Sachs cited in Luscombe 2006)

[C]elebrity humanitarianism [...] is most often self-serving [...] it advances consumerism and corporate capitalism, and rationalizes the very global inequality it seeks to redress; it is fundamentally depoliticizing, despite its pretensions to 'activism'; and it contributes to a 'postdemocratic' political landscape, which appears outwardly open and consensual, but is in fact managed by unaccountable elites.

(Kapoor 2013: 1)

Celebrity philanthropy is a visible and controversial phenomenon, as the opening quotations suggest. According to the Look to the Stars: The World of Celebrity Giving website, which is advertised as 'the web's number one source of celebrity charity news and information' since 2006, there are now more than 3,400 (Hollywood-branded) celebrities involved with over 2,000 charities that aim to 'make a positive difference in the world' ('Look to the Stars: The World of Celebrity Giving' 2006–2015). Besides the apparent upsurge of commentary on celebrity and charity in tabloids, gossip magazines, business and news magazines, and social networking sites, there are a growing number of academic texts on what Dan Brockington (2014: 90) calls the 'charity-celebrity-corporate complex'. These texts chiefly focus on the activities of entertainment celebrities and corporate figures who live and work in developed western societies (Bishop and Green 2008; Brockington 2009; Richey and Ponte 2011; Tsaliki, Frangonikolopoulos and Huliaras 2011; Kapoor 2013).

Although charity and fame are associated historically (Andrew 1989: 80–5), scholars generally agree that entertainment and sports celebrities based in the so-called global

North, and especially in North America and Western Europe, have become increasingly involved with a particular type of philanthropy since the 1990s (Bishop and Green 2008; Littler 2008: 240; Rojek 2014: 127). Figure 1 confirms that there is an empirical basis for this assertion, providing a graphic illustration of the growing publicity given to the subjects of 'celebrity' and 'charity' (the more commonly used term for 'philanthropy') in the world's top media outlets between 1983 and 2013 (with data drawn from the Factiva. com database). A search on the database for the keyword 'charity' obtained over 700 hits in 1983, compared to around 120 for the term 'philanthropy'. The figures for the keyword 'charity' rose to around 22,000 hits in 1993 and 157,000 hits in 2003, reaching a high of more than 353,000 hits in 2013 (compared to a high of around 20,000 for 'philanthropy'). A search for the keyword 'celebrity' obtained just under 600 hits in 1983: that figure rose to nearly 12,000 hits in 1993 and more than 79,000 hits in 2003, reaching a high of more than 166,000 hits in 2013. The results for 'charity' *and* 'celebrity' are considerably lower but demonstrate a steady increase over time: under 20 hits in 1983, more than 500 in 1993, more than 5,000 in 2003, and just over 10,000 in 2013. The results for 'celebrity' and

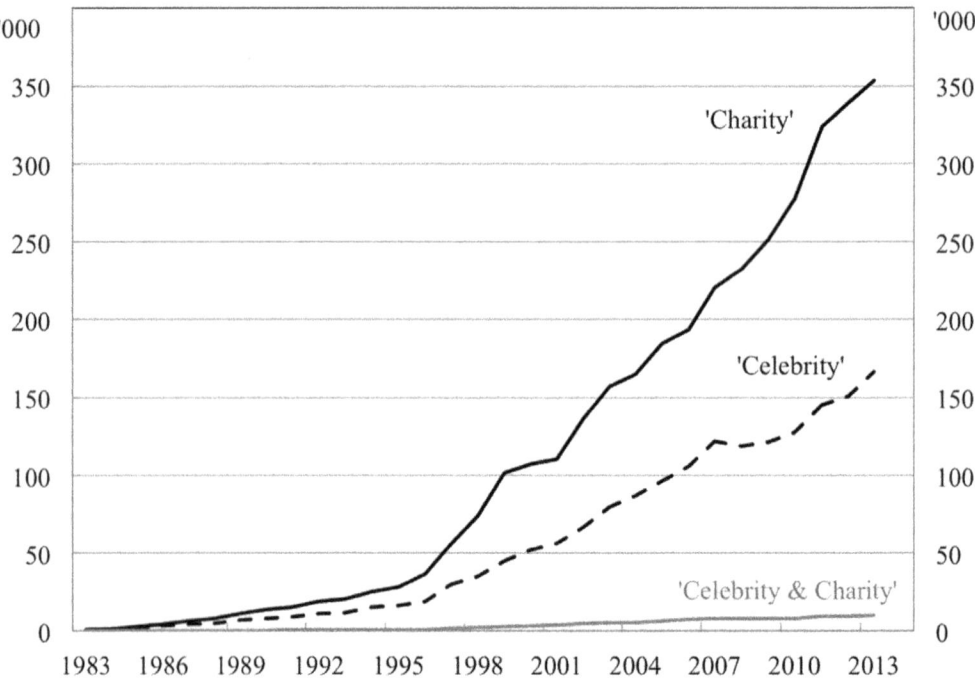

Figure 1: Newspaper Coverage of 'Celebrity' and 'Charity' (1983–2013). Source: Factiva.com (1999–). Accessed 14 August 2014.

'philanthropy' are insignificant by comparison, and hence are not included in the graph: 0 in 1983 and less than 550 in 2013.

Celebrity philanthropy in contemporary western societies is differentiated from the practice wherein the rich and famous 'give back' by cheque-writing at charity galas; celebrities now use their public visibility, brand credibility and personal wealth to promote not-for-profit organizations that are increasingly institutionalized, 'business-like' and transnational in form. The rise of what is sometimes dubbed 'celanthropy' – 'charity projects fronted and, in the public mind, defined by celebrities' (Rojek 2014: 127) – is attributed to a combination of factors. Considerations relating to political change include: the retreat of many governments from providing welfare support or foreign aid; the domination of neoliberal policies; and the failure of those policies to resolve either global inequalities, allocations of risk or suffering. Factors relating to technological change include: the globalization of information technology; widespread media promotion of celebrities as newsworthy; and the competition for funding and donor awareness among not-for-profit organizations, which seems to require ongoing publicity and media interest (Turner, Bonner and Marshall 2000: 166; Cooper 2007: 5–7; Littler 2008: 240–1; Sawaya 2008: 212).

Scholars and other interested commentators praise and condemn celebrity philanthropy for demonstrating the perceived advantages and disadvantages of advanced capitalism and western liberal democracy in action. Supporters argue that leveraging 'fame' helps to popularize humanitarian values and global citizenship by raising the public profile of a given social issues campaign and its host organization, bringing extra media coverage, attracting new audiences, demystifying campaign issues, encouraging sponsorship and raising public awareness (Bishop and Green 2008; 'UNICEF People' n.d.). Critics insist that celebrity-endorsed philanthropy bolsters inequality, consumerism and corporate capitalism because it is driven by media desires for a story and the publicity-grabbing imperatives of the celebrity industry and disguises the exploitative nature of trade and business relationships (Žižek 2006; Nickel 2012; Kapoor 2013; Rojek 2014).

This book explores the controversy surrounding contemporary celebrity philanthropy via critical debates on the politics of charity and philanthropy, capitalism and consumption, celebrity and fandom and development and globalization, with cases studies that span across Europe, Africa, Asia and the Americas. The volume contains 11 chapters, including this introduction, which engage with the subject of celebrity philanthropy from different analytical and cultural perspectives, rather than encouraging a Manichean 'love it or hate it' approach. Viewed as a whole, the book argues for a more nuanced understanding of celebrity engagement with philanthropy – whether referring to celebrity endorsement of public charities, celebrity donors or celebrity-funded private foundations – by exposing the contested nature of the terms 'celebrity' and 'philanthropy', and demonstrating that celebrity philanthropy can take different forms and be viewed differently in different parts of the world.

This introductory chapter proceeds as follows. We first contextualize the keywords 'celebrity' and 'philanthropy'. We then outline the general structure of the book, summarizing the contents and themes of the remaining chapters.

'Celebrity' and 'Philanthropy'

The meaning of the word 'celebrity' may seem self-evident, especially given its increasingly common usage, but it has a long and somewhat chequered history. 'Celebrity' originally referred to the religious observance of rites and ceremonies, and hence pomp and solemnity, and gradually came to mean 'the condition of being much extolled or talked about', that is, being a famous or notorious public character ('Celebrity, n.' 2012 [1989]). Contemporary celebrities are dual objects of 'worship' (media and fan approval) and 'notoriety' (media and fan disapproval/scandal), depending on whether their fame, which is subject to ongoing reassessment, is viewed as being based on innate talents or as an effect of media exposure, especially the media-fed trivia of lifestyle and personality (Turner 2004: 3–4; Redmond and Holmes 2007: 8). Daniel Boorstin (1972: 6), for example, denounces contemporary celebrities on the grounds that 'their chief claim to fame is their fame itself'. Comparing modern-day celebrities in the United States of America (hereafter the US) with former 'heroes', he concludes that 'The hero created himself; the celebrity is created by the media. The hero was a big man; the celebrity is a big name' (Boorstin 1972: 61).

This degenerative conceptualization of celebrity is entwined with the history and 'democratization' of celebrity in the US, with the inventions of silent cinema (late nineteenth century), sound movies (the late 1920s), broadcast television (the 1940s), the Internet (the late 1970s) and social media (the 2000s) being key staging points or phase shifts in the narrative (Jeffreys 2012). The creation of 'talking' pictures ushered in a new age of movie stars, with an accompanying focus on the physical attributes and media-created persona of the star. Broadcast television intensified and extended this process by creating television stars and ultimately making 'ordinary' people temporarily famous through the proliferation of reality television programming and associated interactive formats in the late 1990s and early 2000s. Graeme Turner (2004) has coined the expression 'the demotic turn' to describe the increasing visibility of 'ordinary people in the media' and their apparent desire to celebritize themselves, through reality television shows, talk radio and user-generated materials online.

As indicated by the expansion of types of celebrities and celebrity-making opportunities, defining contemporary celebrity is not a simple task. Some celebrities have extremely high levels of broadcast media visibility and are, arguably, known internationally. Others are celebrated at national or local levels, or transnationally and translocally through ethnic communities and inter-continental diaspora networks and media. Yet others create their own fame through social media and appeal to niche markets/audiences. Attempts to provide a definitive taxonomy of celebrity or a hierarchy of fame are thus complicated by the fact that new technologies are transforming the ways in which celebrity is created, traded and understood; moreover, both 'the celebrity' and 'the function of celebrity' may be conceived of differently in different cultural contexts.

Celebrity is better understood as an industry-coordinated 'media process' and 'the celebrity' as a commodity, sign or text that is 'productively consumed by audiences and

An Introduction

fans' (Turner 2004: 20). The contemporary celebrity is clearly an ambiguous sign with multiple social functions. In western societies at least, the celebrity is a means through which interested audiences think and talk about issues relating to both individual, social and cultural identities, and the nature of political–economic systems (Marshall 1997: x; Turner 2004: 25; see also the contributions to this volume).

The expansion of celebrity forms and celebrity-making opportunities has converged with the 'massification' of philanthropy. Although the English-language words 'charity' and 'philanthropy' are often used interchangeably, both of these terms have complicated histories. The term 'charity', which originally referred to the proclaimed love of God for humanity (c.1200), came to mean Christian love (man's love of God and fellow human beings) and eventually benevolence to one's neighbours, especially to the poor, and more generally love, kindness and natural affection without any specially Christian associations ('Charity, n.' 2012 [1989]). These understandings of the term are largely positive. However, charity as an organized response to human suffering has developed negative connotations, as indicated by phrases such as 'cold as charity' and 'I'd rather die than accept charity'. The first expression refers to 'the perfunctory, unfeeling manner in which acts of charity are often done, and public charities administered' ('Charity, n.' 2012 [1989]). The second phrase highlights the moral taint that was and is still sometimes associated with charity as 'handouts' to groups of people who are presented as socially dependent and inferior to elite providers of charitable aid. Both phrases retain the original imprecise suggestion that 'real charity' stems from an ineffable love rather than being mechanical, obligatory and hierarchical.

The negative connotations of organized charity and its religious associations, explain the growing preference for the synonym 'philanthropy' in some discussions of legal charities or not-for-profit organizations (Payton and Moody 2008). Like charity, the word 'philanthropy' referred originally to God's love of humankind, but now refers to the secular love of humanity as demonstrated through 'the disposition or active effort to promote the happiness and well-being of others', especially by donating time, money, goods and/or services to 'good causes' ('Philanthropy, n.' 2012 [1989]). Practitioners usually describe modern philanthropy in positive terms as referring to the development of the not-for-profit or non-governmental sector, and hence as institutionally channelled and business-style responses to the 'big' issues affecting humankind (Bishop 2007; Payton and Moody 2008). Critics infer that such philanthropies are too impersonal and money-orientated, as indicated by criticisms of not-for-profit CEOs as 'non-profit millionaires' (Bell 2009; see also Badje 2013: 5).

Celebrity endorsement of not-for-profit organizations is often held up as a major example of the perceived inauthentic nature of contemporary philanthropy, especially in leftist critiques put forward by scholars in Cultural and Development Studies. Chris Rojek (2014: 132–5), for example, argues that an enclave of A-list celanthropists is an increasingly notable and 'unelected' part of 'national and trans-national extra-parliamentary politics'. These celebrities use the media to court acclaim and manipulate citizens of western societies into providing resources, which are frequently misappropriated, for private projects that pay lip service to addressing global equality while bolstering vested corporate, government and media interests. Lisa Ann Richey and Stefano Ponte (2011) similarly condemn 'causumerism' – the purchase of a product, usually celebrity endorsed, for which a percentage of the profits goes to a 'good cause' – as a populist co-branding exercise that privileges 'whiteness', consumerism and capitalist accumulation by enabling western celebrities and corporations to 'speak for' and profit from suffering people in developing countries, especially in Africa. Ilan Kapoor (2013: 80) concludes that celanthropy democratizes philanthropy only to depoliticize its assumed traditional emphasis on compassionate benevolence and social change. Instead, celanthropy encourages western consumers to be 'heroes-for-a-day' who think they are delivering salvation to the rest of the world by purchasing the 'right product'.

These criticisms are both affirmed and interrogated in the chapters that make up the rest of this book.

Celebrity Philanthropy: Structure and Contents

The opening chapters, by Elaine Jeffreys and Jonathan Paul Marshall respectively (Part 1), argue for a more nuanced understanding of celanthropy by highlighting the reliance of the leftist critique on idealized conceptions of philanthropy. Elaine Jeffreys (Chapter 2) outlines the arguments 'for' and 'against' celebrity-corporate philanthropy with reference to Andrew Carnegie's 'Gospel of Wealth', Bill Gates' notion of 'creative capitalism' and the United Nations' (UN) celebrity ambassador system, together with the counterarguments of social theorists (Carnegie 1889; Kiviat and Gates 2008; Kapoor 2013; 'UNICEF People' n.d.). Jeffreys argues that the term 'philanthropy' is imbued with debatable, utopian desires to perfect contemporary economic and political structures. While supporters of celanthropy maintain a utopian faith in the ultimate capacity of neoliberal capitalism to bring prosperity to all, critics contend that the goals of international philanthropies are incompatible with media sensationalism, celebrity culture and consumerism. However, reference to history shows that missionaries were celebrated in ethnographic texts and public exhibitions in the nineteenth century as a means to generate public interest in and charitable donations for the 'civilizing mission' (Curtin 1964: 325; Magubane 2007: 374–5). The American Red Cross made use of promotional techniques, movies and celebrities in the early twentieth century to induce millions of 'ordinary' people to purchase goods and services to support wartime relief efforts (Rozario 2003). In other words, humanitarianism only became a mass phenomenon when philanthropy became a commercial marketing venture (Rozario 2003).

Without discounting the critique of celanthropy, Jeffreys points out that critics rarely suggest a viable replacement for the aid they despise. Moreover, despite the proliferation of intellectual complaints about the privileged, superficial and racist nature of celebrity philanthropy in the international arena, there are hardly any empirical studies of how celebrity-involved or celebrity-inspired philanthropy operates in practice in the context of developing countries, what it does for local recipients and how it is viewed and understood by them. Jeffreys concludes that the lack of empirical studies of the operation of celebrity philanthropy in non-western contexts highlights the need for more nuanced applications of both the critical and the enthusiastic accounts.

In Chapter 3, Jonathan Paul Marshall argues that many approaches to celebrity philanthropy refuse to look at the mess of the real world. They foreclose discussion through rushing to apply the categories of 'good' and 'evil', sidestepping the overwhelming magnitude of the problems faced in the world and avoiding the paradoxes of help. In particular, while the left critique of helping is vital and important in pointing out fundamental problems, it leaves any form of practicable help vulnerable to criticisms of oppression, because such help necessarily involves both an unequal exchange and an attempt at maintaining or promoting order. A wider view is needed.

Marshall looks at the different (western) historical varieties of help in order to distinguish these forms in more detail, and follows this survey by looking at the incoherencies found in an interview with Angelina Jolie – international film star, UN Goodwill Ambassador, and currently Special Envoy to the UN High Commissioner for Refugees (UNHCR) (Cooper 2006; 'Goodwill Ambassadors' 2001–2015). Contrary to some critics (e.g. Nickel 2012), Marshall argues that these incoherencies may arise from an implicit awareness of the overwhelming complexity of the situation, and the difficulties involved in any attempt to understand and relate to the culturally different people being helped, however tangentially. Staying with these incoherencies may also allow the possibility of building a fictional but useful and empathetic relationship, thus providing an opening in which less foreclosed, and oppressive, thought and action could occur.

The next four chapters critique the impact of Euramerican-style celebrity philanthropy in the US and in international settings (Part 2). In Chapter 4, Dara Persis Murray explores the different views of female empowerment that inform the brand identity of Tyra Banks, a black US supermodel, media producer and philanthropist. Banks' most popular media program, and her main source of wealth, is *America's Next Top Model*, a global franchise that enjoins young women to embrace and promote capitalist consumer culture as embodied in the fashion and beauty industry (Banks 2003–). The would-be models compete against each other to realize their personal goals of wealth, celebrity and success. In contrast, Banks' main philanthropic effort, the TZONE Foundation, works to support girls and young women from disadvantaged backgrounds and appears representative of classic feminist efforts to empower women, who are understood as an oppressed 'sisterhood'. TZONE recognizes a need for cooperative support to realize change and promote women's social, political and economic rights, whereas *America's Next Top Model* promotes competitive individualism, hegemonic versions of beautiful femininity and success through consumerism. These two conceptions of female empowerment are arguably incompatible.

Although TZONE was established before *America's Next Top Model*, it receives very little publicity and is rarely promoted publicly by Banks, in stark contrast to the high public profile of the Banks franchise. Murray therefore concludes that Banks' philanthropy and self-proclaimed feminism is secondary to her commercial concerns centred on the extension of her reputation and 'brand'. This adds to the general claim, which is normally uncorroborated with empirical evidence, that the mediatized philanthropic activities of celebrities are primarily determined by self-interest, rather than by a genuine desire to help others.

Rob Millington (Chapter 5) examines how UN-advocated Sport for Development and Peace (SDP) programs contribute to the transnational branding of commercial sports and constrict understandings of development issues. Millington undertakes a case study of two specific SDP programs: Right to Play (RTP); a not-for-profit organization based in Canada; and Basketball without Borders (BWB), a corporate social responsibility initiative of the US National Basketball Association (NBA) ('Right to Play' 2014; 'Basketball without Borders' 2015). He argues that sport and sports stars draw the attention of sports fans to social issues, including global poverty and uneven development. The images projected through celebrity involvement in SDP programs also offer a counter-narrative to generalized understandings of poverty in developing economies by showing images of happy, healthy and active children participating in sport. However, the involvement of the sports celebrity within corporate-led and consumer-based development programs may also reduce the effectiveness of aid efforts, marginalize the recipients while enhancing the brands of sports stars and their sponsors, and constrict understandings of development issues by concentrating on individual outcomes such as enhanced self-esteem, confidence and sports-based leadership.

Millington concludes that discourses of philanthropy do not merely reflect social entities and relations but also actively construct those relationships, the problems being faced and those modes of solution that seem obvious. The discourse of 'sports celebrity aid' builds truth claims about what underdevelopment looks like, where it is located, how it can be addressed and who can address it. Because of its success, we rarely hear how the subjects of development conceptualize and understand these endeavours, or indeed, what they think they might need. Interested audiences in the global North are thus deprived of fair evaluations of SDP programs.

In Chapter 6, Hilde Van den Bulck, Nathalie Claessens and Koen Panis analyze a sample of 12 documentaries from Belgium, the Netherlands, the United Kingdom (hereafter the UK) and the US. In these documentaries, celebrity testimonials are used to present development problems and possible solutions, and hence to interpret global relations between 'the West' and 'the Rest' (of the world). Van den Bulck, Claessens and Panis argue that celebrity testimonies fall into four main 'framings'. These are: (1) *The West Saves the Rest: Social Engineering* (including the sub-frame *Social Engineering as the White Man's Burden*); (2) *The West Helps Save the Rest through Western Organizations*; (3) *The West Helps the Rest Save Itself through Local Organizations*; and (4) *The (Diverse) Rest will Save Itself from Problems Caused by the West*. The first three frames are by far the most popular, with 'the West' generally being given a constitutive and dominant role in the development of 'the Rest'.

In the most popular framings, there is little reference to any ideas that might imply that the history of western imperialism and capitalism has helped to create and maintain patterns of underdevelopment, thus depriving the documentaries' audiences of vital information for a deeper understanding of development problems and potential solutions. The framings also present celebrities as transitory figures, passing through and bringing both worlds together in an uneven relationship. Van den Bulck, Claessens and Panis conclude that such celebrity testimonials tend to promote an ideology in which 'civilization' and 'development' are something that 'the West' has and 'the Rest' lacks, and which can be given to 'the Rest' by 'the West'.

Katherine M. Bell (Chapter 7) argues that even in the contemporary world, the model of the 'White Saviour' is still popular in Hollywood film, popular music videos and other mainstream celebrity genres of production. In films such as *Indiana Jones* (dir. Spielberg 2003), *Lara Croft: Tomb Raider* (dir. West 2001) and *Blood Diamond* (dir. Zwick 2006), actors perform roles as heroes who 'save the day' against all odds, usually by thwarting dark and menacing adversaries. Celebrities, such as pop stars Bono and Madonna and actor Angelina Jolie, activate some of the same representations of whiteness when acting as representatives of philanthropy, or as redeemers of 'the Other' in Africa, whether intentionally or not.

Bell examines the publicity and television programs surrounding Madonna's Raising Malawi charity, Bono's Product RED campaign, and Jolie's work for the UN ('Our Story' n.d.; 'Goodwill Ambassadors' 2001–2015; 'Raising Malawi' 2009–2015). Reportage around all three figures as fund-raisers and diplomats for distant causes in Africa, appears to reproduce tropes of primitivism, Christian salvation and motherhood that stretch back to the colonial period. Indeed, media coverage of the role of Madonna and Jolie as celebrity adoptive mothers often implies widespread inadequacies in African motherhood and the salvation of children by white parentage.

As Bell concludes, the mingling of celebrities' personal and professional lives in their humanitarian endeavours generates a powerful form of enculturated authority that enables them to speak for distant others, and to define global problems for the home audience. These social and political problems are usually reduced to hapless circumstance, poor choices or rotten luck. In the cases examined, the problems are resolved through cursory references to African virtues of community and joy, but mainly through the application of North American ideals of individualistic strength, hard work, perseverance and participation in the capitalist economy.

The next three chapters, by Devleena Ghosh, Elaine Jeffreys and Paul Allatson, respectively, examine the politics of celebrity philanthropy as debated in India, mainland China and in Latin American and US Latino settings (Part 3). Devleena Ghosh (Chapter 8) looks at the nexus of celebrity, political activism and philanthropy in the political advocacy of author Arundhati Roy, as found in Roy's comments on the nature of the Indian state, and in India-based reactions against this commentary. Roy, the writer of the Booker Prize-winning novel *The God of Small Things* (1997), has become a global literary celebrity and an icon of social activism through her intervention in local, regional and global politics, her practice of donating her prize monies to humanitarian and environmental causes, and what are seen as her contentious political and social opinions. Roy's main polemics are directed at the Indian state and its attempts to promote development through dams and nuclear power, and what she sees as the ensuing victimization of minorities. These criticisms have, in some people's eyes, led Roy to support dubious anti-state movements such as Maoist insurgents and the Mumbai terrorists (Guha 2000; Parashar 2009).

Although Roy's writings and activism have guaranteed her reputation among left-wing activist circles in Europe and North America, Ghosh concludes that Roy's activism puts her at odds with the more general use of celebrity in India to promote nationalism, modernist discourses of development and the necessity for a homogeneous state. As a result, most of the media coverage that Roy receives in India is negative; her opponents characterize her as naïve, simplistic and anti-Indian (Guha 2000; Parashar 2009). At the same time, Roy rarely gives sophisticated solutions to the problems of India where the state may be the only hope, or means of recourse, for most people. Roy thus promotes a limited form of 'leftist' politics, which both depends on and reinforces her celebrity, by advocating resistance to the Indian state, but failing to provide other viable alternatives to poverty alleviation and development issues.

Elaine Jeffreys (Chapter 9) examines the controversy surrounding celebrity philanthropy in the People's Republic of China (hereafter the PRC) – a rising non-western superpower and authoritarian state. Jeffreys looks at a series of philanthropy-related scandals that arose in 2010 because of celebrity and corporate pledges to disaster-relief funds set up in the wake of the 2008 Sichuan earthquake. The earthquake, which had killed over 70,000 people and left five million homeless, is widely viewed as putting philanthropy 'on the map' in China. Philanthropic donations in 2008 exceeded the documented total for the preceding decade as individuals and corporations responded to the crisis, prompted, in part, by government calls for support (Wang 2008).

In 2010, the internationally acclaimed Chinese actress, Zhang Ziyi, became the focus of public criticism for allegedly defaulting on a pledge to donate CNY 1 million to the disaster-relief efforts (Zhou 2010a; 2010b). The discovery of Zhang's 'failed pledge' led fans and critics in social media forums to reactivate accusations of sexual promiscuity and level new allegations of charity fraud against her. Lack of transparency in Zhang's personal foundation, the Ziyi Zhang Foundation, was also alleged to show that it was a front for personal profiteering. The ensuing controversy obliged Zhang to hire a team of US-based lawyers, give an exclusive interview to the state-run *China Daily* and engage in renewed philanthropic endeavours, in an effort to clear her name (Zhou 2010a; 2010b).

Zhang was neither the first nor the only high-profile casualty of a public backlash against elite philanthropy in the aftermath of the earthquake. Multinational corporations were accused of 'donation-stinginess' in chain letters posted on the Internet and disseminated via mobile phone networks, with accompanying calls to boycott them ('The Story of Donations Gate' 2008). A range of Chinese sports and entertainment stars were also accused of 'dishonest advertising' or failing to deliver on publicized pledges. As Jeffreys concludes, these actions bring into question the assumption that celebrity philanthropy offers an easy, self-serving and 'unaccountable' means of obtaining publicity, and is 'fundamentally depoliticizing' (Kapoor 2013: 1).

Paul Allatson (Chapter 10) counters critiques of celebrity philanthropy when regarded as a problematic form of paternalism imposed on the global South by representatives of the global North, particularly those from the US. Allatson focuses on two internationally famous music stars: the Colombian Shakira and the Puerto Rican Ricky Martin. Key figures in the transnational popularization of Latin(o) American music, both stars are also renowned for their philanthropic work in the Americas. Shakira established her Fundación Pies Descalzos (Barefoot Foundation) in 2003, out of an earlier organization she formed in the late 1990s when she was 18, to enable poor children in Colombia access to education (Fundación Pies Descalzos n.d.). Launching its first initiative in 2004, the Ricky Martin Foundation focuses on supporting children rescued from human trafficking across the world (Fundación Ricky Martin 2014).

Allatson argues that understandings of Shakira's and Martin's celebrity philanthropy must move beyond Northern-centric critiques given the two artists are at home, and are celebritized, in both the global North and global South. Allatson thus locates Shakira's and Martin's celebrity philanthropy in a geospatial construct, the Spanish-speaking Americas, with neither a history of welfare state governance, nor traditions of philanthropy, as would be understood in global North terms. He approaches Shakira's and Martin's celebrity *and* philanthropy as related historical products of transamerican mass-media operations, cultural interchanges and philanthropic-like traditions, as well as the historical legacies of imperialism and capitalist underdevelopment in the Americas. Allatson concludes that Shakira and Martin's fluid relation to a US Latino identification anchored in the global South may in fact challenge readings of celebrity philanthropy as produced in and projected from the so-called global North alone.

Overall, the different chapters that make up this volume suggest that the public involvement of celebrities in charitable causes is likely to continue to expand in national and international settings. What remains to be understood are: the openings celebrity philanthropy can provide; the ways it may be constituted differently in different contexts and places; the unintended effects it may generate; and the reactions of both fans and those being helped. With such a more detailed and nuanced understanding, it may well be possible to gain greater benefit and helpful change from its use. Hence, the Afterword (Chapter 11) outlines some future avenues for research, while also drawing attention to some of the key critical approaches to celebrity philanthropy that are inhibiting more nuanced, and genuinely international, understandings of both celebrity and philanthropy, most notably when theorized and critiqued from North America.

Acknowledgements

This research was supported under the Australian Research Council's Future Fellowship (FT100100238) funding scheme.

References

Andrew, D.T. (1989) *Philanthropy and Police: London Charity in the Eighteenth Century*, Princeton, NJ: Princeton University Press.

Badje, D. (2013) 'Marketized philanthropy: Kiva's utopian ideology of entrepreneurial philanthropy', *Marketing Theory*, 13, 1: 3–18.

Banks, T. (2003–) *America's Next Top Model*, television series, United States: Bankable Productions, http://www.imdb.com/title/tt0363307/. Accessed 9 January 2015.

'Basketball without Borders' (2015) NBA.com, http://www.nba.com/bwb/. Accessed 9 January 2015.

Bell, A. (2009) 'Nonprofit millionaires', *Forbes*, 17 December, http://www.forbes.com/2009/12/17/nonprofits-biggest-salaries-personal-finance-millionaires.html. Accessed 9 January 2015.

Bishop, M. (2007) 'Fighting global poverty: Who'll be relevant in 2020?', Brookings Blum Roundtable, 1 August, http://www.brookings.edu/~/media/Events/2007/8/01sustainable-development/2007bishop.PDF. Accessed 5 March 2015.

Bishop, M., and Green, M. (2008) *Philanthrocapitalism: How the Rich Can Save the World*, New York: Bloomsbury Press.

Boorstin, D. (1972 [1961]) *The Image: A Guide to Pseudo-Events in America*, New York: Atheneum.

Brockington, D. (2009) *Celebrity and the Environment: Fame, Wealth and Power in Conservation*, London: Zed Books.

Brockington, D. (2014) 'The production and construction of celebrity advocacy in international development', *Third World Quarterly*, 35, 1: 88–108.

Carnegie, A. (1889) 'Wealth', *North American Review*, CCCXCL, 391: 653–64.

'Celebrity, n.' (2012 [1989]) *Oxford English Dictionary*, second edition, 1989; online version March 2012, Oxford, UK: Oxford University Press, http://www.oed.com.view/Entry/29424. Accessed 18 August 2014.

'Charity, n.' (2012 [1989]) *Oxford English Dictionary*, second edition, 1989; online version March 2012, Oxford, UK: Oxford University Press, http://www.oed.com.view/Entry/30731. Accessed 18 August 2014.

Cooper, A. (2006) 'Angelina Jolie: Her mission and motherhood', *360 Degrees*, CNN, 23 June, http://transcripts.cnn.com/TRANSCRIPTS/0606/23/acd.02.html. Accessed 9 January 2015.

Cooper, A. (2007) 'Celebrity diplomacy and the G8: Bono and Bob as legitimate international actors', Working Paper 29, The Centre for International Governance, http://www.isn.ethz.ch/isn/Digital-Library/Publications/Detail/?ord516=OrgaGrp&ots591=0c54e3b3-1e9c-be1e-2c24-a6a8c7060233&lng=en&id=39553. Accessed 9 January 2015.

Curtin, P. (1964) *The Image of Africa*, Madison: University of Wisconsin Press.

Factiva.com (1999–) Dow Jones and Company, https://global-factiva-com.ezproxy.lib.uts.edu.au/sb/default.aspx?lnep=hp. Accessed 14 August 2014.

Fundación Pies Descalzos (n.d.) Official website, Spanish-language version, http://www.fundacionpiesdescalzos.com/. Accessed 9 January 2015.

Fundación Ricky Martin (2014) Official website, Spanish-language version, http://www.rickymartinfoundation.org/es/; English-language version, http://www.rickymartinfoundation.org/. Accessed 9 January 2015.

'Goodwill Ambassadors' (2001–2015) UNHCR: The UN Refugee Agency, http://www.unhcr.org/pages/49c3646c3e.html. Accessed 9 January 2015.

Guha, R. (2000) 'The Arun Shourie of the left', *The Hindu*, 26 November, http://www.hindu.com/2000/11/26/stories/13260411.htm. Accessed 9 January 2015.

Jeffreys, E. (2012) 'Modern China's idols: Heroes, role models, stars and celebrities', *PORTAL Journal of Multidisciplinary International Studies*, 9, 1: 1–32, http://epress.lib.uts.edu.au/journals/index.php/portal/article/view/2187/2851. Accessed 9 January 2015.

Kapoor, I. (2013) *Celebrity Humanitarianism: The Ideology of Global Charity*, Abingdon, Oxon: Routledge.

Kiviat, B., and Gates, B. (2008) 'Making capitalism more creative', *Time*, 31 July, http://www.time.com/time/magazine/article/0,9171,1828417,00.html. Accessed 9 January 2015.

Littler, J. (2008) '"I feel your pain": Cosmopolitan charity and the public fashioning of the celebrity soul', *Social Semiotics*, 18, 2: 237–51.

'Look to the Stars: The World of Celebrity Giving' (2006–2015) Look to the Stars, http://www.looktothestars.org/. Accessed 9 January 2015.

Luscombe, B. (2006) 'Madonna finds a cause', *Time*, 3 August, http://content.time.com/time/world/article/0,8599,1222449,00.html. Accessed 9 January 2015.

Magubane, Z. (2007) 'Oprah in South Africa: The politics of coevalness and the creation of a black public sphere', *Safundi*, 8, 4: 373–93.

Magubane, Z. (2008) 'The (Product) Red man's burden: Charity, celebrity, and the contradictions of coevalness', *Journal of Pan African Studies*, 2, 6: 1–25.

Marshall, P.D. (1997) *Celebrity and Power: Fame in Contemporary Culture*, Minneapolis, MN: The University of Minnesota Press.

Nickel, P.M. (2012) 'Philanthromentality: Celebrity parables as technologies of transfer', *Celebrity Studies*, 3, 2: 164–82.

'Our Story' (n.d.) (RED), http://www.red.org/en/about. Accessed 10 January 2015.

Parashar, S. (2009) 'A response to Arundhati Roy: "The heart of India is under attack"', Hariharan's MI blog, Guest Column, Paper No. 3489, 5 November, http://www.southasiaanalysis.org/%5Cpapers35%5Cpaper3489.html. Accessed 13 February, http://hariharansmiblog.blogspot.com.au/2009/11/response-to-arundhati-roy-heart-of.html. Accessed 5 March 2015.

Payton, R., and Moody, M. (2008) *Understanding Philanthropy: Its Meaning and Mission*, Bloomington, IN: Indiana University Press.

'Philanthropy, n.' (2012 [1989]) *Oxford English Dictionary*, second edition, 1989; online version March 2012, Oxford, UK: Oxford University Press, http://www.oed.com.view/Entry/142408. Accessed 18 August 2014.

'Raising Malawi' (2009–2015) Raising Malawi Inc., http://www.raisingmalawi.org/. Accessed 1 January 2015.

Redmond, S., and Holmes, S. (2007) *Stardom and Celebrity: A Reader*, London: Sage.

Richey, L.A., and Ponte, S. (2011) *Brand Aid: Shopping Well to Save the World*, Minneapolis, MN: University of Minnesota Press.

'Right to Play' (2014) Right to Play, http://www.righttoplay.com/International/about-us/Pages/History.aspx. Accessed 14 March 2014.

Rojek, C. (2014) '"Big citizen" celanthropy and its discontents', *International Journal of Cultural Studies*, 17, 2: 127–41.

Roy, A. (1997) *The God of Small Things*, New York: HarperPerennial.

Rozario, K. (2003) '"Delicious horrors": Mass culture, the Red Cross, and the appeal of modern American humanitarianism', *American Quarterly*, 55, 3: 417–55.

Sawaya, F. (2008) 'Capitalism and philanthropy in the (new) gilded age', *American Quarterly*, 60, 1: 201–15.

Spielberg, S. (dir.) (2003) *The Adventures of Indiana Jones: The Complete DVD Movie Collection*, DVD collection, Hollywood, CA: Lucasfilm and Paramount.

'The Story of Donations Gate' (2008) *EastSouthWestNorth*, 29 May, www.zonaeuropa.com/20080529_1.htm. Accessed 9 January 2015.

Tsaliki, L., Frangonikolopoulos, C.A., and Huliaras, A. (2011) *Transnational Celebrity Activism in Global Politics*, Bristol, UK; Chicago, IL: Intellect Press.

Turner, G. (2004) *Understanding Celebrity*, London; Thousand Oaks; New Delhi: Sage.

Turner, G., Bonner, F., and Marshall, P.D. (2000) *Fame Games: The Production of Celebrity in Australia*, Melbourne: Cambridge University Press.

'UNICEF People' (n.d.) UNICEF, http://www.unicef.org/people/people_ambassadors.html. Accessed 9 January 2015.

Wang Zhuoqiong (2008) 'Quake triggers donation deluge', *China Daily*, 5 December, http://www.chinadaily.com.cn/china/2008-12/05/content_7273896.htm. Accessed 9 January 2015.

West, S. (dir.) (2001) *Lara Croft: Tomb Raider*, motion picture, Hollywood, CA: Paramount Home Entertainment.

Zhou, R. (2010a) 'Actress denies charity fraud', *China Daily*, 16 March, http://www.chinadaily.com.cn/china/2010-03/16/content_9593921.htm. Accessed 9 January 2015.

Zhou, R. (2010b) 'Clearing her name', *China Daily*, 16 March, http://www.chinadaily.com.cn/life/2010-03/16/content_9596922.htm. Accessed 9 January 2015.

Žižek, S. (2006) 'The liberal communists of Porto Davos', *In These Times*, 11 April, http://www.inthesetimes.com/site/main/article/2574/. Accessed 9 January 2015.

Zwick, E. (dir.) (2006) *Blood Diamond*, motion picture, US: The Bedford Falls Virtual Studios, Warner Brothers Pictures.

Part 1

Rethinking Celebrity Philanthropy

Chapter 2

On Celebrity Philanthropy

Elaine Jeffreys

Celebrity philanthropy and the socio-political role and impact of the celebrity philanthropist are growing fields of academic inquiry (Tsaliki, Frangonikolopoulos and Huliaras 2011; Kapoor 2013). In 2005, *Time* magazine named rock star Bono and Microsoft co-founder Bill Gates and his wife Melinda as its 'Persons of the Year', citing their philanthropic work and activism aimed at reducing global poverty and improving world health. *Time* also praised Bono and the Gates' for 'being shrewd about doing good, for rewiring politics and re-engineering justice, for making mercy smarter and hope strategic and then daring the rest of us to follow' (Gibbs 2005). This improved version of philanthropy refers to what its exponents describe as 'new philanthropy', 'philanthrocapitalism' or 'creative capitalism' (Bishop 2007; Kiviat and Gates 2008). These terms mark the transformation, which began in late seventeenth-century England and was consolidated in the US in the twentieth century, from 'charity', understood as giving between individuals (Andrew 1989: 197–202; Sulek 2010: 201), to 'philanthropy' – an institutionally channelled humanitarian response to conditions of poverty and social injustice using business-like models of efficiency, transparency and money-making success (Bishop 2007: 5–6; Kiviat and Gates 2008). Celebrities enter into the terrain of new philanthropy by using their public visibility, brand credibility and personal wealth to aid philanthropic activities, defined as 'the planned and structured giving of money, time, information, goods and services, voice and influence to improve the wellbeing of humanity and the community' ('Philanthropy' n.d.).

The involvement of major celebrities in philanthropic work and advocacy on humanitarian issues is not a new phenomenon. Since 1954, the UN has recruited famous people, for example actor Danny Kaye, to obtain funds and support for its causes ('UNICEF People' n.d.; Wilson 2014: 37–9). Popular musicians have also been involved in raising public awareness of humanitarian causes, obtaining funding and lobbying legislators on a wide range of issues. These include civil rights and anti-(Vietnam) war demonstrations in the US during the 1960s and 1970s, and charity concerts, record sales and telethon appeals held in many western nations during the 1980s for poverty alleviation in Africa, such as Band Aid and Live Aid events (Andersson 2007; Huddart 2007; Richey and Ponte 2008: 716).

However, celebrity philanthropy has expanded and altered in character in western societies since the 1990s (Harris 2003: 3; Littler 2008: 240; Traub 2008: 40). Scholars attribute this expansion to a combination of factors. The most important of these are: the post-Cold War triumph of neoliberalism and the decline of the welfare state ideal; the failure of governments to resolve the structural inequalities associated with globalization;

the spread of information technology; the increasing dependence of the not-for-profit sector on marketing, branding and public relations to compete for funds; and the pervasiveness of celebrity culture in everyday life (Turner, Bonner and Marshall 2000: 166; Cooper 2007b: 5–7; Littler 2008: 240–1; Sawaya 2008: 212).

Celebrity philanthropy and activism in the twenty-first century is differentiated from the practice wherein the rich and famous 'give back' by cheque-writing at gala charity functions because of its increasingly institutionalized, business-like and transnational form. Celebrity philanthropy now occurs through the establishment of foundations that employ professional philanthropic advisers and operate based on transparency and public performance analysis (Traub 2008: 40). Celebrities act as image ambassadors for large not-for-profit organizations using their profiles to shape public opinion and lobby governments and for-profit companies to support their chosen causes (Cooper 2007a, 2007b; Bishop and Green 2008: 73, 78; Dieter and Kumar 2008: 259). Celebrities have also emerged as a new type of transnational advocate in debates about development goals through their involvement in global humanitarian causes associated with the UN, which expanded its celebrity ambassador system in the 2000s to include over 400 people (Alleyne 2005: 176–8; Wheeler 2011: 55). Indeed, the Look to the Stars: The World of Celebrity Giving website – advertised as 'the web's number one source of celebrity charity news and information' – claims that as of January 2015, there were over 3,400 (Hollywood-branded) celebrities involved with more than 2,000 charities that aim to 'make a positive difference in the world' ('Look to the Stars: The World of Celebrity Giving' 2006–2015).

Scholars and other interested commentators both praise and condemn the phenomenon of contemporary celebrity philanthropy – its manifestations in international contexts, in particular – for demonstrating the perceived benefits and drawbacks of advanced capitalism and western liberal democracy in action. It is lauded for popularizing humanitarian values and global citizenship (Cooper 2007b: 16–18; Kiviat and Gates 2008; Traub 2008). Conversely, it is criticized for affirming neoliberal capitalism and undermining philanthropy's potentially transformative emphasis on the need for social change (Alleyne 2005; Weiskel 2005; Fullilove 2006; Nickel and Eikenberry 2006; Dieter and Kumar 2008; Nickel 2012; Kapoor 2013).

While supporters may overstate the transformative capacity of celebrity philanthropy, critics tend to unify different types of celebrities, philanthropic activity, and even the motivations of individual celebrities and their fans, under the overarching framework of 'bad capitalism and consumer culture at work'. Clearly celebrity philanthropy, and the individual motivations of celebrities and their fans for philanthropic advocacy and engagement, can take very different forms: 'no grand, one-size-fits-all interpretation is sufficient' ('t Hart and Tindall 2009: 257). Further case studies and typologies are required to comprehend the nature and effects of the different kinds of celebrity-mediated philanthropy and activism that exist in the world today (Stewart 2007: 19).

This chapter examines the controversy surrounding contemporary celebrity philanthropy as follows. It first details the arguments provided by supporters and critics of celebrity philanthropy, in order to highlight their organizing concerns. The debate is largely related to the question of whether mediatized celebrity philanthropy contributes to the goals of international humanitarianism and the expansion of democratic politics or not. The chapter then questions claims by critics that celebrity-mediated philanthropy is the antithesis of humanitarian values and progressive politics. It shows that the development of international humanitarianism, like celebrity, has itself been closely tied to the historical development of capitalism and the mass media. It also shows that the social and political impact of celebrity philanthropy is not reducible to the intentions and actions of individual celebrities. In conclusion, I argue that empirical studies of the development and impact of celebrity philanthropy in contexts other than the US and the UK are required, in order to provide a comparative framework for analysis and to redress the western and Anglophone focus of existing studies. This point is demonstrated with reference to the example of the PRC – a non-western country that has only recently begun to develop a market economy, a commercial celebrity culture and concepts of philanthropic citizenship.

In Praise and Blame of Celebrity Philanthropy

> The problem of our age is the proper administration of wealth, so that the ties of brotherhood may still bind together the rich and poor in harmonious relationship.
> (Carnegie 1889: 653)

Supporters of new philanthropy, and by extension both corporate and celebrity philanthropy, often maintain a utopian conviction that the free-market economy offers a solution to the problems posed by worldwide growing inequalities of wealth, rather than being the cause of such problems (Bishop and Green 2008). Andrew Carnegie (1835–1919), a Scottish-born rags-to-riches US industrialist and one of the richest men in history, was an early proponent of this claim. In a famous essay titled 'Wealth', Carnegie (1889: 653–64) argues that 'the law of competition' has revolutionized the condition of human life. Instead of living in universal squalor, considerably more people than previously have access to vastly improved standards of living and education, albeit especially the wealthy. Thus, the task posed for modern human society is to work out how to spread the advantages of the free-market economy more equitably. Carnegie's solution to this problem, which he describes as involving the 'proper administration of wealth', justifies the free-market economy and prescribes a philanthropic asceticism for the entrepreneurial new rich as a kind of 'middle way' between material individualism and state socialism.

Carnegie (1889) believed that inequalities between the rich and the poor were temporary and could be eliminated under what we now refer to as capitalism, so long as people with the ability and energy to produce wealth assumed responsibility for the 'proper' recirculation of their money back into society. In his view, successful entrepreneurs were duty-bound to set an example of modest, unostentatious living; provide moderately for the legitimate needs of their dependents; and use all their surplus revenues during their lifetime in a manner best calculated to benefit the community, rather than leaving large sums of money to be squandered by heirs or ineffective charitable organizations. At the same time, Carnegie (1889) disapproved of what he saw as 'alms-giving' – charity that maintained the poor in an impoverished state and created welfare dependency. Instead, he argued that charitable organizations should help those with the desire to improve themselves and therefore society as a whole.

Carnegie (1889) called his idealistic solution to the problem of social inequalities 'The Gospel of Wealth'. While disavowing organized religion until late in his life, Carnegie's solution is influenced by the Protestant work ethic and an accompanying view of human nature, social obligations and the role of government, a view that might now be described as conservative liberalism. Successful people in Carnegie's opinion are hard-working and frugal entrepreneurs who deserve to be rewarded for their industry, rather than having their energy and innovation restricted by heavy government taxes. Successful entrepreneurs are also willing to continue producing surplus wealth to be redistributed as social welfare throughout their lifetime, even though they are not elected officials with an obligation to do so, because of their love of humanity and love of self (ego). According to Carnegie (1889), charitable entrepreneurs will be rewarded for their actions by being praised in life and after their death, whereas those who die leaving unspent and unassigned millions will be 'unwept', 'unhonored', 'unsung' and 'disgraced'. In short, Carnegie believed that late nineteenth-century US entrepreneurs had the capacity to overcome the problem of poverty and generate future social harmony by continuing to do what they did best – accumulating private wealth under a free-market economy, while ensuring that their surplus wealth was disposed of during their lifetime in a way that promoted the welfare, happiness and culture of humankind.

Billionaire-philanthropist Bill Gates similarly expounds the benefits of 'creative capitalism' as a twenty-first-century solution to the problem of global as opposed to national social inequalities (Kiviat and Gates 2008). In a modern-day echo of Carnegie, Gates asks, 'How can we most effectively spread the benefits of capitalism and the huge improvements in quality of life it can provide to people who have been left out?' He argues that market incentives and supportive government policies should be used to harness the creativity, technical skills and profit-maximizing desire of corporations, in order to spread the benefits of capitalism more quickly, and speed up the traditional and slower work of governments and not-for-profit organizations in assisting the socially vulnerable (Kiviat and Gates 2008). Providing an example of creative capitalism at work, Gates notes that companies that sell RED-branded products, such as Dell, Gap, Hallmark and Microsoft, donate a portion of their profits to fight AIDS (Kiviat and Gates 2008). Since it was launched by rock star Bono in 2006, Product RED has generated USD 300 million for the Global Fund to Fight AIDS, tuberculosis and malaria – a public-private financing organization that works in partnership with donor-country governments, helping over 13 million people, mostly in Africa, through HIV and AIDS programs ('Our Story' n.d.).

Gates concludes that creative capitalism can resolve the problems associated with inequalities in wealth because it draws on 'two great forces of human nature: self-interest and caring for others' (Kiviat and Gates 2008). Unlike the reactive response of traditional corporate philanthropy to grant requests from unrelated not-for-profit organizations, creative capitalism generates a virtuous cycle of philanthropy by encouraging socially responsible companies to grasp new opportunities and profits while 'serving the people who have been left out' (Kiviat and Gates 2008). It also draws in consumers who want to be associated with good causes and employees who want to work for organizations that they can feel good about in both their private and public lives. In 2008, Gates stopped working on a day-to-day level at Microsoft to spend more time at the Bill and Melinda Gates Foundation, a foundation that has distributed around USD 31.6 billion since 1994 in grants that aim to improve health and alleviate poverty in developing countries, and provide equal education opportunities in the US ('Foundation Fact Sheet' 1999–2015). In 2010, Gates also launched a Carnegian-style campaign called The Giving Pledge with business magnate Warren Buffett. The Giving Pledge invites the world's wealthiest individuals to commit to giving the majority of their wealth to effective philanthropic organizations/causes of their choice either during their lifetime or immediately after their death (http://givingpledge.org/).

Supporters of new philanthropy typically praise the involvement of celebrity CEOs and entertainment celebrities in international humanitarian causes on pragmatic grounds. The use of their money and public reputation promotes philanthropic objectives, irrespective of their individual motivations, which may be altruistic, self-interested or a combination of both. As development economist and philanthropist Jeffrey Sachs puts it,

> In the very noisy and complicated world that we have, people that reach large numbers of people, like Madonna does, have an extraordinarily important role to play. When they're devoting their time, their money, their name, a lot of effort, a lot of organization skill to all of this, it makes a huge difference. The cynics are just wrong. They don't get it.
> (Sachs cited in Luscombe 2006)

Celebrity philanthropy is therefore praised by supporters for raising the public profile of a given social issues campaign and its host organization, bringing extra media coverage, attracting new audiences, demystifying campaign issues, encouraging sponsorship and raising public awareness ('UNICEF People' n.d.).

Supporters of new philanthropy also often praise celebrity philanthropists as exemplary citizens who 'can act as prisms through which social complexity is brought back to the human level' (Turner, Bonner and Marshall 2000: 166). Nancy Gibbs (2005), for example, endorses *Time* magazine's naming of Bono and the Gates' as its 'Persons of the Year' in 2005, by arguing that rock stars and billionaires are expected to be shallow, extravagant and removed from everyday social concerns because of their fame and wealth. The decision of certain celebrities to 'care about' causes that are neither sexy nor dignified 'in the ways that celebrities normally require' leaves no one with a valid reason to sit on the sidelines. New philanthropy, according to Gibbs (2005), not only encourages and demands active citizenship, but also promotes political passion, as opposed to passive pity, by building on the hope that the poor and socially vulnerable 'are fully capable of helping themselves if given the chance'.

Supporters of new philanthropy further praise celebrity involvement in international development issues for promoting global citizenship and extending democratic values. The concept of global citizenship is philanthropic insofar as it refers to a form of cosmopolitan and ethical citizenship that is motivated by both local interests (love of family, communal fairness, self-interest) and global interests (care for humanity and an active responsibility to tackle socio-economic inequality and safeguard the environment) ('What is Global Citizenship?' 1997; Noddings 2005). Celebrity involvement in development issues arguably promotes these goals by reaching new audiences, especially young voters in western-liberal democracies who may feel that the current political system not only denies them adequate representation, but also has failed to deliver an effective solution to the problem of dire poverty (Cooper 2007b: 6; Duvall 2007: 2). For example, the invitation extended to rock stars Sir Bob Geldof and Bono to speak about poverty in Africa at two G8 summits may constitute a positive response to the legitimacy problems associated with the G8 – an organization criticized at extensive mass protests in developed nations for being an exclusive club composed of elite representatives from wealthy countries and being negligent on its promise to address the structural imbalances in globalization (Cooper 2007b: 2–4). Celebrity advocacy is thus praised for its inclusiveness and democratizing potential, for its perceived capacity to break 'the hold of established elites on political agendas and the discourse about policy' and lend 'powerful voices to the disenfranchised in society and at the world stage' ('t Hart and Tindall 2009: 271).

Conversely, critics of new philanthropy, whether referring to celebrity philanthropy or corporate social responsibility, insist that it undermines the transformative potential of the discourse of humanitarian assistance – its promotion of the need for positive social change – by relying on market forces, that is, the economic system that arguably creates inequality, poverty and the need for philanthropy in the first place (Nickel and Eikenberry 2006: 5–6; Nickel 2012: 165). Viewed from this neo-Marxist perspective, new philanthropy is a false or bastardized form of philanthropy in that it promotes consumption, profit and media celebration as the best means to demonstrate care for humanity. Such marketized philanthropy celebrates a continued culture of global capitalism, and disguises the exploitative nature of big business by advancing the notion of 'giving back' through increased consumption – buying celebrity-endorsed products from which a portion of the profits are donated to humanitarian organizations – without acknowledging that it means giving back that which has already been taken away (Nickel and Eikenberry 2006: 9). It is not a discourse of social change, but rather a celebration by the privileged of the status quo. Hence, Slavoj Žižek (2006) describes Bill Gates as a paradigmatic figure of our times, both a ruthless entrepreneur and the greatest philanthropist in the history of humankind.

Celebrity philanthropy is further decried by critics for turning global citizenship into theatre (show business) and undermining the goals of the UN Charter – to create a world without war and a world that has respect for human rights, international law and social and economic progress (Alleyne 2005: 176; de Waal 2008; Nash 2008). Celebrity involvement with the UN is undoubtedly increasing. The UN's Department of Public Information ran two conferences for the UN's growing ranks of celebrity advocates between 2000 and 2002, calling the second conference *Celebrity Advocacy for the New Millennium* (Alleyne 2005: 177–9). At the start of 2015, 13 celebrities held the title of UN Messengers of Peace, a program that began in 1997, and around 170 famous people were involved in the Goodwill Ambassadors program, which began in 1953 ('Goodwill Ambassadors' n.d.; 'The United Nations Messengers of Peace' n.d.). The UN's adoption of celebrity advocates, as with that of many other non-governmental organizations (NGOs) and humanitarian agencies, aims to achieve brand awareness by distinguishing such organizations in the public eye from other competitors (Cottle and Nolan 2007: 865). Abandoning the former use of crisis imagery, the UN and other international organizations, such as Oxfam, have made celebrities the visual focus of campaigns that are designed to shape the global citizens of tomorrow by promoting public awareness of humanitarian issues, and the need to final lasting solutions to poverty and related injustice around the world (Alleyne 2005: 179; Fain 2008: 1).

For critics, the use of celebrities to promote global citizenship and humanitarian concerns is problematic because the aims of international aid organizations are potentially compromised by their growing reliance on 'the practices and predilections of the global media' (Cottle and Nolan 2007: 862, 865). This convergence is accused of leading to shallow and questionable media coverage of important social issues (Cottle and Nolan 2007: 869, 874), diverting money and organizational resources away from the work of aid, distorting agenda-setting through a focus on 'safe' international issues while indulging 'a more palatable liberalism that operates at a safe remove from controversial issues at home' (Magubane 2008: 19), and guiding fans towards ill-conceived solutions to complex problems (Cooper 2007b: 11–13; Littler 2008: 242). It is further condemned for exacerbating existing regional inequalities between North and South or developed western nations and 'the rest of the world' by promoting wealthy western celebrities and first-world hegemony, eliding the faces and voices of indigenous aid workers and the non-western poor, and positioning the non-destitute, non-celebrity consuming subject as a kind of neutral in-between (Cooper 2007b: 13; Cottle and Nolan 2007: 870; Duvall 2007; Fain 2008: 4; Littler 2008: 246; see also the collection of articles in a special issue of the *Third World Quarterly*, 35, 1 [2014]).

Critics further condemn the mediatized use of celebrities to promote global citizenship and humanitarian concerns for undermining the principles of representative democracy. A standard complaint is that celebrity advocacy and politics thrive on admiring fans, not on discriminating citizens, and enable a form of leadership that is driven by fame, admiration and dramaturgy, rather than by election, representation and accountability ('t Hart and Tindall 2009: 256; Kapoor 2013: 1, 115; Rojek 2014: 128). On the one hand, celebrity involvement in humanitarian-philanthropic causes is accused of hijacking the political process, replacing real substance with 'pseudoevents' and 'pseudoleadership' (Weiskel 2005: 399), or bringing 'more superficiality and less substance in our political process', and potentially skewing 'civil discourse towards solutions that may not represent effective long-term remedies for complex policy problems'

(West 2007: 1, 2; see also Jagger 2005: 13; Weiskel 2005; Fullilove 2006; Collier 2007: 4; Dieter and Kumar 2008). On the other hand, it is accused of providing an attractive yet problematic new vehicle for counter-consensus that not only detracts from more radical protest and political mobilization, but also obliterates alternative, progressive voices (Cooper 2007b: 13).

Last, but not the least, celebrities are tarred with the taint of false consciousness or even blatant hypocrisy because their philanthropic activism acts as a kind of brand extension, and is therefore a part of the process of making and consolidating a celebrity (Kapoor 2013: 19–25). Celebrity philanthropists not only get to 'stay in the news even when they have no new movie or CD to promote' (West 2007: 5), but also get to pull their personas out of the crude zone of narcissism and extravagant consumption and into the quasi-religious and heroic realm of altruism, compassion and caring (Harris 2003; de Waal 2008: 44; Littler 2008: 239, 241). Critics consequently present celebrity philanthropy as a contradiction in terms. Stars cannot be true philanthropists because of their vested interests as stakeholders in the capitalist system. They can only 'play' at being the saviours of the disadvantaged because of their advantaged status as the personalized embodiment of wealth and privilege gained from the systematic exploitation of the poor (Harris 2003; Littler 2008; Nickel and Eikenberry 2009; Rojek 2014: 133).

In short, critics conclude that celebrity philanthropy has transformed the perceived traditional emphasis of philanthropy on compassionate benevolence and social change into a racist form of humanitarian voyeurism and individualistic commercialism (de Waal 2008: 54; Fain 2008: 6–12; Nickel and Eikenberry 2009: 3–6; Rojek 2014: 130). Far from creating active global citizens, new philanthropy (re)creates a privileged class of western consumers who believe that they can deliver salvation to the rest of the world by consuming the 'right product' (see Collier 2007: 4; Magubane 2008: 13). Philanthropy allegedly is no longer focused on the sufferers and their plight, but rather on the personal philanthropic experiences of celebrities and donors (Fullilove 2006). Celebrity philanthropy consequently is condemned as symptomatic of the individualistic, overly commercialized and unequal nature of modern (western) societies (Harris 2003: 5).

Rethinking Philanthropy and Celebrity

Criticisms of celebrity as a means to market philanthropy and international humanitarian organizations are often well founded. Celebrity marketing per se is a risky business as numerous examples of individual perversity attest. In 1994, supermodel Naomi Campbell appeared naked in a People for the Ethical Treatment of Animals (PETA) campaign advertisement featuring the tag line 'We'd rather go naked than wear fur'. Much to PETA's dismay, she went on to disregard the informing ethos of the campaign by wearing a fur coat while walking down the runway at a Fendi fashion show in March 1997 (Destries 2007). Christian Dior in China, one of the world's strongest-growing cosmetics markets, suffered major setbacks when its celebrity endorser, Sharon Stone, implied that the millions of victims of the Sichuan earthquake in 2008 got what they deserved because of China's treatment of the Dalai Lama (Rein 2009). Both examples support the claim that celebrities are more concerned about their own agendas than the products and causes they endorse, and therefore constitute inadequate spokespersons for serious humanitarian issues. Examples can also be found that support claims that celebrity philanthropy as promoted through governments, big business, the UN and other international humanitarian agencies, should be abandoned or, at the very least, could be better managed. For example, the Band Aid phenomenon has been criticized for inadvertently prolonging the war in Ethiopia through the 'indiscriminate supply of humanitarian aid to the Mengistu government', which some people claim was diverted to purchase arms (de Waal 2008: 52; Rojek 2014: 130).

Yet, it is equally clear that adopting an attitude of blanket cynicism towards celebrity philanthropy is often not only 'unhelpful and likely undeserving' (Stewart 2007: 5), but also analytically misdirected. Negative examples of celebrity involvement in philanthropic work and activism can be countered with reference to positive, albeit contested, examples of the same. Just as the work of Bono and Geldof is credited with bringing the issue of poverty relief in Africa to the attention of audiences on a previously unimagined global scale (Cooper 2007b), so too actor Angelina Jolie's work with the UN Refugee Agency has received enormous publicity on celebrity Internet sites and in women's magazines (Duvall 2007; see also Bell and Marshall, in this book).

The United Nations Children's Fund (UNICEF), for example, contends that singers, actors and athletes are ideally situated to perform certain roles for the organization because leveraging fame can introduce social justice issues to large sectors of the population who might otherwise not have been interested. According to UNICEF, the use of fame or star power is 'positive' because:

> Celebrities attract attention, so they are in a position to focus the world's eyes on the needs of children, both in their own countries and by visiting field projects and emergency programmes abroad. They can make direct representations to those with the power to effect change. They can use their talents and fame to fundraise and advocate for children and support UNICEF's mission to ensure every child's right to health, education, equality and protection.
>
> ('UNICEF People' n.d.)

This conclusion is premised on the simple fact that celebrity gossip tabloids have vast readerships comprising both people who admire celebrities and those who 'love to hate' them. *People* magazine, for example, has a weekly circulation base of more than 3.5 million and its online version has estimated website traffic of 50 million page views per day (Lulofs 2013). Viewed from this perspective, some argue that it is not the superficiality of celebrity philanthropy and humanitarian activism that 'needs closer examination but the superficiality of the dismissal by its critics' (Cooper 2007b: 17).

Claims by critics that celebrity-mediated involvement in humanitarian causes has corrupted a 'better' form of global humanitarianism are especially problematic. Simon

Cottle and David Nolan (2007: 862) maintain that the NGO practice of using celebrities to 'brand' themselves in the media jeopardizes 'the very ethics and project of global humanitarianism that aid agencies historically have done so much to promote'. Daniel Harris (2003: 10–11) contends that celebrity philanthropy 'damages the effectiveness of relief agencies' because it undermines the integrity of philanthropic organizations as something that 'transcends the forces of capitalism'. New philanthropy obviously is not a 'cure-all' for the geo-political and socio-economic inequalities associated with economic globalization. However, the claim that consumption-based and celebrity-mediated philanthropy undermines 'authentic' humanitarian values is brought into question if we acknowledge that the development of international humanitarianism, like celebrity, has itself been closely tied to the historical development of capitalism and the mass media.

Reference to some historical examples undermines the implied dichotomy between philanthropy/international humanitarianism – understood as among the highest and noblest expressions of human civilization – and media sensationalism/celebrity culture – construed as evidence of the trivial and deplorable nature of contemporary consumer society. To cite Zine Magubane (2007: 374–5), during the nineteenth century the 'ideology of the "White Man's Burden"', with its emphasis on "Christianity, Civilization, and Commerce", married philanthropy, entertainment, and consumerism', turning imperial progress into a 'mass produced *consumer spectacle*' (original emphasis). The history of organized philanthropy and international humanitarianism is enmeshed with the history of European and US colonial projects, and thus the development of global capitalism.

Entertainment, spectacle and publicity were intrinsic components of western missionary work in South Africa during the mid-1800s, for example. Unlike colonial government officials and traders, the missions and missionaries relied on voluntary contributions from 'home', which meant that publication was crucial to their survival (Curtin 1964: 325). The strategic packaging and disseminating of images of African suffering and 'noble savagery' was an acknowledged way of generating public interest in and charitable donations for the 'civilizing mission'. Ethnographic texts and public exhibitions of native peoples and customs were not only extremely popular, but also made frequent reference to famous missionaries and their work in Africa (Magubane 2007: 374–5). Hence, 'consumption philanthropy' in the humanitarian arena and the associated 'othering' of the non-west is not exactly a new phenomenon, even though it now occurs on a different scale and in different forms.

The American Red Cross offers another example of the historical links between international humanitarianism and mass/consumption-based philanthropy. Kevin Rozario (2003: 427) describes how World War I and the imperatives of funding wartime relief turned amateur charity organizations such as the American Red Cross into national and professional fund-raising entities that resembled efficient corporations. These organizations set about 'hiring directors, recruiting teams of trained canvassers, planning campaigns, employing strict accounting methods, and developing the sort of door-to-door solicitation strategies' that make it difficult for 'ordinary' members of the public to avoid donating small amounts of money to worthy causes. They also began to pay attention to the 'science of publicity' and the question of 'how to appeal' in such a way as to be appealing to broad sectors of the population who might not be motivated by any such presumed universal human sentiment as 'compassion' (Rozario 2003: 427–8; see also Zunz 2012: 58–9).

Contrary to idealized conceptions of philanthropy as a *natural* affective response to the sufferings of strangers, charity organizations during the period of World War I began to exploit the opportunities presented by an emerging 'mass culture of movies and mass-circulation newspapers' to 'beguile' millions of people of modest means into 'acts of benevolence' (Rozario 2003: 423, 429). The American Red Cross, 'which was initially granted exclusive control over the distribution of government war films', began to promote international humanitarianism alongside often racist wartime propaganda and scenes of violence and human suffering (Rozario 2003: 432). It recruited stars from Broadway and Hollywood to promote mass fund-raising drives and publicized its activities in romantic, wartime motion pictures such as *The Spirit of the Red Cross* (dir. Flagg 1918). The *American Red Cross Magazine* also dramatically boosted its sales by running 'red-blood stories of suffering and want, of valor and sacrifice' alongside advertisements urging its readers to serve humanity by buying products from its sponsors, which included 'Wrigley's chewing gum, Jell-o, Lucky Strike cigarettes, beauty products, and even marital guides' (Rozario 2003: 437, 439). As these examples suggest, the claim that contemporary humanitarian organizations are compromised by their growing reliance on marketing and the media may be overstated. International aid organizations as we know them have always devoted as 'much attention to advertising as to ethics, and to "entertainment" as to education' (Rozario 2003: 429), because they depend on mass philanthropy.

Also contrary to understandings of philanthropy as the disinterested expression of a 'love of mankind' (Sawaya 2008: 203), it appears that successful philanthropic organizations are those that generate 'interested expressions' of humanitarian concern. The mediatized marketing exercises of the early American Red Cross were undoubtedly effective. Its membership swelled from 20,000 in 1914 to 20 million, with an additional 11 million 'junior' members, by the declaration of Armistice on 11 November 1918. In addition, the American Red Cross raised USD 400 million during the same period (Rozario 2003: 433). Although the vast majority of new members joined the organization after the US entered the war in April 1917, the Red Cross flourished not simply by selling patriotism and 'anti-Hun' sentiment, but also by competing with commercial ventures through the creation of consumer 'wants' and the provision of 'thrills' (Rozario 2003: 444). The organization's publications, films and fund-raising efforts aimed to elicit compassionate benevolence by combining the act of feeling good in the moral and political sense with the act of feeling good in the pleasure sense. Charity consequently may be a longstanding feature of human society. However, as Rozario (2003: 419) concludes, humanitarianism only became a mass phenomenon when philanthropy became a commercial marketing venture, and 'donors began to be treated and courted as consumers who had to be entertained', in order to meet the funding requirements of wartime relief efforts (see also Thompson 2002).

Successful philanthropic organizations inevitably exploit individual ego and desire to obtain 'interested' resources because they trade in compassion, an emotion that implies a social relation, with the emphasis being placed on what the privileged spectator *over here* feels and does in practice for the suffering 'other' *over there* (see Berlant 2004). The term 'compassion' derives from 'the Latin *com*, together with, and *pati*, to suffer'. From the fourteenth century to the start of the seventeenth century the term described suffering together with one another, participation in suffering, or fellow feeling between equals, *and* an emotion felt 'when a person is moved by the suffering or distress of another, and by the desire to relieve it by offering succor' ('Compassion, n.' 2012 [1989]). However, the first sense of the term has become obsolete.

Compassion in the contemporary sense of the word is an emotion felt on behalf of someone in distress by someone who is free from it, and who is in this respect their superior, and has the surplus resources required to ameliorate another's suffering, *if* they wish to or feel obliged to do so ('Compassion, n.' 2012 [1989]). The modern association of philanthropy with voluntarism and/or moral obligation is indicated by the draft inclusion in the *Oxford English Dictionary Online* in 2002 of a new term 'compassion fatigue' – 'apathy or indifference towards the suffering of others or to charitable causes acting on their behalf' ('Compassion, n.' 2012 [1989]). Reference to notions of voluntarism and moral obligation suggest that the compassionate actor has to be induced to 'give' by receiving something in return – a commercial product and/or the individual pleasure/relief of knowing that one has helped to meet the expressed needs of the 'deserving' as relayed through the public entreaty of an humanitarian organization, perhaps with public acknowledgement. Both forms of recognition or 'reward' are based to varying degrees on the hierarchical categorization of human suffering in terms of deserving recipients of donations and those who are deemed to be less deserving by default.

In short, there is no 'authentic' form of organized philanthropy that can be held up as a mirror to reveal a set of problems specific to the new phenomenon of celebrity philanthropy (see also Marshall, in this book). Philanthropy per se is an ethically complicated business because it thrives on the interaction between two forms of socio-political inequality that are tied to modern conceptions of 'good' citizenship. This is the assumed obligation and benevolence of those who have '(the power of the rich)', and the assumed rights and entitlement of those who need '(the power of the poor)' (Garber 2004: 26).

Claims by critics that mediatized celebrity involvement in humanitarian causes encourages social and political apathy are also problematic. Kapoor (2013: 1) argues that 'celebrity humanitarianism' is 'fundamentally depoliticizing' and 'contributes to a "postdemocratic" political landscape, which appears outwardly open and consensual, but is in fact managed by unaccountable elites'. Harris (2003: 12, 10) contends that the professionalization of philanthropy, as exemplified by celebrity philanthropy, has helped to create an 'apathetic, uninvolved society' because 'it reinforces the notion among the general public that charity is the exclusive province of the fabulously rich who are the sole members of the community capable of solving social problems'. Another common criticism, as noted by Paul 't Hart and Karen Tindall (2009: 256), is that celebrity politics, including celebrity activism on international humanitarian causes, thrives by virtue of the public behaving as 'admiring fans' rather than 'discriminating citizens'. Consequently what celebrity activism offers those who follow it is a leadership of the 'well-known' rather than a leadership of the 'well-qualified', echoing Boorstin's (1972: 57) famous dismissal of celebrities as people who are known merely for their 'well-knownness'.

This style of criticism is misdirected for at least two reasons. First, the 'well-knownness' of celebrities may empower them to talk to an extraordinary range of audiences and political leaders on subjects about which they are not 'official experts'. However, it does not empower them to act with impunity or without restraint because they are subject to constant media surveillance and public scrutiny (Stewart 2007). Far from constituting an easy, self-serving and 'unaccountable' means to stay famous (Kapoor 2013), celebrity philanthropists and activists are subject to forms of public scrutiny that equal, if not exceed, 'the accountability regime of parliamentary scrutiny and political journalism' ('t Hart and Tindall 2009: 273). Celebrity philanthropy and the engagement of fans with such activism could therefore function to stimulate public involvement in humanitarian endeavors and/or demand greater transparency from relevant policymakers ('t Hart and Tindall 2009: 271). This has certainly proved to be the case in the authoritarian PRC, where repeated accusations of celebrity charity fraud in Internet chat rooms have forced A-list celebrities – international film star Zhang Ziyi, for example – to make the financing of their philanthropic activities more transparent (see Jeffreys, in this book).

Second, the use of social media by fans to mobilize their peers to engage with humanitarian causes in the symbolic name of a given celebrity is a development that challenges understandings of celebrity-related philanthropy as fundamentally a top-down media-led exercise that encourages social alienation and political apathy. In China, for example, fans of pop music and film stars have sidestepped both the mainstream media and government organizations by establishing philanthropic initiatives in the name of specific celebrities. These initiatives typically begin as transient communities built around celebrity and contexts provided by the recent expansion of social media in China, rather than as registered charities with legal support. Despite the time and energy required to organize them, they usually have no connection initially to a real-life celebrity other than the symbolic community created by the use of their name and they provide little or no financial benefit to the individual fans concerned.

The successful nature of some fan-driven philanthropic initiatives has prompted their named celebrities to subsequently offer them different forms of support. Pop star Li Yuchun now actively endorses the fund created by her fans – the Fans of Li Yuchun Charity Fund (*Yumi aixin jijin*) – when she won a Chinese reality television music competition, the most-watched TV show in Chinese history, in 2005. Li Yuchun, or Chris Lee as she is known in English, has since released more than 50 number-one singles in the PRC and is the first mainland Chinese pop star to have won multiple international music awards, including topping superstar Justin Bieber to win the award for Best Worldwide Act at the 2013 MTV

European Music Awards gala, with 'a total of more than 100 million global votes' (Li 2013). Since 2006, fans of Li Yuchun have worked with the Chinese Red Cross Foundation to raise funds of around CNY 10 million to help children with leukemia and improve rural health care. Fans have also established an online charity auction site and six health centres in poor rural regions of China that are run mostly by volunteers ('Yumi aixin jijin' 2011; 'Yumi aixin jijin 2013 niandu juanzeng kuan' 2014).

These forms of social activism are neither a direct product of celebrity egoism, nor the imperatives of branded corporate capitalism. This suggests the need for different approaches to the analysis of the development and impact of celebrity philanthropy. A more nuanced approach would pay attention to how celebrity and celebrity-related philanthropy operates in cultural contexts other than the US and the UK (see Allatson, in this book). In addition, it would consider how new forms of media have changed the way in which celebrities can aid philanthropic causes.

Conclusion

The term 'philanthropy' is imbued with critical and utopian – and hence debatable – 'longings for transcendence of the contemporary economic and political scene' (Sawaya 2008: 203), which are exacerbated by the addition of the term 'celebrity'. Supporters of new philanthropy, including celebrity involvement in humanitarian causes, maintain a utopian faith in the ultimate capacity of neoliberal capitalism to bring prosperity to all (Bishop and Green 2008; Kiviat and Gates 2008). Critics, by contrast, suggest that new philanthropists are 'the enemy of every true progressive struggle today' (Žižek 2006), precisely because they promote the expansion of the free-market economy (see also Nickel 2012; Kapoor 2013; Rojek 2014). Celebrities enter into this debate as the branded faces of humanitarian causes who also embody individual wealth and privilege.

Neither point of view engages with the phenomenon of new philanthropy and its prominent offshoot of celebrity philanthropy in a constructive manner. The utopianism of proponents of new philanthropy is easily brought into question. While the expansion of the capitalist economy may lead to ongoing increases in wealth, there is no reason to assume that the wealth that is created will be distributed equally or 'fairly', or even in a way which allows all participants to live. It is also unrealistic to assume that those with wealth, whether CEOs or entertainment celebrities, will always make correct and socially responsible decisions about how that wealth can be used to the 'greater benefit of humankind', and that those decisions will necessarily improve upon the welfare initiatives of not-for-profit organizations and nation states.

However, the arguments of critics of new philanthropy are underpinned by an equally implausible utopianism – that the free-market economy can and must be dismantled and the welfare state ideal can and must be revitalized (Kapoor 2013: 124–7). This option is problematic because the redistribution of wealth via a centralized state system and/or heavier taxes has proved to be unpopular historically, being associated with unwieldy, rigid, ineffective and corrupt modes of governance. Likewise, it discounts examples of nations, such as those in Latin America, which have no history of welfare state governance as would be understood in western European or North American terms, and no significant traditions of philanthropy as understood in western capitalist and state terms. Rather, scholarship on philanthropy in Latin America and among Latinos in the US indicates instead a long history of religious giving within the Catholic Church apparatus and via mutual-aid organizations, and an established tradition among the continent's class elites of funding building projects and donating to causes relating to disaster relief, children, education and the arts ('Latino Philanthropy Literature Review' 2003; Sanborn and Protocarrero 2005; see also Allatson, in this book).

Given the impracticality of effecting system-wide changes in the immediate future, critics of celebrity involvement in humanitarian causes are obliged to suggest how organized philanthropy might be done otherwise, and none does this convincingly. They offer criticism tinged with moral outrage, but little in the way of concrete suggestions. Moreover, despite the proliferation of intellectual complaints about the privileged, superficial and racist nature of celebrity philanthropy in the international arena, there are hardly any *empirical* studies of how celebrity-involved or celebrity-inspired philanthropy operates in practice in the context of developing countries, and what it does for local recipients and how it is viewed and understood by them. Such studies are vital to any informed critique. As the example of China would suggest, empirical studies of the local development and impact of celebrity philanthropy in developing countries are required, in order to provide a comparative framework for analysis, to redress the western and Anglophone focus of existing analyses, and to understand the possibilities that may arise from different forms of organized and enculturated philanthropy.

Acknowledgements

This research was supported under the Australian Research Council's Future Fellowship (FT100100238) funding scheme.

References

Alleyne, M.D. (2005) 'The United Nations' celebrity diplomacy', *SAIS Review*, 25, 1: 175–84.
Andersson, J. (2007) 'Pop-culture icons as agents of change? The roles and functions of celebrity activists in peace- and development-related global issues', MA thesis, Växjö University, School of Social Sciences, Department of Peace and Development Studies, http://urn.kb.se/resolve?urn=urn:nbn:se:vxu:diva-1710. Accessed 9 January 2015.
Andrew, D.T. (1989) *Philanthropy and Police: London Charity in the Eighteenth Century*, Princeton, NJ: Princeton University Press.

Berlant, L. (2004) 'Compassion (and withholding)', in L. Berlant (ed.) *Compassion: The Culture and Politics of an Emotion*, New York: Routledge, pp. 1–14.

Bishop, M. (2007) 'Fighting global poverty: Who'll be relevant in 2020?' Brookings Blum Roundtable, 1 August, www.brookings.edu/events/2007/~/media/Files/Programs/Global/brookings_blum_roundtable/2007bishop.pdf. Accessed 1 April 2012.

Bishop, M., and Green, M. (2008) *Philanthrocapitalism: How the Rich Can Save the World*, New York: Bloomsbury Press.

Boorstin, D. (1972 [1961]) *The Image: A Guide to Pseudo-Events in America*, New York: Atheneum.

Carnegie, A. (1889) 'Wealth', *North American Review*, CCCXCL, 391: 653–64.

Collier, P. (2007) *The Bottom Billion: Why the Poorest Countries Are Failing and What Can Be Done About It*, Oxford, UK: Oxford University Press.

'Compassion, n.' (2012 [1989]) *Oxford English Dictionary*, second edition, 1989; online version March 2012, Oxford, UK: Oxford University Press, http://www.oed.com/view/Entry/37475. Accessed 29 March 2012.

Cooper, A. (2007a) *Celebrity Diplomacy*, Boulder; London: Paradigm Publishers.

Cooper, A. (2007b) 'Celebrity diplomacy and the G8: Bono and Bob as legitimate international actors', Working Paper 29, The Centre for International Governance, http://www.isn.ethz.ch/isn/Digital-Library/Publications/Detail/?ord516=OrgaGrp&ots591=0c54e3b3-1e9c-be1e-2c24-a6a8c7060233&lng=en&id=39553. Accessed 9 January 2015.

Cottle, S., and Nolan, D. (2007) 'Global humanitarianism and the changing aid-media field', *Journalism Studies*, 8, 6: 862–78.

Curtin, P. (1964) *The Image of Africa*, Madison: University of Wisconsin Press.

de Waal, A. (2008) 'The humanitarian carnival: A celebrity vogue', *World Affairs: A Journal of Ideas and Debate*, Fall: 43–55.

Destries, M. (2007) 'Naomi Campbell lashes out at PETA, still sounds lame', *Ecorazzi*, 13 September, http://www.ecorazzi.com/2007/09/13/naomi-campbell-lashes-out-at-peta-still-sounds-lame/. Accessed 9 January 2015.

Dieter, H., and Kumar, R. (2008) 'The downside of celebrity diplomacy: The neglected complexity of development', *Global Governance*, 14: 259–64.

Duvall, S.-S. (2007) '"Ambassador mom": Angelina Jolie, celebrity activism, and institutional power', paper presented at the annual meeting of the International Communication Association, San Francisco, 11 December, http://www.allacademic.com/meta/p172714_index.html. Accessed 18 January 2011.

Fain, S. (2008) 'Celebrities, poverty and the mediapolis: A case study of the ONE Campaign', paper presented at the *London School of Economics Media and Humanity Conference*, September, London, http://voices.yahoo.com/the-one-campaign-celebrity-poverty-mediapolis-3097851.html. Accessed 20 March 2014.

Flagg, J. (dir.) (1918) *The Spirit of the Red Cross*, motion picture, US: Committee of the National Association of the Motion Picture Industry.

'Foundation Fact Sheet' (1999–2015) Bill and Melinda Gates Foundation, http://www.gatesfoundation.org/about/Pages/foundation-fact-sheet.aspx. Accessed 9 January 2015.

Fullilove, M. (2006) 'Celebrities should stick to their day jobs', *Financial Times*, 1 February.

Garber, M. (2004) 'Compassion', in L. Berlant (ed.) *Compassion: The Culture and Politics of an Emotion*, New York: Routledge, pp. 15–28.

Gibbs, N. (2005) 'The good Samaritans', *Time*, 19 December, http://www.time.com/time/magazine/article/0,9171,1142278,00.html. Accessed 9 January 2015.

The Giving Pledge (n.d.) Givingpledge.org, http://givingpledge.org/. Accessed 5 March 2015.

'Goodwill Ambassadors' (n.d.) United Nations Messengers of Peace, http://outreach.un.org/mop/goodwill-ambassadors/. Accessed 9 January 2015.

Harris, D. (2003) 'Ladies among lepers: The nonprofit celebrity', *Southwest Review*, 88, 2: 291–300.

Huddart, S. (2007) 'Do we need another hero? Understanding celebrities' roles in advancing social causes', *McGill-McConnell Papers*, The Centre for Voluntary Sector Research and Development.

Jagger, B. (2005) 'Real people power, or pernicious platitudes?', *New Statesman*, 11 July, 13, http://www.newstatesman.com/200507110006. Accessed 29 March 2012.

Kapoor, I. (2013) *Celebrity Humanitarianism: The Ideology of Global Charity*, Abingdon, Oxon: Routledge.

Kiviat, B. and Gates, B. (2008) 'Making capitalism more creative', *Time*, 31 July, http://www.time.com/time/magazine/article/0,9171,1828417,00.html. Accessed 9 January 2015.

'Latino Philanthropy Literature Review' (2003) Donor Research Project, Center on Philanthropy and Civil Society, City University of New York, http://www.philanthropy.org/programs/literature_reviews/latino_lit_review.pdf. Accessed 9 January 2015.

Li, S. (2013) 'Chris Lee wins MTV EMA Worldwide Act', China.org.cn, 11 November, http://www.china.org.cn/arts/2013-11/11/content_30560519.htm. Accessed 9 January 2015.

Littler, J. (2008) '"I feel your pain": Cosmopolitan charity and the public fashioning of the celebrity soul', *Social Semiotics*, 18, 2: 237–51.

'Look to the Stars: The World of Celebrity Giving' (2006–2015) Look to the Stars, http://www.looktothestars.org/. Accessed 9 January 2015.

Lulofs, N. (2013) 'The Top 25 U.S. consumer magazines for June 2013', Alliance for Audited Media, 6 August, http://www.auditedmedia.com/news/blog/2013/august/the-top-25-us-consumer-magazines-for-june-2013.aspx. Accessed 9 January 2015.

Luscombe, B. (2006) 'Madonna finds a cause', *Time*, 3 August, http://content.time.com/time/world/article/0,8599,1222449,00.html. Accessed 9 January 2015.

Magubane, Z. (2007) 'Oprah in South Africa: The politics of coevalness and the creation of a black public sphere', *Safundi*, 8, 4: 373–93.

Magubane, Z. (2008) 'The (Product)Red man's burden: Charity, celebrity, and the contradictions of coevalness', *Journal of Pan African Studies*, 2, 6: 1–25.

Nash, K. (2008) 'Global citizenship as show business: The cultural politics of Make Poverty History', *Media, Culture & Society*, 30: 167–81.

Nickel, P.M. (2012) 'Philanthromentality: Celebrity parables as technologies of transfer', *Celebrity Studies*, 3, 2: 164–82.

Nickel, P., and Eikenberry, A. (2006) 'The discourse of marketized philanthropy in fast capitalism', unpublished, Center for Public Administration and Policy, Virginia Tech, Blacksburg.

Nickel, P., and Eikenberry, A. (2009) 'A critique of the discourse of marketized philanthropy', *American Behavioral Scientist*, 52, 7: 974–89.

Noddings, N. (ed.) (2005) *Educating Citizens for Global Awareness*, New York: Teachers College Press.

'Our Story' (n.d.) (RED), http://www.red.org/en/about. Accessed 10 January 2015.

'Philanthropy' (n.d.) Philanthropy Australia, http://www.philanthropy.org.au/about-us/vision-and-mission/. Accessed 9 January 2015.

Rein, S. (2009) 'Celebrities and China: Marketing hell', *Forbes*, http://www.forbes.com/2009/02/11/china-phelps-drugs-leadership_0211_marketing.html. Accessed 9 January 2015.

Richey, L.A., and Ponte, S. (2008) 'Better (RED)™ than dead? Celebrities, consumption and international aid', *Third World Quarterly*, 29, 4: 711–29.

Rojek, C. (2014) '"Big citizen" celanthropy and its discontents', *International Journal of Cultural Studies*, 17, 2: 127–41.

Rozario, K. (2003) '"Delicious horrors": Mass culture, the Red Cross, and the appeal of modern American humanitarianism', *American Quarterly*, 55, 3: 417–55.

Sanborn, C., and Protocarrero, F. (eds) (2005) *Philanthropy and Social Change in Latin America*, Cambridge, MA: Harvard University Press.

Sawaya, F. (2008) 'Capitalism and philanthropy in the (new) gilded age', *American Quarterly*, 60, 1: 201–15.

Stewart, D. (2007) 'Celebrity led humanitarian interventions: Blanket cynicism vs. a framework for success', 29 November, http://www.winstonchurchillbc.org/images/PDF/2008%201st%20Prize%20paper%20-%20Drew%20Stewart.pdf. Accessed 10 October 2010.

Sulek, M. (2010) 'On the modern meaning of philanthropy', *Nonprofit and Voluntary Sector Quarterly*, 39, 2: 193–212.

't Hart, P., and Tindall, K. (2009) 'Leadership by the famous: Celebrity as political capital', in J. Kane, H. Patapan, and P. 't Hart (eds) *Dispersed Democratic Leadership: Origins, Dynamics, and Implications*, Oxford, UK: Oxford University Press, pp. 255–78.

'The United Nations Messengers of Peace' (n.d.) United Nations Messengers of Peace, http://outreach.un.org/mop/. Accessed 9 January 2015.

Thompson, A.S. (2002) 'Publicity, philanthropy and commemoration: British society and the war', in D. Omissi and A.S. Thompson (eds) *The Impact of the South African War*, New York: Palgrave, pp. 511–27.

Traub, J. (2008) 'The celebrity solution', *New York Times Magazine*, 9 March, p. 38.

Tsaliki, L., Frangonikolopoulos, C.A., and Huliaras, A. (2011) *Transnational Celebrity Activism in Global Politics*, Bristol, UK; Chicago, IL: Intellect Press.

Turner, G., Bonner, F., and Marshall, P.D. (2000) *Fame Games: The Production of Celebrity in Australia*, Melbourne: Cambridge University Press.

'UNICEF People' (n.d.) UNICEF, http://www.unicef.org/people/people_ambassadors.html. Accessed 9 January 2015.

'What is Global Citizenship?' (1997) Oxfam Education, http://www.oxfam.org.uk/education/gc/what_and_why/what/. Accessed 20 March 2014.

Weiskel, T.C. (2005) 'From sidekick to sideshow: Celebrity, entertainment, and the politics of distraction. Why Americans are 'sleepwalking towards the end of the Earth', *American Behavioral Scientists*, 49, 3: 393–403.

West, D.M. (2007) *Angelina, Mia, and Bono: Celebrities and International Development*, Washington, DC: The Brookings Institution.

Wheeler, M. (2011) 'Celebrity politics and cultural citizenship: UN Goodwill Ambassadors and Messengers of Peace', in L. Tsaliki, C.A. Frangonikolopoulos, and A. Huliaras (eds) *Transnational Celebrity Activism in Global Politics*, Bristol, UK; Chicago, IL: Intellect Press, pp. 45–62.

Wilson, J. (2014) 'Stardom, sentimental education, and the shaping of global citizens', *Cinema Journal*, 53, 2: 27–49.

'Yumi aixin jijin' [Fans of Li Yuchun Charity Fund] (2011) *Zhongguo Yulewang*, 1 August, http://news.67.com/cishanquan/2011/08/01/279827.html. Accessed 9 January 2015.

'Yumi aixin jijin 2013 niandu juanzeng kuan wu shou zhi qingkuang shenji baogao' [Fans of Li Yuchun Charity Fund Annual Financial Report 2013] (2014) Chinese Red Cross Foundation, 19 August, http://new.crcf.org.cn/html/2014-08/24784.html. Accessed 12 January 2015.

Žižek, S. (2006) 'The liberal communists of Porto Davos', *In These Times*, 11 April, http://www.inthesetimes.com/site/main/article/2574/. Accessed 9 January 2015.

Zunz, O. (2012) *Philanthropy in America: A History*, Princeton; Oxford, UK: Princeton University Press.

Chapter 3

Philanthropy, Celebrity and Incoherence

Jonathan Paul Marshall

Aid, and celebrity philanthropy in particular, is often criticized as if such help was always a simple matter of it defending, or governing, those structures of power and order that produce the need for philanthropy in the first place (Eikenberry 2006; Kapoor 2013). This argument should not be downplayed; however, it might not be the only line to the story. Criticisms of celebrity philanthropy might equally stem from a desire for tidiness and order in the world that does not acknowledge the complexities of the situation or human motivation, or of the difficulties of virtue or of unintended effects, and itself does little to fix the situation. Indeed, demands for order and for divisions into good and evil may also lead to significant problems in dealing with the difficulty, magnitude and 'horror' of the troubles facing the world.

This chapter explores 'incoherence' as a response that, if stayed with, has the potential to produce an opening that may allow us to deal with overwhelming mess, chaos, divergence and despair, and to build empathy without foreclosing those possibilities into premature order, certainty or condemnation. The term 'incoherence' refers to disorder of speech, disorder of argument and disorder of intent and results, that is, to a general lack of congruence and coherence. The argument proceeds by looking at the relationships between help, exchange and empathy, moving into a brief history of 'help' (primarily in the UK) and finally exploring an interview with Angelina Jolie – film star, Goodwill Ambassador for the UNHCR, and Special Envoy to the current High Commissioner of the UNHCR. I argue that incoherencies are inevitable and often useful if not dismissed, and emulation of celebrity may be preferable to attempted compulsion or control.

Help, Exchange and Empathy

Help always involves a potential inequity of exchange, an incoherence that can produce tensions. When the helper helps, the suffering people helped receive, and may never be able to make equal return. This is the prime dynamic of 'charity', where the giving directly invokes deference, praise, status or a sense of virtue received by the giver, in exchange for their charitable gift. As the well-known anthropological theory of the 'gift' implies, such inequality contributes to maintaining power and status differentials while simultaneously allowing the forging of bonds (Mauss 1969; Cheal 1988). Inequality also disrupts communication, as the receiver can no longer completely tell their truth without risking loss of the exchange and is likely to resent, or attempt to manipulate, the giver.

Not all forms of gifting are the same and, as an initial proposal, we may be able to distinguish the following types of help/exchange:

1. *'kindness'*, gifts of help without ties
2. *'charity'*, usually, but not always, semi-random gifts of help that imply or demand recognition of status differential by the helped. Charity builds up both separation and bonds
3. *'meritorious charity'*, the main official function of charity is spiritual benefit to the giver
4. *'charity of compulsion'*, in which people are restrained or forced to labour for charity – the obligation expected from charity is violent and formalized
5. *'philanthropy'*, organized 'kindness' or 'charity' usually involving visible or public gifts of money to an organization that raises, publicizes, administers and allocates the funds. Any help received can be distanced from the givers
6. *'demand obligation'*, in which the helped have a socially recognized ability to demand recognition from those with more
7. *'impersonal welfare'*, in which people have a recognized right to certain types of aid, usually from an impersonal source such as the state.

Some of this help may primarily be aimed at 'social control' and some at maintaining 'community'. However, maintaining community usually involves some attempt to maintain order and control, and attempts at social control are often aimed at maintaining an ideal of community; hence, an ambiguity, or incoherence, in the functions and consequences of help is always possible. Incoherence is further emphasized, as we cannot completely predict the consequences of all acts of help, and so what is intended to help community or to maintain control may have unintended, disorganizing or beneficial effects that differ with a person's social position. This lack of precise control is a feature of all acts in complex interactive systems, and is magnified by the possibility of human reflection upon the consequences of acts and the acts of others (Prigogine 1996; Soros 2011). Similarly, demand obligation or impersonal welfare lowers the status differential built into unequal exchange, diminishes obligation, and allows the possibility that the receiver can criticize the giver and their gifts. However, it can also demotivate the givers. The givers may start to feel put upon as relationships become onerous or tenuous, and there is little reward or acknowledgement. We cannot make a simple division of all acts of help into 'good' and 'bad' so as to salve our conscience, or the consciousness of our privilege.

As well as involving exchange, help also involves a degree of empathy or fellow feeling; a feeling that something should be done to help. Humans generally seem to be more compassionate towards those they know, identify with, or classify as similar to themselves (Berreby 2006; Marshall 2006). While empathy is a 'natural' feature of human life, it has to be built, as do other human capabilities like language. Empathy towards people outside a person's immediate acquaintance, especially towards those a person may have reason to dismiss or condemn, is not guaranteed. What is classified as 'like us' can be extended by membership of empires, religions, appearances of intimacy or making other people seem to have similar features to us and be part of our wider group. Such similarities appear weaker the more distant, opposed or inferior the other groups and cultures are classified as being (Turner et al. 1987). With foreign aid, as there are few personal relationships, empathy has to become almost impersonal. This sets up another incoherence. Empathy, in being extended where there are few personal contacts, can override the significant differences (which would make the person not one of us) through fictional similarity, and in doing so almost guarantee misunderstanding and lack of precision in the help provided. Again, while impersonal welfare makes help more equitable (and less prone to 'charity begins at home'), it further diminishes the status accrued from putting those being helped into debt or obligation, so rendering the impulse less rewarding and less easy to motivate.

In the information society, in which people are continually asked to be compassionate towards people they do not know and do not identify with, empathy is stretched and resistances to it arise (Höijer 2004). What is known as 'compassion fatigue' may prevail when the scale of the problems begin to dawn upon us ('no matter what we do it will never end'), there is little self-identification between the sources of charity and those who receive the charity, and little local payoff for giving.

One solution for this problem may be emulation. Societies often have exemplars and 'culture heroes' whose (often fictionalized) lives show people how to live: Kings and Queens, founders of Empire, heroes of the Republic, revolutionaries, founding fathers, soldiers, saints, composers, poets, and so on (Cubitt and Warren 2000). One way of building empathy or benevolence and compassion, especially over classificatory distance, is by putting forward exemplars of such acts, so that people may come to emulate them in a socially reinforced manner. This requires 'celebrity'; namely that the exemplars be publicized, well-known and admired. Emulation is a major feature in all help, including celebrity philanthropy.

In summary, the connection between help, gifting and obligation makes help problematic. Receiving a gift implies obligation, inferiority or dependence on the part of the receiver, and hence can undermine accurate communication, and set up inequalities and the preservation of what maintains the inequality (see also Jeffreys, in this book). Conflict can arise between help as maintaining order and help as maintaining community, or between serving one's self and serving community. Building empathy can delete the recognition of important differences, and while impersonal giving can be freeing for the recipient, it can also delete motivation from the giver, and a new motivation, such as emulation, is needed. These incoherencies shape the paradoxical dynamics of helping, and are common throughout history, with motivation being built from spiritual reward, compulsion, gaining a sense of control, or through emulation.

A Short History of Incoherent Help

Donna Andrew (1989) suggests that 'pre-modern' charity in Britain was primarily meritorious, focusing on the religious benefits to the donor more than on the help given to the recipient. Giving was an act of devotion that compensated for sin and demonstrated faith (Andrew 1989: 197). It was promoted 'that thereby they might render the deity propitious to them', with the poor praying for their benefactors in return (Burn 1764: 3). Tales of saints, and the strength of their relics, acted as exemplars of Christian charity and its rewards. Charity was also given from the tithes compulsorily paid to the local Bishop (Burn 1764: 2–5). Such charity was not separated from obligation and deference, and might be considered self-oriented as it benefitted the giver socially and spiritually. While it may have produced communal bonds, it did not produce the fixed communal order that the dominant classes desired, with charity supposedly being abused by wandering vagabonds (Burn 1764: 5).

Over time, meritorious charity both clashed and combined with acts of Parliament that attempted to make local authorities responsible for their indigents, punish wandering beggars, scholars or folk healers, and set up workhouses, with the apparent intention of making being unable to support oneself or one's family as unpleasant and punitive as possible; empathy was to be broken. A vagrant would be stripped and publicly whipped 'till his body be bloody' (Burn 1764: 27). Meritorious charity given to such people could result in heavy fines (Burn 1764: 17–20, 57), making kindness guilty and covert and threatening the community order it was supposed to defend (see Lord Hale in Burn 1764: 137). Vagabonds could also be enslaved and, from Charles II onwards, enslaved and transported to overseas plantations (Burn 1764: 32). Houses of correction were established for able-bodied poor: 'there to be straightly kept, as well in diet as in work, and also punished from time to time' (Burn 1764: 82). This charity of compulsion is clearly intended as social control. However, these laws also failed to keep people bound to their community, as self-sufficiency was broken, there was little work available and the local 'poor taxes' resented or misappropriated – there was an incentive to expel the poor. People continued to flood into the cities from the country, providing the cheap semi-starving labour that helped form capitalism (Marx 1954: 671–701). The larger the city, the less obvious the vagabond; impersonality became freedom of a sort. Charity of compulsion attempted to forcibly preserve social 'order' in the face of its ongoing failure.

With a growing recognition of this failure during the eighteenth century, older communal forms of charity were supplemented by organized private charities aimed at resolving or suppressing social problems (the two actions are hard to distinguish). These efforts aimed at 'reforming immorality', changing the workforce into docile workers and improving the wealth of the nation. In '1650 London had few if any privately organized and financed charitable institutions, by 1800 it had dozens' (Andrew 1989: 1). Writing in the eighteenth century, Richard Burn (1764: 129) states that the 'ancient laws' were 'to prevent enormities; the present laws are to encourage industry. Anciently, the *maintenance* of the poor was principally intended; their *employment*, at present, merits equally our regard'.

While Michel Foucault (2003: 242–63) appears to emphasize that in France these concerns over the quality of national populations ('biopolitics') originated with the emergence of modern forms of government, Andrew's focus (1989) suggests these changes, in the UK, began in private philanthropy. Civic-minded merchants formed the 'joint stock or "associated" charity' that raised money for foundling hospitals, orphanages and educational facilities, which provided work training for impoverished youth, 'penitent Magdalens' and criminals (Andrew 1989: 49, 122–7). These facilities resembled workhouses and prisons. The philanthropies targeted wealthy donors through charity balls and bazaars, charity sermons and dinners and benefits at theatres and operas (Andrew 1989: 80–5). Philanthropy was entangled with both entertainment and imposition of social order from the beginning. It intertwined charity with displays of wealth and generosity before other wealthy people who emulated each other in competition of gifting. The 'worthiness' of such causes was shown, not so much by their effects on the recipients, but by transparent management and accounting practices (money was not to be wasted), and by ensuring that the recipients were seen as 'deserving' rather than 'undeserving' of assistance (Andrew 1989: 83–5). Presumably, the cause's 'worth' also relied on it not upsetting those who sponsored it. This is always a problem for help; it will usually aim at pleasing its giver's sense of order, which may not be the sense of order possessed by the helped.

However, in organized philanthropy donors do not receive personal genuflection from the receivers of gifts of help; the receivers may not even know who the donors are, other than their generalized 'betters'. Charity becomes more impersonal. As an unintended and incoherent consequence, this growth in impersonality could have made the ability of the working class to demand help in hard times as a right, rather than a discipline, not be heard as completely unreasonable, during the struggles for what came to be called the welfare state in the late nineteenth and early twentieth centuries. The virtuous condescension of the visiting donor, faced with a less connected underclass able to make demands, began to appear uneasy and ineffective (Siegel 2012).

These philanthropic organizations were primarily devoted to local or national philanthropy. As Elaine Jeffreys argues in Chapter 1 of this book, celebrity came into internationalized philanthropy as a necessary part of its growth. Missionaries, such as Dr. Livingstone (1813–1873), became exemplars of help in the nineteenth century. This again emphasizes the paradoxical nature of help: the imperialistic forces that might trivialize, or even destroy 'foreign' self-sufficiency, are also those that bring the issues to the fore.

Celebrities provided a focus and bridge with which to build empathy. The first modern, truly international, celebrity philanthropist might be Albert Schweitzer (1875–1965), the German theologian, missionary, doctor, philosopher and music theorist, who set up a hospital in Lambaréné in Africa (Picht 1964). People such as Schweitzer gave up considerable wealth and success in order to help others in fairly dangerous conditions. They risked anger from establishment forces that considered the people they worked with to be mere brutes, or in need of violent governing, and later risked anger from those who thought they treated the locals patronizingly, or who thought they had no business protesting against war (Picht 1964: 22). This was also the case with people like General Booth (1829–1912), who founded the Salvation Army, and who, like Friedrich Engels (1820–1895, the friend of Karl Marx), Henry Mayhew (1812–1887, the journalist and publisher), and the largely anonymous factory inspectors, drew middle-class attention to the desperate lives of the British working and proletarian classes under nineteenth-century capitalism (Mayhew 1968; Engels 1972).

While these reformers may have been incoherent because they were largely unsympathetic to cultural values other than those of their own group and were often heavy handed and repressive in their proposals for reform, they also attempted to draw 'injustices' to wider attention, and engendered change. Their cross-cultural incoherence was an opening.

Later in the nineteenth century, celebrity capitalists such as Andrew Carnegie (1889) spent vast amounts of money on philanthropy. With Carnegie (who set out to be someone for other rich people to emulate via his 'gospel of wealth'), it is debatable how much of that money was seen by the poor as opposed to the relatively well off, as he was certain that those 'worthy of assistance, except in rare cases, seldom require assistance' (Carnegie 1889: no page). His philanthropy automatically classified most of the poor as unworthy of help or of being questioned as to their needs. However, such wealthy donors, through the scale of their acts, again inculcate impersonal welfare. They cannot give personally to everyone they benefit, and hence cannot expect a submissive, or obligated, response to them personally from individual receivers of charity. They help build up the idea of public works and public rights to assistance, irrespective of moral approbation and praise of the giver. Hence, they indirectly undermine some of the power and control aspects of charity. At least Carnegie's gifts did not directly demand whipping or imprisoning the poor.

Max Weber (1930) suggested that a distinctive notion of early Protestant capitalism was the breaking of human relationships:

> [The Protestant] divided from the eternally damned remainder of humanity by a more impassable and in its invisibility more terrifying gulf, than separated the monk of the Middle Ages from the rest of the world about him, a gulf which penetrated all social relations with its sharp brutality. This consciousness of divine grace of the elect and holy was accompanied by an attitude toward the sin of one's neighbour, not of sympathetic understanding based on consciousness of one's own weakness, but of hatred and contempt for him as an enemy of God bearing the signs of eternal damnation.
>
> (Weber 1930: 121)

Poverty and misfortune became evidence of sin, and association with sin risked salvation (Weber 1930: 163, 177; Tawney 1938: 262). Lack of spending on enjoyment or the support of others allowed the accumulation of capital rather than mandating the distribution of excess wealth amongst kin and community. This accumulation then became the practice by which virtue was measured. Impersonal philanthropy attacks (from within) this notion that the collection of capital is the absolute aspiration of virtuous capitalists and to be pursued at all costs. Such philanthropy has the potential of its incoherence to break the breakage that Weber (1930) points to, even while it is attempting to support the order that its wealth grows out of.

In the twentieth century, the hard-fought-for welfare state was seen by left-wing critics (who refused to acknowledge incoherence as anything other than bad) to be a mode of control, acting on behalf of dominant groups, turning out docile rather than revolutionary workers, and not immediately ending inequality or the system in which hardship arose (Harris 1961; Miliband 1982). With this approach, it was hard to defend the welfare state against neoliberals who argued that state representation was inherently oppressive and inefficient, and should be abandoned with support going to successful people, to let the 'trickle down' effect, hard work and charity remedy all. An acceptance of incoherence may have benefitted left-wing politics.

Summarizing this brief history, there appears to have been a set of overlapping stages in the social organization of formal acts of help, in the UK at least. The first stage is *meritorious charity*, where giving primarily functions as an act of devotion or building relationships. This fails to stop movement of people and generates a *charity of compulsion* aimed at controlling and punishing the poor and curtailing empathy. Faced with the failure of compulsion, there comes a more private and perhaps gentler *philanthropy* that attempts to persuade wealthy people to give to organizations that then 'manage' supervised recipients, with the primary aim of quelling vice or social unrest and generating docile labourers. This leads into a more impersonal giving, which naturalizes *impersonal welfare* based on class demand, and mutual obligation as fellow nationals, to cushion misfortune. During the fight for impersonal welfare in the nineteenth century, international help grows, along with colonialism, as both missionary charity and philanthropy. International aid serves both as a mode of control *and* as a mode of extension of empathy, through exemplary figures.

In the late twentieth century, under neoliberal ordering regimes, a tendency arises to return to charities of control and discipline: 'work for the dole'; time periods on payment; constant purges of people on welfare; extensions of working life; 'green armies'; and so on. The idea that poorer citizens should be able to demand help is no longer relevant to contemporary states, as the wealthy and the poor separate again and 'downwards' empathy is broken. Neoliberal policies are generally accompanied by an argument that private charity is more flexible, transparent, effective and reliable than government-based charity as is, supposedly, all non-government activity. It is claimed that NGOs can distribute resources more effectively than national governments (Zunz 2012: 286). In keeping with neoliberal ideology, this assumes that wealth and the powers it allocates should not face interference by the government, or by the people that government supposedly represents.

We might expect private funds to take up these claims as part of a rhetorical strategy to justify and prolong their existence. On the other hand, NGOs may not act completely coherently with neoliberal theory. As Olivier Zunz (2102: 5) suggests, there is an ongoing political struggle over the governance of help and its functions. Some strands of contemporary philanthropy, say Oxfam and other 'aid' organizations, seem focused on the question of 'what kind of philanthropy is valued by those receiving it?' These strands are more prone to treat those benefiting as fellow humans with rights and opinions that are worth paying attention to. They recognize 'demand obligation' where the privileged have an obligation to listen and give to the demands of those being helped or gifted. This requires the humanization of those receiving, and the recognition that they belong in the community. Thus, we cannot say because an organization may fit in with neoliberal ideology it necessarily serves that ideology coherently.

Celebrity may even play a role in the escape from neoliberalism within neoliberalism. Successful 'helping' organizations, in particular those who are helping people who are classified as 'different', may need to cultivate an 'artificial' empathy and humanitarian concern. They may need to build a following by allowing *some* givers to attempt at gaining status or legitimacy through visibly helping, and hence becoming exemplars of help. In the information society, living well-known exemplars may be able to make direct appeals to their audience and establish 'virtual' relationships that extend the possibilities of personal contact, empathy and discussion. However, as such processes are rarely coherent, these exemplars, and 'gifting properly' may then become foci of competitive exchange or of gift denigration ('your gifts are not good enough, not as good as ones "we" *might* make'), in a political contest for power, which can further distract from offering actual help.

Celebrities play on our sense of relationship with them, but we do not have a relationship with them, nor do most of us have a relationship with those people we might be required to help. Therefore, the celebrity in going to the field and having experiences provides a possible transitional object, a fiction that allows the formation of an apparent connection to people not just to facts. By engaging with unspeakable events, celebrities can set up being generous and giving help to outsiders (often radically different outsiders), as an exemplar of modelable behaviour, even if the unspeakability is too soon resolved. People may want to be like them and help (or donate) without being personally involved themselves, thus generating impersonal welfare, which helps free the helped of indebtedness and promotes the ability to demand obligation from the givers.

As untrained people, these celebrities may offer escape from the assurance of neoliberalism, celebrity capitalists or bourgeois revolutionaries, through some suspension of articulateness and foreclosure of certainties, as we shall see when Angelina Jolie displays awkwardness around her obligation to others, her privilege and the help she gives, or can give. What Jolie establishes, deliberately or otherwise, is a sense of relationship between viewers and helped, based in difference and incomprehension. This messy classificatory relationship, however inadequate or fictional, may be better than none. It allows and cultivates empathy, while being open to more responsiveness than relations of charity, deference or compulsion.

Celebrity Incoherence

In 2006, Angelina Jolie gave an interview about her experiences with refugees, which is almost a locus classicus for critics of celebrity philanthropy (Cooper 2006; Nickel 2012; see also Bell, in this book).

It is a long interview, and I want to focus on her lacunae and stumblings; the points in which ease of language use breaks down, without seeing these as irrelevant. They are the moments where we might hear something being built, or build something ourselves. She is being interviewed on Cable News Network (CNN) by Anderson Cooper, who has also visited refugees. Cooper starts awkwardly:

Philanthropy, Celebrity and Incoherence

COOPER: At a certain point, it's – some people need to block it out. I mean, how do you – you go repeatedly and you see this repeatedly. And that – I mean, takes a toll. How do you get to a place where you can function in that environment?

JOLIE: It does, but, I mean – and you know this – it's that you get – I am so inspired by these people. And they are the greatest strength.

So, it's not – you have that memory. You have that moment – I have had it – where, even just today, I was, you know, breast-feeding, and tired, and thinking, God, I really don't know how I'm going to get myself together to be thinking for this interview.

But you think, Jesus, the things these people go through. I owe it to all of them to get myself together, to stop whining about being tired, and get there and get focused, and, because God, it's the least I can do, with what they live with and what they can – you know, they pull themselves out of the most horrible despair. And they're able to smile and get on with it and survive. And, so, you don't – it's that same thing. You don't – you don't think, poor me, what I have seen. You just think, like, Jesus, thank God I – I'm not experiencing it […]

And it was kind of just this area of people who had been – who had had their limbs cut off from the violence. And it was an amputee camp. And it was probably to this day the worst camp I have ever seen.

And I knew I was changing as a person. I was learning so much about life. And I was – so, in some ways, it was the best moment of my life, because it… […] changed me for the better. And I was never going to be never going to be – going to want for more in my life or be… […]

And then, suddenly, you see these people who are really fighting something, who are really surviving, who have so much pain and loss and things that you have no idea.
(Cooper 2006)

Both Jolie and the interviewer clearly do not know what to say. In Cooper's words 'And then you come back, and especially in this world that you live in, it's got to be such a strange – it's got to be surreal'. Is that not the point here? That there is no easy conception of this, of what has been witnessed? That 'we', Jolie and *most* of the audience, do not have daily experience of camps of war amputees, or of human endurance at the limits, or of war trauma. That we complain and 'whinge' about tiredness, when other people carry on with suffering and lives we *cannot* imagine realistically. Moreover, how dare we express that tiredness? And then, she clearly does not want to risk patronizing these people; they get on with life in the midst of the inconceivable 'they're able to smile and get on with it and survive.' We may also note the intrusions of God at these points (as an expressive marker) as conception, expression and identification break down, but are maintained. Jolie, despite her later claims to youthful troubles, has no pain to share with them equally; nothing to share other than through classifying herself as human and opening empathy. However, how do we as viewers/readers empathize in such a situation? Again, how dare we? How does anyone not make the attempt incoherently, without breakage of smooth talk? The breaks allow something to happen. This is not all foreclosed in neat categories; the audience has to participate to make the broken speech meaningful. By listening and making it out, if attentive, they can become involved.

Jolie sketches how she got into this, through reading a book from the UN:

> And it said almost 20 million people are displaced. And it showed pictures of Rwanda and pictures of all these – and I was kind of – and I was just shocked.
> I thought, how is that possible, that I have known nothing about this, and I'm 20-something years old, and there are this many people displaced in the world?
> So, I knew it was something that had to be discussed, and wasn't being discussed.
>
> (Cooper 2006)

Her ignorance excuses the audience's ignorance, but she knows something 'must' be done and points to the lack of discourse, the silence; the lack of action. Analysts of celebrity philanthropy, journalists or politicians and even the aid workers, have not crashed through this silence that is perhaps a cultivated protective shield to shelter us from the storm of suffering we know is present and to allow us to break empathy. Indeed, over the last 15 years in Australia aid workers, advocates and journalists have not broken through the political cultivation of self-righteousness about refugees, as self-righteousness is a defence against the suffering and is so much easier to speak through (McKenzie and Hasmath 2013; Toohey 2014). Hatred is directed against an imagined and *resolved* Other who is made meaningful in that hatred. Empathy, in these circumstances of distance, is indirect and largely gained through relating to the reactions of exemplary others who have made an empathetic leap into difference.

Cooper (2006) attempts the classifications of empathy, making commonality: 'But, in fact, they – I mean, they are everyone. We all could be refugees at one point or another in our lives.' But this is threatening too. Cooper discusses his own feelings after being in Somalia:

> COOPER: And then I felt like I was going through phases, the more wars I would go to, of anger, and then confusion…
> JOLIE: Yes.
> COOPER: … and then outrage, and then sort of resignation, then sort of an open feeling that allows me to continue doing it. But do…
> JOLIE: Yes.
> COOPER: Do you go through those phases?
> JOLIE: I did. Yes. I don't know which phase I'm in now.
>
> (Cooper 2006)

Again we are faced with incoherence, confusion and feeling. Hopefully, the audience could be building a feeling of some of this complexity as well; some of this anguish, which cannot be compared with the anguish of the suffering, but is a reaching towards it, and the impossibility and possibility of help. It exemplifies the confusion: we know and we do not really know. We do not know how to react when it is so big. We might oscillate between concern and retreat, outrage and resignation. We do not know which phase we are in now. Jolie says that she felt she could save the world, but 'And then I was – and then I did feel helpless and just angry' (Cooper 2006). This is a familiar sentiment: we can also feel angry and helpless, and realistically too. What *do* we do? There is very little that is inflated or over-optimistic here; resigned but exemplifying not giving up, still striving, not stopping at the point of 'what do we do?'

Cooper and Jolie are not certain, this we can see and perhaps feel ourselves. They talk about legislation in Washington, how the bill was passed, and yet it was not funded, so it meant nothing. This too may tell the audience something about politics and the ways that 'help' actually works in neoliberal capitalism. It might provoke some action whether protest or kindness. There is no reward being offered here for empathy, except feeling the enormity along with Jolie and Cooper, building an empathy with otherness, recognizing both that otherness and the humanity, and coming to possibly think about the unthinkable, unfeelable and unactable rather than stay avoiding it.

The conversation moves to the situation in Darfur at the time. Jolie says,

> I hear people talking about Darfur on the news now. And they're talking about, what are we going to do? And they're starting to discuss solutions. And you're starting – the solutions that you heard field officers begging to be addressed three years ago, you know?
>
> And you just, God, feel like, you know, how many times are we going to let these things go on this long? Or when are we going to finally be united internationally to be able to handle these things immediately and…
>
> (Cooper 2006)

It is not Jolie who provides the solutions, but those people on the ground who have been ignored. Again, we are dealing with horror and silence. Political silence, the silence originating in power, and some sign of indignation at this state of affairs, perhaps felt in the audience too as we react along with the two of them.

The interview continues, but we shall stop here, in the hope that something has been intimated of the constructive force of staying with this incoherence. Complexity of reaction, expression and a sense of being overwhelmed (all real) are being built up as the interviewer and the interviewee grapple with fundamental issues, without (yet) foreclosing into simple solutions or too complex solutions. Hopefully, the audience is lured into feeling empathy and the desire to help, despite the complexity, and then take some action – neither Cooper nor Jolie can compel. The incoherence and gaps allow the audience to do its own sense-making, or make its own empathy, and not just accept or reject the meanings being made for it by analysts.

Patricia Nickel in her article, 'Philanthromentality: Celebrity parables as technologies of transfer' (2012: 165), hacks into the interview, first pointing to incongruities in Cooper's remark about using 'the very picture of Hollywood glamour' to talk about refugees. This ignores the point that we, as audience, may not expect film celebrities to be concerned, real, or anything other than trivial. This could be an incoherence that acts to bridge our lack of concern: if she can feel and act, then why not me? It is a move that might draw people in. Nickel (2012: 174) criticizes Jolie for focusing on herself and the 'best moment' in her life. She claims this manifests what development theorist Kapoor calls '"narcissistic samaritanism" [...] an "act of self-glorification and gratification"' (Nickel 2012: 174), perhaps missing again the reasons and hesitations around that moment of shock, empathy and opening, which takes Jolie out of her established life, however temporarily, and perhaps allows us to go with her, if only imaginably. Can many people be pure and act without any self-interest or any forced compulsion?

Nickel (2012: 175, 179) also argues that the interview justifies Jolie's wealth and privilege; but focusing on that justification means not grasping the whole story. The interview witnesses rather than justifies. Her wealth allows the travel and direct involvement. We know she could be wealthy and do nothing and remain silent; that is not impossible. However, it also allows the audience to be involved without feeling they have to rush to Darfur themselves, as they do not share that wealth, and they probably would not be welcome. They do not have to give everything they own; it opens them to do what they can, to the extent they can.

Nickel (2012: 175) also berates the attempt not to patronize the helped; 'those who suffer are celebrated by Jolie, as they were by Carnegie [...] for their willingness to help themselves, to "smile and get on with it and survive", their toughness, vibrancy and readiness to live'. Does this criticism imply that the only people who deserve help are those who are crushed and unable to live, who are completely and pleasingly abject? Presumably not. The celebrity is caught, they are either said to show no respect or it is said that the respect shown is belittling, without the critic ever considering the difficulty of showing respect or comprehension across cultures, or the differences in sophistication between celebrity analyses. Jolie says of people in the Congo, 'All the people, [...] they're so different. And they're passionate. And they're tough. And they're vibrant. And ready to live' (Cooper 2006). The idea that people can be strong and still need help, contradicts common US ideas of the worthless or whining poor (as seen in Carnegie). It helps build empathy in its prime audience; it may help build respect for others.

Jolie is also accused of not opposing the regime. It is true she is not a revolutionary, but she is also not without criticism of political process, the ignoring of aid workers or the silence in the media and general discussion. Is it better *not* to point out, as Cooper (2006) does, that 'When the donations don't get there, the food aid gets cut', in the hope that we can agitate for donations not to be cut while waiting for the revolution to occur? Jolie herself has been politically active, not only in promoting the bill mentioned earlier, but focusing on 'unaccompanied minors' who arrive in the US and 'basically find themselves in the legal system without representation'. This is a political situation, as was the charity of compulsion 'solution', of locking them up, that she was opposing. Is the implication that it might be better to do nothing than to protest as Jolie does? Jolie is also blamed for choosing 'whose suffering she will observe and draw attention to as an aesthetic source of emotion and satisfaction in her own life' (Nickel 2012: 175), as if there was not always a choice of who was to be heard or helped, and as if such deciding did not affect our lives. At least some are being heard, and some involvement might begin. While Jolie may not be held to account by elections, she is subject to criticism by media, the Right, the Left and academics. Her failings are not hidden; they are more public than those of most organizations.

Such criticism of celebrity encounters with suffering and pain in the world ignores the possibility that such encounters are difficult, or that the celebrity could both be disturbed (or overwhelmed) by what they see, and possibly transformed by it (in wanting to help somehow), and this might cause them problems in maintaining their position or attitude to life. Is it the case that Jolie's life is more comfortable because of her actions? Some celebrities may be playing games for publicity; they may also be genuinely torn by experiential comparisons between their wealth and fortune, and the poverty of others. A kinder approach may lead us to notice Jolie's incoherence as a real response centred on her inability to phrase what she feels, her sense of obligation, the inadequacy of what she can do without wanting to put people down, and the sense that she might want people (including the helped) to participate, rather than have her tell them what to do. Those attentive to her incoherence may also empathize with her, and through her with the people she has seen, and may move to act. Nickel's approach, although making many telling points, removes complexity through a rush to condemn. Even when Nickel (2012) presents transcripts of the interview, she does not touch on what was not sayable; the incoherence is ignored, the pauses, the self-questionings are all downplayed, so as to get to the fact that we were talking about Jolie rather than the people of Sierra Leone – as if Jolie could talk as a person of Sierra Leone, or as if the capitalist media would give such a person a lengthy interview. Again, this is not saying that some celebrities, or others, may not avoid the pain of incoherence and rush into quick solutions and quick condemnations. It is saying that the incoherence is important and may lead people somewhere if they can stay with it and not foreclose.

Conclusion

This chapter has argued that more emphasis on the paradoxical and incoherent nature of help in general, and celebrity philanthropy in particular, would be useful to understanding how 'attempts to help' work in practice. Philanthropy and help are always going to be focal points of dispute. They attempt to build both order and help. Either they aim at changing things, assuming they understand the situation perfectly and know exactly what to do, and thus produce unexpected results that may or may not benefit those being helped; or they work towards improving order in which case they can be said to help maintain the conditions that produce the need for help, unless again unforeseen effects intrude, which is not improbable as the brief history given earlier implies.

Modes of help are often not either entirely good or bad, but both simultaneously. They can be both noble and self-undermining, or complex and awkward. Recognizing the awkwardness could clearly allow us to acknowledge the difficulties presented by celebrity philanthropists as well as recognize the possible openings they might engender, and the need we might have for them.

The mess of Jolie's interviews shows a real response to the immensity and inconceivability of the problems, as do her floundering and relations back to herself in her search for meaning (Cooper 2006). The pauses presented by incoherence might even allow us to think, and to imagine a relation between people and experience, or generate some kind of bond felt in us that respects the incompatibilities and inconceivabilities between people. This could be deeply necessary given that most of the intended audience do not have a 'real' or experiential relation to the problems of the peoples being discussed, or even to the presence of those problems. Such incoherence before the immensity of disorder and hardship, perhaps allows the fiction of relationship, empathy and understanding to be seen as complex or fraught rather than being taken as real and understood. Trying to build coherence and certainty in this disorder might lead even more to overriding local conditions with oppressive goodness and the demands of charity of compulsion.

The incoherence and the contradictions laid bare by Jolie point to possibilities of complex relationships of gifting without expecting obligation, and should not be ignored. They could mark the paradoxes and contradictions of help, and perhaps of empathy, and lead us into a space of contemplation, action and dialogue, with the knowledge of inadequacy before us, and not removed by compulsive certainty. In this situation, incoherence is a valid mode of response, not just an indicator of triviality.

Acknowledgements

Without the help, encouragement and criticism of Elaine Jeffreys, this chapter would not exist. However, any stupidities are my own. Some of the arguments in this chapter grew out of research supported under the Australian Research Council's Discovery Project (DP0880853) funding scheme.

References

Andrew, D.T. (1989) *Philanthropy and Police: London Charity in the Eighteenth Century*, Princeton, NJ: Princeton University Press.
Berreby, D. (2006) *Us and Them: Understanding Your Tribal Mind*, London: Hutchinson.
Burn, R. (1764) *The History of the Poor Laws*, London: A. Millar.
Carnegie, A. (1889) 'Wealth', *North American Review*, CCCXCI, June, http://www.swarthmore.edu/SocSci/rbannis1/AIH19th/Carnegie.html. Accessed 9 January 2015.
Cheal, D. (1988) *The Gift Economy*, London: Routledge.
Cooper, A. (2006) 'Angelina Jolie: Her mission and motherhood', *360 Degrees*, CNN, 23 June, http://transcripts.cnn.com/TRANSCRIPTS/0606/23/acd.02.html. Accessed 9 January 2015.

Cubitt, G., and Warren, A. (eds) (2000) *Heroic Reputations and Exemplary Lives*, Manchester: Manchester University Press.

Eikenberry, A.M. (2006) 'Philanthropy and governance', *Administrative Theory & Praxis*, 28, 4: 586–92.

Engels, F. (1972) *The Condition of the Working-Class in England*, Moscow: Progress Publishers.

Foucault, M. (2003) *Society Must be Defended: Lectures at the Collège de France, 1975–1976*, New York: Picador.

Harris, N. (1961) 'The decline of welfare', *International Socialism*, 1, 7: 5–14, https://www.marxists.org/history/etol/writers/harris/1961/xx/welfare2.htm. Accessed 9 January 2015.

Höijer, B. (2004) 'The discourse of global compassion: The audience and media reporting of human suffering', *Media, Culture & Society*, 26, 4: 513–31.

Kapoor, I. (2013) *Celebrity Humanitarianism: The Ideology of Global Charity*, Oxford, UK: Routledge.

Marshall, J.P. (2006) 'Categories, gender and online community', *E-Learning and Digital Media*, 3, 2: 245–62.

Marx, K. (1954) *Capital: Volume 1*, Moscow: Progress Publishers.

Mauss, M. (1969) *The Gift: Forms and Functions of Exchange in Archaic Societies*, London: Routledge & Kegan Paul.

Mayhew, H. (1968) *London Labour and the London Poor*, Volumes 1–4, New York: Dover.

McKenzie, J., and Hasmath, R. (2013) 'Deterring the "boat people": Explaining the Australian government's people swap response to asylum seekers', *Australian Journal of Political Science*, 48, 4: 417–30.

Miliband, R. (1982) *Capitalist Democracy in Britain*, Oxford, UK: Oxford University Press.

Nickel, P.M. (2012) 'Philanthromentality: Celebrity parables as technologies of transfer', *Celebrity Studies*, 3, 2: 164–82.

Picht, W. (1964) *The Life and Thought of Albert Schweitzer*, New York: Harper & Row.

Prigogine, I. (1996) *The End of Certainty: Time, Chaos and the New Laws of Nature*, New York: Free Press.

Siegel, D. (2012) *Charity and Condescension: Victorian Literature and the Dilemmas of Philanthropy*, Athens; Ohio: Ohio University Press.

Soros, G. (2011) 'My philanthropy', in C. Sudetic (ed.) *The Philanthropy of George Soros: Building Open Societies*, New York: Public Affairs, pp. 1–57.

Tawney, R.H. (1938) *Religion and the Rise of Capitalism*, London: Pelican.

Toohey, P. (2014) *That Sinking Feeling: Asylum Seekers and the Search for the Indonesian Solution*, Quarterly Essay, 53, Collingwood: Black Inc.

Turner, J., Hogg, M., Oaks, P., Reicher, S., and Wetherall, M. (1987) *Rediscovering the Social Group: A Self-Categorization Theory*, Oxford, UK: Blackwell.

Weber, M. (1930) *The Protestant Ethic and the Spirit of Capitalism*, London: George Allen and Unwin.

Zunz, O. (2012) *Philanthropy in America: A History*, Princeton, NJ: Princeton University Press.

Part 2

Branding and Development

Chapter 4

Tyra Banks' Celebrity Philanthropy: *Top Model*, TZONE and the Communication of Female Empowerment

Dara Persis Murray

The brand identity of Tyra Banks – supermodel, media mogul and philanthropist – conveys complex meanings of female empowerment by merging messages of postfeminist individualism and feminist solidarity. Banks' most popular work, *America's Next Top Model* (hereafter ANTM), promotes a neoliberal, postfeminist conception of the female subject. It enjoins young women to embrace consumer culture (as embodied in the fashion and beauty industry) and to compete against each other in order to realize personal goals of wealth and celebrity. In contrast, Banks' main philanthropic effort, the Tyra Banks TZONE Foundation, draws on the insights provided by the US–Anglophone liberal strand of feminism. It recognizes the need for social change to realize women's social, political and economic rights, and supports initiatives designed to liberate women as a collective from oppressive cultural norms.

This chapter explores the different views of female empowerment that inform the Banks brand and its organizing projects as follows. The first section explains how Banks rose to fame as a black supermodel in the 1990s, and details her more recent and transformed celebrity image as a media producer and the CEO of Bankable Productions. I note how the Banks brand, which promotes Tyra Banks as an inspiring and achievable role model, targets diverse consumers through commercial messages of female empowerment that simultaneously cultivate selected groups of young women as aspiring model-celebrities and enhance Banks' celebrity. The second section examines the production of ANTM contestants as branded commodities, as these young women may become minor celebrities by being connected to the Banks brand, thereby demonstrating its claim to reveal the star-like quality of women via the directed consumption of mass-produced fashion and beauty products. The third section looks at the ways in which the TZONE Foundation, Banks' philanthropic initiative, works to support girls and young women from disadvantaged backgrounds and is representative of classic feminist efforts to empower women understood as an oppressed 'sisterhood'. I conclude by discussing how the tensions between the different conceptions of female empowerment that inform ANTM and TZONE make Banks' philanthropic endeavours appear to be merely an extension of the Banks brand.

Tyra Incorporated

Tyra Banks (b. 1973) achieved celebrity status as a black supermodel in the late 1990s. This feat was acclaimed by numerous commentators for 'shatter[ing] one of modeling's glass ceilings' (Penrice 2010) and 'open[ing the] doors for people of color, in a very exclusive industry' (JRAJ9 2012). In 1996, Banks became the first African American woman and fashion model to appear on the cover of the Victoria's Secret catalogue, alongside model Valeria Mazza (Penrice 2010). Also in 1996, Banks was the first African American woman and fashion model to be featured alone on the cover of the *GQ* (Norment 1997). In 1997, she appeared solo on the cover of the *Sports Illustrated*'s swimsuit issue, becoming the first African American model to appear unaccompanied on this coveted media text (Kris 2007). The same year, she received a VH1 award for Supermodel of the Year (Proscout 2009).

The fashion industry recognized and simultaneously racialized Banks' emerging celebrity status as early as the mid-1990s by calling her the 'new Naomi Campbell', referring to the British supermodel of Jamaican heritage who had dominated runways in the 1980s and early 1990s (Allan 2006). The comparison reportedly miffed Campbell, who prevented the young and upcoming model from appearing with her at a Chanel show. Of her early experiences in the fashion industry, Banks told a reporter for *Essence* magazine, 'No model should have to endure what I went through at 17 [...] It's very sad that the fashion business and press can't accept that there can be more than one reigning black supermodel at a time'. Banks further stated, 'It's long overdue that black models receive the same benefits as white models [...] But I still don't make as much as the white supermodels do' (Brennan and Pendergast 2012).

Banks' interpretation of the fashion industry as having racist and classist undertones perhaps spurred her entrepreneurialism and desire to control her own image and financial future. In 1992, she founded Ty Girl Corporation, which was headed by Banks as the CEO and managed by her mother (Hill 2009: 18). In 2003, Banks set about creating a media empire by establishing Bankable Enterprises, a film and television production company focused on beauty and entertainment texts targeted at female audiences (Hirschberg 2008), which she heads in the position of President and Chief Creative Officer ('Tyra Banks' n.d.).

The creation of Bankable Enterprises has shifted Tyra Banks' celebrity image away from being primarily a supermodel towards being a producer of television shows that both enhance her celebrity and cultivate selected groups of young women as aspiring model-celebrities. Banks (2008) explained this move in a *Newsweek Magazine* profile as follows: 'I've had my glory in the modeling world. I want to use the power I have now to cultivate new talent in front of the camera and behind the scenes' (Banks 2008).

The latter claim illuminates the core branding strategy behind Banks' commercial operation, which trades on her personal success story as a young black woman who achieved fame against the odds, and who simultaneously embodies characteristics that 'all young women can aspire towards and eventually, ostensibly, possess' (Joseph 2009: 238, 242). As global brands are created via the cultivation of various stories, symbols and values into a consistent message about a cultural entity (Klein 2002), consumers of Banks' branded products are unified across diverse backgrounds and cultural contexts as they self-identify with Banks' own story of female empowerment, which is communicated across different genres and industries (see also Millington, in this book).

Bankable's first and most successful text, ANTM, is a reality television program that premiered in 2003 as a breakout hit for United Paramount Network (UPN) (Banks 2003–).

When UPN merged with the WB Television Network to form the CW Television Network (hereafter the CW) in 2006, ANTM became the highest rated series for the new network's 2006 to 2007 launch season with a 2.51 demographic average. In other words, an estimated 2.51 per cent of the total number of television households in the US watched the show based on the Nielsen Ratings system ('Spotted Ratings: *America's Next Top Model*' 2010). ANTM's most watched cycle was its second, which was broadcast on UPN with a 3.01 demographic average. The show enjoyed a consistent viewership from Cycle 3 in autumn 2004 through to Cycle 9 in autumn 2007 with demographic averages between 2.35 and 2.51. Since then, ratings have steadily dropped. In 2010, ANTM had a demographic average of only 1.30. However, despite the drop in viewing audiences, the show was renewed for Cycles 10 to 20, with Cycle 20 airing in August 2013 ('*America's Next Top Model*: Guys, Girls' 2013; Gorman 2011), as it retains strong viewing averages among women aged between 18 and 34 years, a coveted demographic for advertisers. Cycle 21 aired in August 2014, and as per Cycle 20, it also featured aspiring male models ('*America's Next Top Model*: Apply for Cycle 21' 2014).

Top Model is now a global franchise that is licensed in 120 countries. There are also approximately 50 national versions of *Top Model* airing in a variety of cultural contexts around the world ('*Top Model*' 2015). Local versions of *Top Model* are produced in Australia, China, Denmark, France, Finland, Germany, Hungary, Israel, Mexico, the Netherlands, Norway, the Philippines, Russia, Slovakia, Spain, Sweden, Thailand, Turkey, Vietnam and the UK.

Bankable's other texts have proved to be less enduring than ANTM. Although the *Tyra Banks Show* (TBS), which aired between 2005 and 2010, won two Daytime Emmy awards in the new category of 'informative program' in 2008 and 2009 (Silverman 2008; Hinckley 2009), the CW stopped producing the program because of 'so-so ratings' (Adalian 2009). *True Beauty*, a televised 'inner' beauty competition produced by Tyra Banks and actor Ashton Kutcher, was cancelled in 2010 after only two seasons. *Stylista*, a reality television series based on fashion magazines, only ran for one season in 2008. Moving away from its sole focus on television in 2010, Bankable Enterprises launched Bankable Studios, a film production company that reportedly will present 'positive images of women [on] the big screen' and enable Banks to 'follow her longtime dream of film producing' (Keith 2009).

Tyra Banks' financial and cultural capital has been acknowledged in multiple media outlets. In 2006, *Time* magazine described Banks as a 'Supermogul with a Business Model' and included her on their list of '100 People Who Shape Our World'. Also in 2006, *Forbes* magazine placed Banks on their annual list of 'The World's Most Powerful Celebrities' with a 'power ranking' of number 84, a ranking system based on a combination of celebrity status and financial success ('The Celebrity 100: The World's Most Powerful Celebrities 2006' 2006). Banks' ranking on the *Forbes* list rose to number 61 in 2007 before falling to number 68 in 2008, and she has not been placed on the list since ('The Celebrity 100: The World's Most Powerful Celebrities 2007' 2007; 'The Celebrity 100: #68 Tyra Banks' 2008). However, Banks' financial power has remained steady. In 2008 and 2009, Banks' estimated earnings of USD 23 million and USD 30 million, respectively, placed her at the top of the *Forbes* list of 'Primetime TV Top-Earning Women' (Rose 2009), and she was number 2 on that list in 2010 with estimated earnings of USD 25 million (Rose 2010). Tyra Banks had an estimated net worth of 90 million in 2013 ('Tyra Banks Net Worth' n.d.).

Banks has expressed a desire for even more financial and cultural capital in order to realize positive social change, in a similar fashion to her professed role model, female media mogul and philanthropist, Oprah Winfrey. In an interview with the *New York Times Magazine*, Banks states, 'I want power … The power to make change' (Hirschberg 2008). Banks has also said that she envisions herself as a 'Gen-X Oprah' and wants 'an empire like Oprah's' (Chase 2006: 62). Popular publications have taken notice. The cover of a February 2008 edition of *Entertainment Weekly* stated, 'Tyra Inc: She's Building an Empire. Just Don't Call her Oprah Jr' (Banks 2008).

The Banks brand – its media texts and organizing projects, including the philanthropic TZONE organization – is unified by a message emphasizing 'the attainable fantasy' of 'girl empowerment' in a style that is 'not preachy' (Stack 2008). In 1999, Banks established the Tyra Banks TZONE Foundation, an organization that provided summer camps for girls. In the mid-2000s, the organization began promoting itself as the TZONE Foundation and became a grant-giving organization. TZONE is described as a 'national public charity dedicated to empowering girls and young women to make positive choices by supporting outstanding community-based organizations that share the same vision that Tyra is passionate about – encouraging girls to be leaders, not followers; in control, not out of control; powerful, not powerless' ('Tyra Banks and TZONE Foundation Celebrate Girls in the Game' 2008).

In a note called 'Tyra's Message', Banks claims that her philanthropic work and media texts share the same goal of empowering girls and young women through positive example. In the words of Banks,

> I launched the Tyra Banks TZONE Foundation with my own money because I feel I have a responsibility to lead by example and bring attention to the issues facing girls and young women. That's the purpose of *The Tyra Show* and *America's Next Top Model* – to inspire women to take positive action to realize their ambitions.
>
> ('Tyra's Message' 2009)

Although the professed aim of TZONE and ANTM is female empowerment, the Banks brand turns on two competing strands of feminist communication that may be loosely described as 'feminist' and 'postfeminist'. The feminist position refers to the US–Anglophone liberal strand of feminism that began as part of the second wave of the women's movement, and centered on the liberation of women as a collective from the oppression of patriarchal norms and structures (Siegel 1997: 55–82). The North American and North European Anglophone feminist movement is generally characterized as composed of three waves, although the dates and orientations of each of these 'waves' may vary according to the views of different historiographers (Siegel 1997: 55–82). Broadly speaking, the First Wave took place at the end of the nineteenth and the beginning of the twentieth century, and aimed to realize women's suffrage. The second wave occurred between the 1960s and the 1980s, and concentrated on achieving equal rights for 'women', understood as a collective group. It is associated with the publication in the US of Betty Friedan's *The Feminine Mystique* in 1963, which questioned the relegation of women to the private domain via the sociocultural assumption that women's sole and highest purpose was to be a housewife and mother (Friedan 1963). Although the second wave of the feminist movement refers to different strands of feminist theorizing and activism – liberal feminism, socialist feminism and radical feminism – these three political positions were unified by a belief that women as a collective group were equal to men and should be treated accordingly (Jeffreys 1991: 2 –3). The third wave of the feminist movement began in the 1990s and continues to the present time. It also promotes actions in support of equal rights for women while recognizing that women as individuals are marked by racial, sexual, age and body differences, and therefore has encouraged a focus on women as opposed to Woman, and feminisms as opposed to Feminism (Jeffreys 1991: 6–11).

As part of the second wave feminist movement, the advertising industry was criticized by scholars and activists for producing objectifying, sexualized and demeaning representations of women (Talbot 2000). Many advertisers responded to the associated declining sales of products by shifting their marketing strategies towards what sociologist Robert Goldman (1992) calls 'commodity feminism' (see also Fox 1984; Craig 2003). Commodity feminism refers to the different ways in which feminist concepts and symbols are appropriated for commercial purposes, such as the way television networks and media products conflate consumption with empowerment. Along these lines, the British all-female pop group the Spice Girls promoted the slogan of 'girl power' as agency through the consumption of fashion and beauty products and the presentation of a sexual, hyper-feminine appearance. These commercialized communications of feminism run counter to classic second wave feminist arguments in that they minimize the meanings of feminist politics to mass audiences.

Commodity feminism and notions of girl power flooded popular culture around the same time that Tyra Banks rose to fame in the mid-1990s. These popular views of feminism align with 'postfeminism', a view of the convergence between feminism and neoliberal free markets that also emerged in the 1990s. Proponents argue that gender equality has been achieved in contemporary western culture, and embrace consumer culture by emphasizing the promotion of individualism through a lexicon of choice, self-management and personal responsibility. Others argue that the postfeminist emphasis on individual economic power and support for consumerism 'works to commodify feminism via the figure of woman as empowered consumer' (Tasker and Negra 2007: 2). Some scholars criticize postfeminism for complicating the feminist meanings of social change and liberation in popular culture (Gill 2007). The concepts of 'girl power' and 'postfeminism' also refer to a tension between an affirmation and disavowal of feminist principles, a consideration of 'the individual pleasures of consumption and the social responsibilities of solidarity' (Banet-Weiser 2007: 111; see also Gill 2007).

These different understandings of female empowerment underpin the Banks brand, the Tyra Banks celebrity persona, and Banks' role as a celebrity philanthropist. Her most popular media text, ANTM, promotes a postfeminist message of individual female empowerment based on the promotion of celebrity and consumerism. In contrast, TZONE is organized around a feminist message of collective empowerment for women understood as an oppressed sisterhood.

Top Model

Banks' brand and celebrity are closely related to ANTM. In this text, young women compete for the title of 'America's Next Top Model' and a chance to realize their dreams of becoming working A-list models, thereby achieving wealth and celebrity just like Tyra Banks, whom the title of the show implies is America's 'top model'. ANTM was created and is hosted by Banks, who serves as its executive producer and as a judge. Information about the show on the CW Network website augments Banks' celebrity by directing interested viewers to Banks' websites and Twitter accounts ('*America's Next Top Model*' n.d.). At the same time, Banks has posted items about ANTM contestants on her former official website, tyra.com, and on a weblink called 'Tyra's Inner Circle' (2010), thereby reinforcing the links between the Banks brand and ANTM contestants for audiences. The contestants are thus branded commodities, as they can achieve minor celebrity chiefly because of their connection to the Banks brand.

ANTM presents Banks as a success story and guide who shows contestants with the required drive, passion and ostensibly unrealized star quality how to achieve the attainable fantasy of becoming a 'top model' too. In the words of Banks,

> *America's Next Top Model* is about dreams, plain and simple. And it's about accomplishing these dreams through hard work, talent, and passion. I worked my butt off to get to the top of the modeling industry so I know exactly what it takes to make a star.
>
> (Banks 2004)

Banks further emphasizes her ability to notice the unnoticeable woman and turn her into a star in mere months.

> I want to make a Top Model in eight weeks. I want to take someone from obscurity to fame and I want to chart the entire process and show America how it happens [...] Some of these girls you would not look at twice in the streets. But I'll know when I can make them into something [...] This is a once in a lifetime opportunity, a life-changing opportunity. What I'm looking is for a star – that's all.
>
> (Banks 2003)

The initial episodes of each cycle and the discourse throughout every cycle emphasize that the contestants are lucky to have been selected from among thousands of applicants to experience 'the dream of a lifetime'. That dream involves the proclaimed life-changing opportunity of being a part of ANTM, having access to Banks and her team of experts, and achieving the ultimate prize of stardom via ANTM and in post-ANTM life. As Banks noted in the first episode of Cycle 7 of ANTM in 2006, 'Our finalists have blasted into success, on the runway, in magazines, on television, and in every fashion capital on the globe'.

ANTM clearly trades on the American (now celebrity) Dream, promising that it will pluck deserving contestants from obscurity, and often low-income work, and show them 'the good life'. Adrianne Curry, the winner of Cycle 1 of ANTM in 2003, highlights the assumed transformative potential of ANTM when responding to the news of her success. To use Curry's words, 'Screw serving [waitressing] ever again. I'm going to have a good life now. A lot is going to change. And it kicks so much ass' (cited in Weber 2009: 140).

Banks' and ANTM's textual claims regarding the transformative celebrity-making potential of ANTM are not unfounded, a consideration that has no doubt contributed to the longevity of the show. None of the winners of the 21 cycles of ANTM that aired in the US to date have become superstars. However, Adrianne Curry appeared in her own reality television show, *My Fair Brady*, which aired on VH1 between 2005 and 2008, along with her then-husband, a former child star of the 1970s US sitcom *The Brady Bunch* (prod. Stevens 2005–2008). Curry also had a role on the ABC sitcom *Hot Properties*, and was a model for *Beverly Hills Choppers* and *Playboy* ('Adrianne Curry Biography' n.d.). Yoanna House, the winner of Cycle 2 of ANTM in 2004, hosted a Style Network show (prod. Simon 2005–2012), and Cycle 5's Nicole Linkletter hosted segments for VH1 reporting on New York Fashion Week in 2006 (*Fashion Week* 2006). Eva Pigford, the winner of Cycle 3 of ANTM in 2004, secured a recurring role on the now-defunct television program *Kevin Hill*, a US legal drama that aired on UPN between 2004 and 2005 (created by Reyes 2004–2005). Several winners have also had their ANTM prize of a cosmetics contract renewed, including Cycle 6's Danielle Evans, Cycle 7's CariDee English and Cycle 8's Jaslene Gonzalez (Mosthof 2011; Cherry n.d.). In 2011, Analeigh Tipton from Cycle 11 appeared in minor roles in feature films, including the *Green Hornet*, *Crazy Stupid Love* and *Damsels in Distress*, and selected episodes of television series such as *Hung* and *The Big Bang Theory* ('Analeigh Tipton' n.d.).

Aspiring contestants can apply to access the dream of becoming a Top Model by going to the CW Network website, filling out an ANTM application, sending in their photographs, and meeting certain eligibility requirements – consistent with Tyra Incorporated's message of female empowerment. The aspiring contestant must be a female citizen of the US who resides in the US. She must also be between 18 and 27 years of age, have excellent physical and mental health, be at least five feet and seven inches in height (1.7 metres), and have no record of professional experience as a model in the preceding five years ('*America's Next Top Model* Cycle 9 – Eligibility Requirements' 2007). These requirements do not vary in a substantial manner, as demonstrated by the aim of discovering a 'shorter' model in Cycle 13: the winner was Nicole Fox, who is five feet and seven inches in height ('Nicole Fox of Louisville Wins *America's Next Top Model*' 2010). The aspiring contestants must also agree to live in specified accommodations during production with between nine and 14 female strangers, and with minimal privacy – the accommodations are 'outfitted with video and audio devices which will record, broadcast, and exhibit [the contestants'] actions and voice at all times, twenty-four hours a day, seven days a week' ('*America's Next Top Model* Cycle 9 – Eligibility Requirements'). Aspiring contestants must also accept that they may be 'required to pose and be photographed or videotaped while clothed, partially clothed, or naked' ('*America's Next Top Model* Cycle 9 – Eligibility Requirements' 2007).

Throughout the course of approximately 13 episodes per cycle, contestants undertake a series of challenges and are eliminated via a process of judging until the winner is crowned ('*America's Next Top Model* Episode List' n.d.). The eliminations involve photography, runway and television challenges that test contestants' aptitude for being photogenic, particularly under difficult conditions; for example, contestants have modelled with spiders on their faces and in wind tunnels. Contestants must excel at providing photographs that reflect beauty and personality, act as potential spokesmodels and perform runway work in a manner that meets the judges' approval. The only constant judge has been Banks; other judges of textual importance are a runway coach, ANTM's creative director and a photographer. There are also alternating guest judges such as fashion designers, models, casting agents and magazine editors.

The winner of each cycle achieves the promised, albeit often temporary, dream of becoming an A-list fashion model through the award of a modelling contract with a mass cosmetics company, representation by a prestigious modelling agency and a spread in a popular women's magazine. The prize has remained the same over the show's more than 20 cycles, although different companies are involved. Winners of ANTM have received a modelling contract with cosmetics giants such as Revlon, Sephora or Cover Girl, been represented by modelling agencies such as Wilhelmina, IMG, Ford and Elite, and been featured in fashion and beauty magazines such as *Marie Claire, Jane, Elle, ElleGirl, Seventeen* and *Italian Vogue*.

While the prize is a modelling contract, Banks consistently stresses the alignment of the aspiring Top Models' narratives and values with the Banks brand. Many of the contestants carry their own stories of impoverishment, disadvantage and low self-esteem. Past ANTM contestants include teenage mothers (Cycle 15's Liz Williams), homeless vagrants (Cycle 14's Angelea Preston slept in bus depots), survivors of domestic violence (Cycle 18's Ashley Brown) and women who have had difficult childhoods (Cycle 14's Naduah Rugley was born into a cult that allegedly molested children). Participation in ANTM is presented as a means to become empowered, and the prize presents an opportunity for these women to transform their identities, leaving their difficulties behind to realize their dreams.

Throughout the course of each cycle, Banks stresses that contestants are not just marked by their outer physical beauty: they are positive role models for female audiences because of their 'inner beauty'. These inner qualities are demonstrated by the their ability to communicate effectively with all the participants in the show – Banks, the judges, and fellow contestants. Eva Pigford, a contestant on Cycle 3 in 2004, explains her relationship with another contestant as follows: 'we both know to be enemies here is so pointless'. Announcing Pigford as the winner, Banks' voiceover declared, 'Eva has vitality, she has sass and spunk that make her relatable to young girls everywhere. Eva is a true Cover Girl'. Pigford responded, 'Tyra Banks just told me that I'm about to be a star! Watch out world, here comes Eva!'

ANTM as a competition also inevitably fosters an environment of postfeminist individualism among its contestants. Banks and the other judges highlight the purpose of the show by repeatedly declaring that 'there is only one Top Model'. The understanding that one woman will 'be on top of the competition' and rise above the rest is also reiterated in the theme song and played out through the various challenges and judging scenarios that comprise each episode. This encourages relations between the contestants that often present them as self-monitoring and competitive based on negative forms of comparison, rather than promoting self-confidence based on collective support.

The contestants appear well aware of the contradictory obligation to be sisterly while protecting their own interests. When talking about Shandi Sullivan's elimination in Cycle 2 in 2004, Yoanna House states, 'I love her dearly as a friend, but she's my competitor and it's like, this [elimination] just gets me one step closer to having my dream fulfilled'. Likewise, in Cycle 4 in 2005, Naima Mora explains her relationship with Kahlen Rondot as follows: 'I've been very supportive of Kahlen and Kahlen has been very supportive of me. Right now, Kahlen is not my friend. She's a girl I have got to outshine. I've got to do better than her by a lot'. Jaslene Gonzalez similarly says in Cycle 8 in 2007, 'I'm just not letting Natasha get to me. You never know what strategy she might have'. The interactions of the contestants across the series reflect a statement made by CariDee English in Cycle 7 in 2006. As English put it, 'Now this house just feels like pure competition. It's the battle of the blondes'.

The contestants' pursuit of the ANTM moniker is also articulated through their conformity with the dictates of the fashion industry, and the program's narrative suggests that their acceptance of such values will result in enhanced personal and cultural power. The contestants' physical and affective 'makeover' regime reinforces dominant conceptions of female beauty and behaviour. Contestants become branded commodities through a series of makeovers, involving haircuts, hairstyling and clothing choices, as well as through adopting behavioral modifications such as diet, exercise and even emotional changes. Through these challenges, ANTM promotes a normative message to the contestants and viewers regarding hegemonic femininity in western culture. As the messages of the ANTM brand are exported to the various countries in which it airs, an important site for future audience research would consider the translation of ANTM's meanings of beauty into local versions of *Top Model*.

In addition to shaping female bodies, the desired 'star-making' subjectivities of female contestants, as described by Banks and the other judges, often promote problematic stereotypes of women, and especially women in the fashion industry, as psychologically out of control. In Cycle 7 of ANTM in 2006, a judge makes the following remark to Banks and the other judges at the final evaluation of CariDee English:

Let's think about this business, guys. The fashion industry loves extremes. CariDee, she's an extreme; and there are designers out there that would say, she is cookoo crazy nuts and I want that for my show. She becomes a star.

(Banks 2006)

While arguably the opinion of an individual judge, this comment nevertheless communicates messages to audiences about what constitutes a female celebrity and acceptable female behavior in the context of ANTM. After all, CariDee won.

Furthermore, Banks and the judges discipline contestants who are women of colour for failing to erase markers of ethnic difference or for failing to perform stereotyped racial identities (Hasinoff 2008; Joseph 2009). As Ralina Joseph explains,

> This is a show where a brown-skinned African American woman is maligned for the 'ethnic' gap in her teeth and her working class, black southern accent. This is a show where a Latina contestant is told to 'work it' as 'Cha Cha' or risk elimination. This is a show where a mixed-race Asian-American contestant is eliminated because she fails to perform Asianness in a way the judging panel deems 'authentic,' and another Asian-American contestant is reprimanded because she reveals that she has not dated Asian-American men.
>
> (Joseph 2009: 242)

Messages about both the removal and promotion of racial and ethnic difference is ironic given Banks' personal history and her associated claim that Tyra Incorporated is about challenging 'industry and universal standards by featuring and celebrating non-traditional beauty, and stressing that true beauty is both inside and out' (Jill 2010). Rather than recognizing the complexities of representing race and ethnicity in media texts and working towards a more nuanced portrayal, Banks offers the same reductive stereotypes as other media properties.

In short, ANTM and its postfeminist claim to empower women are tied to the promotion of individualism and consumption practices as a core component of Banks' expanding brand. In 2008, Banks inked a deal with corporate giant Walmart for a line of ANTM-branded clothing aimed at 'teens and tweens', which is described as 'enabl[ing] women to explore a world in which creativity and individuality are valued' (Balser 2008). In 2011, Banks launched an online venture with Demand Media called typeF.com, a community reportedly inspired by Tyra Banks and her mission to redefine beauty as 'built on the celebration of diversity and the ideal of empowering women to be their very best' through creating their own 'unique personal style' ('About Us' 2011). A 'magaline' on typeF.com called 'Tyra: Beauty inside and out' enjoins viewers to 'get your top model behind-the-scenes here!' and to join the 'revolution' by exploring the website ('Tyra's Inner Circle' 2010).

The Banks brand promises to empower young women by helping them to realize the bifurcated goal of youth culture, as they can display their uniqueness through their (mass-produced) sartorial style while remaining a part of the 'in' crowd. Much like other earlier media properties that repackaged feminism through a commercial message, the Banks brand similarly commodifies feminism. In the process, its brand messaging arguably co-opts and depoliticizes the second wave feminist focus on social change and the collective liberation of women from oppressive cultural norms and forms of social organization.

Top Model's claim to empower girls and young women through particular consumption practices has consequently met with mixed responses. Both ANTM and Banks have been praised by some media commentators; ANTM for transforming women as aspiring models into professional model-celebrities; and Banks for being 'a positive, self-empowered role model for all women particularly for younger black women' (Bailey 2008: 4; Hill 2009). Conversely, both ANTM and Banks have attracted criticism from academic and media commentators for promoting stereotypical conceptions of female beauty and behaviour, and postfeminist ideals under 'the guise of sisterhood' (Joseph 2009: 247).

TZONE

The Tyra Banks TZONE Foundation turns on a model of feminism organized around second wave feminist conceptions of solidarity in sisterhood, resulting in individual self-awareness and the capacity to succeed. Predating ANTM, it was founded in 1999 with the mission of providing a summer camp where 'girls would create a sisterhood, learn about themselves, and gain the self-confidence to become successful and powerful young women' ('About Us' 2009). The idea for a girls' camp reportedly grew out of 'countless letters' sent to Banks from young women 'seeking guidance about body image, self-doubt and pressures from boys' ('Tyra Banks Establishes Girls' Camp' 2002). The resulting TZONE camp was an all-expenses paid, 'one-week overnight summer camping experience' for girls between 11 and 16 years of age ('Take Great Pictures: Tyra Banks' n.d.) that took place annually between 2000 and 2004 in California. Reinforcing her commitment to the camp's goals of creating a sisterhood and providing leadership by example, Banks was directly involved with the girl campers. She ate the camp food, slept in a cabin and made efforts to bond with them ('Tyra Banks Discusses Camp' 2002; 'Tyra Banks' 2011).

Drawing on feminist pedagogy, the aim of the TZONE summer camps was to empower young women from diverse cultural backgrounds by providing safe, supportive, female-only spaces for them to discuss, in directed ways, the issues affecting them. Banks claims to have personally selected every girl at each camp, in part to ensure that the final group was composed of young women from varied racial and ethnic backgrounds. To use Banks' words, 'I actually read every single application and I choose every single applicant' to ensure that TZONE is 'as diverse as possible' ('Tyra Banks Discusses Camp' 2002). Banks concludes that bringing girls from different backgrounds together is important for breaking down stereotypes and encouraging girls to 'realize that they all have the same problems' ('Tyra Banks Discusses Camp' 2002).

TZONE campers were encouraged to enhance their self-esteem and bond with one another while attending art, dance and photography classes, performing in talent shows, testing their physical fitness, and participating in nightly staff-led discussion groups about friendship, sex, dating and relationships, and body image ('Take Great Pictures: Tyra Banks' n.d.; 'TZONE Camps at Scripps' 2011). On the first evening, campers discussed the meaning and importance of friendship by talking through the reasons why adolescent girls are often cliquey and competitive with each other. The second evening, campers engaged in role-playing about their mostly negative experiences of 'sex, dating and relationships' ('Tyra Banks Discusses Camp' 2002). On the third evening, they discussed 'beauty and body image', what they expressed was 'the most beautiful part of themselves ... [and what] part of their body that they wish would just go away' ('Tyra Banks Discusses Camp' 2002). Banks describes the latter issue as extremely emotional, with campers being moved to tears as they discussed their body image.

The underlying impetus of these supervised discussions was reinforced through activities emphasizing female solidarity and personal growth. For example, campers chanted a song penned by Banks before engaging in morning art classes or physical exercise. The words of this cheer are,

> My T-Zone sister, what's up, what's up, what's up? I got your back, girl, you know I'll back you up. I'll be there for you, no ifs, no ands, no buts. T-Zone sister, what's up, what's up, what's up? T-Zone sister, what's up, what's up, what's up?
>
> ('Tyra Banks Discusses Camp' 2002)

The girls at the TZONE camp were also encouraged to adopt 'fun' new names such as 'Chocolate Shortcake', in order to put aside their insecurities and reimagine themselves. Post-camp mentoring and fund-raising activities further aimed to ensure that the camp experience was more than a week-long event ('Tyra Banks Discusses Camp' 2002). In other words, TZONE campers were encouraged to develop self-confidence, establish friendships and become strong women in the future by engaging in educational activities designed to highlight the shared nature of many of their experiences and concerns, and subsequently learn how to resist social pressures associated with female adolescent body image, sexuality and relationships.

In 2005, the Tyra Banks TZONE Foundation was reorganized as a public charity with the expressed mission of honouring the TZONE's camp origins by creating a 'larger sisterhood' among underprivileged girls and young women ('TZONE Story' 2009). Described as a 'fierce cause for girls', the Foundation's mission is 'to build a sisterhood movement among women and girls by raising funds and making grants to community-based non-profits that serve low-income, disadvantaged girls' ('About Us' 2009). As with Banks' other projects, this mission is described as empowering 'girls and young women to live their dreams' and 'building self-esteem and confidence, launching leaders, showing the world that girls can do and be anything they set their minds to' ('Our Mission' 2009). In its current form, TZONE has a broader reach than in its original form as a summer camp. It aims to help girls and women aged between 13 and 35 years old rather than girls aged between 11 and 16 years of age. It is also national, rather than localized, in scope.

TZONE awards grants of up to USD 10,000 to non-profit organizations across the US that are dedicated 'to fostering long-term, supportive female relationships through innovative programs and services that promote personal accountability, self-esteem, goal-setting, [and] healthy lifestyles' ('Tyra Banks' TZONE Foundation' 2015). Grants to date have been awarded to organizations in the cities of Chicago, New York and Los Angeles. Chicago-based grantees include the Young Chicago Authors, whose GirlSpeak project uses writing as a gateway to encourage young women to 'empower young artists to change the world' ('GirlSpeak' n.d.), and Girls in the Game, a non-profit organization that encourages young women to engage in 'sports and fitness opportunities, nutrition and health education and leadership development to enhance the overall health and well-being of girls' ('About Us' 2008). Grant recipients in Los Angeles include a mentoring program called Motivating Our Students through Experience, which aims to reduce gang involvement, teen pregnancy rates, substance abuse and school drop-out rates for inner city girls, and the Downtown Women's Center in Los Angeles, which provides resources to local women who are homeless or surviving on low incomes.

TZONE grant recipients in New York include the Ifetayo Cultural Arts Academy, the Lower Eastside Girls Club, the Sadie Nash Leadership Project and the Girls Project. The Ifetayo's Sisters in Sisterhood Rites of Passage program 'leads girls through a two-year process of learning about health and sexuality, building awareness of their African cultural heritage, and making connections with a local and international community of women' ('TZONE Network' 2009). The Lower Eastside Girls Club offers a space for girls and young women to engage in an array of programs (leadership, science, art, etc.) to gain confidence and skills, and the Sadie Nash Leadership Project promotes female leadership and advocacy on issues such as domestic violence and human and civil rights. The Girls Project works with 'public schools and community organizations, providing materials, curricula and training on the core issues of health and wellness, nutrition and positive body image for girls' ('TZONE Network' 2009).

Taken together, the TZONE Foundation expresses a commitment to empowering girls and young women in ways that convey feminist-activist values concerning the need to liberate women as a collective group from oppressive cultural norms and achieve socio-economic equality. First, it supports organizations that raise awareness of and help girls to overcome issues that they face in contemporary society, such as low self-esteem and a negative body image. Second, TZONE supports organizations that promote gender equality by encouraging public discussion of these topics and listening to the views of girls and young women, which are often unheard. Finally, it aims to increase public awareness of and support for TZONE's grantee organizations, and for the needs, goals and achievements of girls and young women from 'at-risk urban communities' ('Tyra's Message' 2009).

A message by Banks on the former TZONE Foundation website – the site was revamped in 2014–2015 – encourages viewers to support the foundation and the community groups that it endorses in personal and collective feminist terms. Banks begins by drawing connections between her celebrity status and brand messaging of female empowerment. As Banks puts it, 'I feel I have a responsibility to lead by example and bring attention to the issues facing girls and young women. That's the purpose of *The Tyra Show* and ANTM – to inspire women to take positive action to realize their ambitions' ('Tyra's Message' 2009). Banks concludes by asking viewers to join her, stating, 'We all stand to benefit from doing this for our sisters, our mothers, our daughters. Please join me in this fierce cause' ('Tyra's Message' 2009).

While she draws connections between ANTM and TZONE in the above instance, Banks has only recently used her celebrity to actively promote TZONE. In 2014, information was posted on the revamped version of the TZONE Foundation's website about a fund-raising gala for TZONE, the Flawsome Ball; its host committee included Banks' fashion industry colleagues such as Ann Shoket (editor-in-chief of *Seventeen* magazine) and Steven Meisel (a fashion photographer) ('Immersive Events: Changing Lives' 2014). Prior to this occasion, TZONE was solidly situated among non-profit organizations. In May 2012, it was announced that TZONE would be a leadership development centre within the Lower Eastside Girls Club ('MAY 2012 – The TZONE Takes Residence in New York City' 2009–2012). TZONE's support for the Ifetayo Cultural Arts Academy is mentioned on the Academy's website in 2007 ('Tyra Banks' TZONE Foundation Announces Its Expansion of Grant Program to NYC Community' 2007); and TZONE's support for the Young Chicago Authors program GirlSpeak is noted on their website between 2007 and 2008 ('GirlSpeak' n.d.). Interestingly, TZONE's mission is cited on the Look to the Stars: The World of Celebrity Giving website, which claims to be 'the web's number one source of celebrity charity news and information, covering what the top stars are doing to make a positive difference in the world' ('About Us' 2006–2015). However, the Look to the Stars website has no information or news about TZONE other than its mission statement, and a search for 'Tyra Banks' on that site receives no hits for any charity-related activities or events related to TZONE ('TZONE Celebrity Supporters and Events' n.d.).

Conversely, as the preceding examples suggest, the existence of TZONE enhances the legitimacy of the Banks brand messaging of female empowerment, even though it operates at first glance as a separate philanthropic initiative and provides much-needed services for girls and young women. As such, TZONE is part of Banks' brand management strategy in that it fosters a value for feminist-activist communication that becomes associated with Banks' brand. This value operates as knowledge about the brand for audiences (Arvidsson 2006), and likely feeds into their ideological and material consumption of the brand. Thus, while ANTM markets the message of empowering women via individualism and consumerism in commercial media spaces, TZONE serves to 'prove' Banks' commitment to female empowerment through feminist practices in non-mediatized, personal and even grassroots spaces. Viewed from this perspective, TZONE can be viewed as one of the range of products that make up the Banks brand.

Although messages about TZONE are rare in mass-media texts, when they are present, they reinforce Banks' brand messaging. For example, in 2002, Banks appeared with a number of girls from the TZONE camp on *Life Moments*, a reality television series distributed by Paramount, which claimed to show 'relevant and inspirational stories by and about women and the pivotal moments in their lives' ('Super Model Tyra Banks and Her TZONE Camp for Girls to be Featured on *Life Moments*' 2002). While mentioning the TZONE camp, associated media publicity emphasized Banks' celebrity and her brand. In 2007, Saleisha Stowers, the winner of Cycle 9 of ANTM, was accused of winning based on an unfair advantage because she had met Banks as a TZONE camper. Both Banks' team and Stowers adamantly rejected accusations of partiality, stressing that ANTM and TZONE are two unrelated initiatives. As Stowers explained, TZONE 'wasn't a modeling camp […] It was more like for girls who [had] low self-esteem. Girls like that. It had nothing to do with modeling' (Rocchio 2007). However, this crossover illustrates that the target audiences for TZONE and ANTM are ultimately the same, as both offer (oftentimes disadvantaged) girls and young women the dream of overcoming personal and socio-economic obstacles to achieve adult success. This message is offered to girls and women of different ages in different forms and spheres of sociocultural experience.

Conclusion

When brands originated in the late nineteenth century, they were labels that identified the manufacturer or distributor responsible for the product's quality (Strasser 1989). Today, although branding continues to trademark corporate identity through logos and so forth, the value of branding strategies lies in their ability to act as a means of social communication that draws people together through their shared knowledge of the values associated with a brand. Indeed, a demonstrated way for corporations to build an iconic brand is to merge capitalist and political messages (Holt 2004: 220; see also Millington, in this book).

The Banks brand may aspire to an iconic stature through its communication of a feminist principle: female empowerment. Yet, the ways in which this message is executed suggests that the brand itself conveys a 'postfeminist sensibility,' primarily through its 'entanglement of feminist and anti-feminist ideas' (Gill 2007: 255). Although the TZONE Foundation is a potential site for collective female empowerment and social activism, ANTM's focus on individual female empowerment oppresses women by shaping them into Bankable cultural products to benefit Banks' bottom line.

As a neoliberal entrepreneurial subject who has professed liberation from her own obstacles to become a celebrity and a philanthropist, Tyra Banks appears to present a positive role model for girls and young women. While her stated aim is 'empowering women to utilize their resources, achieve their goals and pursue their passions' ('Empowerment' 2012), this chapter has argued that Banks' brand messaging primarily stimulates women to desire celebrity as a route for their own personal power and to be ardent advocates of consumer culture. Banks perpetuates a value system that is not conducive to the realization of positive social change for girls and young women.

To sum up, TZONE's advocacy of collective female empowerment is undermined by the success of ANTM, which communicates postfeminist individualism to global audiences. These dynamics create an impression that Banks' philanthropy is an extension of the Banks brand. Whether this tension is the result of a cynical corporate strategy or simply a conceptual failure, it underscores why the mediatized philanthropic activities of A-list celebrities are often criticized as self-serving. One thing is certain, however: for the uncritical consumer of Banks' brand messaging, the problematic conflation of TZONE and ANTM values disseminates dangerous misconceptions about the meanings and practices of female empowerment in popular culture.

References

'About Us' (2006–2015) Look to the Stars, http://www.looktothestars.org/about#ixzz1rEWO14EC. Accessed 1 January 2015.
'About Us' (2008) Girls in the Game, https://www.girlsinthegame.org/content/index.asp?s=475&t=About-Us. Accessed 9 January 2015.
'About Us' (2009) TZONE Foundation, http://tzonefoundation.org/about-us. Accessed 6 April 2012.
'About Us' (2011) Typef.com, http://www.typef.com/about-us/. Accessed 20 March 2014.
Adalian, J. (2009) 'Tyra Banks' daytime talk show cancelled', *The Wrap*, 28 December, http://www.thewrap.com/tv/column-post/tyra-banks-daytime-talk-show-cancelled-12267. Accessed 9 January 2015.
'Adrianne Curry Biography' (n.d.) M&C, http://www.monstersandcritics.com/people/Adrianne-Curry/biography/. Accessed 9 January 2015.
Allan, H. (2006) 'When Tyra met Naomi', *Bitch Magazine*, http://bitchmagazine.org/article/when-tyra-met-naomi. Accessed 9 January 2015.
'America's Next Top Model' (n.d.) The CW: TV to Talk About, http://www.cwtv.com/shows/americas-next-top-model. Accessed 9 January 2015.
'America's Next Top Model Cycle 9 – Eligibility Requirements' (2007) The CW Network, 28 February, http://www.cwtv.com/images/topmodel/antm_cylce9_eligibility.pdf. Accessed 9 January 2015.
'America's Next Top Model Episode List' (n.d.) Internet Movie Database, http://www.imdb.com/title/tt0363307/episodes. Accessed 9 January 2015.
'America's Next Top Model: Apply for Cycle 21' (2014) The CW, http://www.cwtv.com/thecw/topmodel-cycle21-casting. Accessed 20 March 2014.
'America's Next Top Model: Guys, Girls' (2013) The CW, http://www.cwtv.com/shows/americas-next-top-model/episodes/2001. Accessed 20 March 2014.
'Analeigh Tipton' (n.d.) Internet Movie Database, http://www.imdb.com/name/nm3006818/. Accessed 20 March 2014.
Arvidsson, A. (2006) *Brands: Meaning and Value in Media Culture*, New York: Routledge.
Bailey, E. (2008) *Black America, Body Beautiful: How the African American Image is Changing Fashion, Fitness, and Other Industries*, Westport, CT: Praeger.
Balser, E. (2008) 'Walmart to sell *America's Next Top Model* clothing', Crushable.com, 2 December, http://crushable.com/entertainment/walmart-to-sell-americas-next-top-model-clothing/. Accessed 20 March 2014.

Banet-Weiser, S. (2007) *Kids Rule! Nickelodeon and Consumer Citizenship*, Durham: Duke University Press.

Banks, T. (2003–) *America's Next Top Model*, television series, US: Bankable Productions, http://www.imdb.com/title/tt0363307/. Accessed 9 January 2015.

Banks, T. (2003) 'The girl who wants it so bad', *America's Next Top Model*, television series, 20 May, US: Bankable Productions.

Banks, T. (2004) 'The girl who overslept', *America's Next Top Model*, television series, 13 January, US: Bankable Productions.

Banks, T. (2006) 'The girl who becomes America's Next Top Model', *America's Next Top Model*, television series, 6 December, US: Bankable Productions.

Banks, T. (2008) 'An empire behind the scenes: Tyra Banks, talk-show host and producer, on her life in front of and behind the camera', *Newsweek Magazine*, 4 October, http://www.newsweek.com/id/162338/page/2. Accessed 6 April 2012.

'Black History Month: Tyra Banks' (n.d.) Gale Cengage Learning, http://www.gale.cengage.com/free_resources/bhm/bio/banks_t.htm. Accessed 6 April 2012.

Brennan, C., and Pendergast, S. (2012) 'Tyra Banks biography – grounded in family love, entranced the Paris runways, spotted by influential director', *Net Industries*, http://biography.jrank.org/pages/2497/Banks-Tyra.html. Accessed 12 January 2015.

Chase, L. (2006) *Totally Tyra: An Unauthorized Biography*, New York: Price Stern Sloan.

Cherry, A. (n.d.) '*America's Next Top Model* winners', HubPages, http://abigailcherry.hubpages.com/hub/Americas-Next-Top-Model-Winners. Accessed 20 March 2014.

Craig, S. (2003) 'Madison Avenue versus the feminine mystique: The advertising industry's response to the women's movement', in S.A. Inness (ed.) *Disco Divas: Women and Popular Culture in the 1970s*, Philadelphia: University of Pennsylvania Press, pp. 13–23.

'Empowerment' (2012) *Bakersfield Magazine*, http://www.bakersfieldmagazine.net/features/women-in-business/606-empowerment. Accessed 20 March 2014.

Fashion Week (2006) television series, US: VH1.

Fox, S. (1984) *The Mirror Makers: A History of American Advertising and Its Creators*, New York: William Morrow and Company.

Friedan, B. (1963) *The Feminine Mystique*, London: Penguin Group.

Gill, R. (2007) *Gender and the Media*, Malden, MA: Polity Press.

'GirlSpeak' (n.d.) Young Chicago Authors, http://www.youngchicagoauthors.org/girlspeak/2008/about/history.html. Accessed 26 August 2014.

Goldman, R. (1992) *Reading Ads Socially*, New York: Routledge.

Gorman, B. (2011) '*The Vampire Diaries, Gossip Girl, 90210, Supernatural, & America's Next Top Model* renewed by the CW' TV By the Numbers, 26 April, http://tvbythenumbers.zap2it.com/2011/04/26/'the-vampire-diaries'-'gossip-girl'-'90210'-'supernatural'-americas-next-top-model-renewed-by-the-cw/90700/. Accessed 20 March 2014.

Hasinoff, A.A. (2008) 'Fashioning race for the free market on *America's Next Top Model*', *Critical Studies in Media Communication*, 25, 3: 2324–43.

Hill, A.E. (2009) *Tyra Banks: From Supermodel to Role Model*, Minneapolis, MN: Lerner Publications Company.

Hinckley, D. (2009) 'Daytime Emmy Awards 2009 winners: Rachel Ray, Tyra Banks on top, Ellen DeGeneres dethroned,' *NY Daily News*, 31 August, http://articles.nydailynews.com/2009-08-31/entertainment/29435967_1_ellen-degeneres-show-awards-ceremony-daytime-emmy-awards. Accessed 28 April 2011.

Hirschberg, L. (2008) 'Banksable', *New York Times Magazine*, 1 June, http://www.nytimes.com/2008/06/01/magazine/01tyra-t.html. Accessed 9 January 2015.

Holt, D.B. (2004) *How Brands Become Icons: The Principles of Cultural Branding*, Boston: Harvard Business School Press.

'Immersive Events: Changing Lives' (2014) TZONE Foundation, http://tzonefoundation.org/view/tzone-events. Accessed 9 January 2015.

Jeffreys, E. (1991) 'What is "difference" in feminist theory and practice?', *Australian Feminist Studies*, 14: 1–15.

Jill (2010) '*America's Next Top Model*: Tyra gets fiercely real', The CW Source, 1 February, http://weblogs.baltimoresun.com/network/cwsource/2010/02/americas_next_top_model_tyra_g.html. Accessed 9 January 2015.

Joseph, R.L. (2009) '"Tyra Banks is fat": Reading (post-)racism and (post-)feminism in the new millennium', *Critical Studies in Media Communication*, 26, 3: 237–54.

JRAJ9 (2012) 'Top 10 most influential black supermodels', The Top Tens, http://www.the-top-tens.com/lists/influential-black-supermodels.asp. Accessed 9 January 2015.

Keith, A.E. (2009) 'Tyra Banks says goodbye to talk show', People.com, 28 December, http://www.people.com/people/article/0,,20421592,00.html. Accessed 20 March 2014.

Klein, N. 2002, *No Logo: No Space, No Choice, No Jobs*, New York: Picador.

Kris (2007) 'Tyra Banks: Reliving the *Sports Illustrated* cover milestone', BuddyTV, 15 February, http://www.buddytv.com/articles/americas-next-top-model/tyra-banks-reliving-the-sports-4109.aspx. Accessed 20 March 2014.

'May 2012 – The TZONE Takes Residence in New York City' (2009–2012) TZONE Foundation, http://tzonefoundation.org/tzone-updates/. Accessed 12 February 2014.

Mosthof, M. (2011) 'CariDee English is ANTM's most ambitious former winner', *Wetpaint Entertainment*, 3 January, http://www.wetpaint.com/americas-next-top-model/articles/caridee-english-is-antms-most-ambitious-former-winner. Accessed 20 March 2014.

'Nicole Fox of Louisville Wins *America's Next Top Model*' (2010) *The Huffington Post*, 18 March, http://www.huffingtonpost.com/2009/11/18/nicole-fox-of-louisville_n_362931.html. Accessed 9 January 2015.

Norment, L. (1997), 'Tyra Banks: On top of the world – African American fashion model', *Ebony*, May, http://findarticles.com/p/articles/mi_m1077/is_n7_v52/ai_19383832/?tag=mantle_skin;content. Accessed 5 May 2011.

'Our Mission' (2009) TZONE Foundation, http://tzonefoundation.org/our-mission. Accessed 14 March 2014.

Penrice, R.R. (2010) 'TheGrio's 100: Tyra Banks, a model who's breaking the mold', TheGrio.com, 1 February, http://2010.thegrio.com/black-history/thegrios-100/thegrios-100-tyra-banks.php. Accessed 10 May 2011.

Proscout (2009) 'Former supermodel named one of the world's most influential women', ProScout: Talent Discovery Blog, 15 July, http://www.proscoutblog.com/former-supermodel-named-one-of-the-worlds-most-influential-women/. Accessed 17 May 2011.

Reyes, J. (creator) (2004–5) *Kevin Hill*, television series, US: United Paramount Network.

Rocchio, C. (2007) '*Top Model* Saleisha Stowers defends prior Tyra Banks relationship', Reality TV World, 14 December, http://www.realitytvworld.com/news/top-model-saleisha-stowers-defends-prior-tyra-banks-relationship-6264.php. Accessed 12 January 2015.

Rose, L. (2009) 'Prime-time TV's 20 top-earning women', *Forbes*, 9 February, http://www.forbes.com/2008/08/28/television-actresses-hollywood-biz-media-cx_lr_0902tvstars.html. Accessed 20 March 2014.

Rose, L. (2010) 'Prime-time's top-earning women', *Forbes*, 10 December, http://www.forbes.com/2009/10/09/prime-time-actresses-business-entertainment-tyra.html. Accessed 20 March 2014.

Siegel, D.L. (1997) 'Reading the waves: Feminist historiography in a "postfeminist" moment', in L. Heywood and J. Drake (eds) *Third Wave Agenda: Being Feminist, Doing Feminism*, Minneapolis, MN: University of Minnesota Press, pp. 55–82.

Silverman, S. (2008) 'Ellen DeGeneres, Tyra Banks win daytime Emmys', People.com, 21 June, http://www.people.com/people/article/0,,20208186,00.html. Accessed 20 March 2014.

Simon, R. (prod.) (2005–2012) *The Look for Less*, television series, US: Style Network and Planet Style Productions.

'Spotted Ratings: *America's Next Top Model*' (2010) Spottedratings.com, 11 August, http://www.spottedratings.com/2010/08/war-of-18-49-americas-next-top-model.html. Accessed 20 March 2014.

Stack, T. (2008) 'Tyra Banks: America's next top mogul', *Entertainment Weekly*, 10 March, http://www.ew.com/ew/article/0,,20178169,00.html. Accessed 20 March 2014.

Stevens, L.A. (prod.) (2005–2008) *My Fair Brady*, television series, US: VH1.

Strasser, S. (1989) *Satisfaction Guaranteed: The Making of the American Mass Market*, Washington, DC: Smithsonian Institution Press.

'Super Model Tyra Banks and Her Tzone Camp for Girls to be Featured on *Life Moments*' (2002) Prnewswire.com, 30 October, http://www.prnewswire.com/news-releases/super-model-tyra-banks-and-her-tzone-camp-for-girls-to-be-featured-on-life-moments-76544187.html. Accessed 20 March 2014.

'Take Great Pictures: Tyra Banks' (n.d.) Takegreatpictures.com, http://www.takegreatpictures.com/photo-tips/celebrities-who-shoot/tyra-banks. Accessed 9 January 2015.

Talbot, M.M. (2000) 'Strange bedfellows: Feminism in advertising', in M. Andrews and M.M. Talbot (eds) *All the World and Her Husband: Women in Twentieth-Century Consumer Culture*, New York: Cassell, pp. 177–91.

Tasker, Y., and Negra, D. (2007) 'Introduction: Feminist politics and postfeminist culture', in Y. Tasker and D. Negra (eds) *Interrogating Postfeminism: Gender and the Politics of Popular Culture*, Durham, NC: Duke University Press, pp. 1–25.

'The Celebrity 100: The World's Most Powerful Celebrities 2006' (2006) *Forbes*, 16 June, http://www.forbes.com/2006/06/15/richest-celebrities-powerful_cx_lg_06celebrities_0615celebrityintro.html. Accessed 20 March 2014.

'The Celebrity 100: The World's Most Powerful Celebrities 2007' (2007) *Forbes*, 14 June, http://www.forbes.com/lists/2007/53/07celebrities_The-Celebrity-100_Rank_3.html. Accessed 20 March 2014.

'The Celebrity 100: #68 Tyra Banks' (2008) *Forbes*, 11 June, http://www.forbes.com/lists/2008/53/celebrities08_Tyra-Banks_L5FY.html. Accessed 20 March 2014.

'*Top Model*' (2015) Wikipedia, http://en.wikipedia.org/wiki/Top_Model_series. Accessed 9 January 2015.

'Tyra Banks' (n.d.) Blackentrepreneurprofile.com, http://www.blackentrepreneurprofile.com/profile-full/article/tyra-banks/. Accessed 20 March 2012.

'Tyra Banks' (2011) Kim's Amazing Blog, 9 March, http://kimscs15.edublogs.org/2011/03/09/tyra-banks. Accessed 6 April 2012.

'Tyra Banks and TZONE Foundation Celebrate Girls in the Game' (2008) Girls in the Game, http://www.girlsinthegame.org/news/article.asp?p=242&s=496&t=Tyra-Banks-and-TZone-Foundation-Celebrate-Girls-in-the-Game. Accessed 9 January 2015.

'Tyra Banks Discusses Camp' (2002) CNN, 28 August, http://edition.cnn.com/TRANSCRIPTS/0208/28/lt.04.html. Accessed 9 January 2015.

'Tyra Banks Establishes Girls' Camp' (2002) Teenhollywood.com, 9 September, http://www.teenhollywood.com/2002/09/09/tyra-banks-establishes-girls-camp. Accessed 9 January 2015.

'Tyra Banks Net Worth' (n.d.) The Richest, http://www.therichest.com/celebnetworth/celeb/model/tyra-banks-net-worth/. Accessed 9 January 2015.

'Tyra Banks' TZONE Foundation' (2015) GuideStar, http://www.guidestar.org/organizations/20-3118514/tyra-banks-tzone-foundation.aspx. Accessed 9 January 2015.

'Tyra Banks' TZONE Foundation Announces Its Expansion of Grant Program to NYC Community' (2007) Ifetayo Cultural Arts Academy, 8 May, http://www.ashayproductions.com/ifetayo/news/tzone.shtml. Accessed 26 August 2014.

'Tyra's Inner Circle' (2010) Typef.com, http://tyra.typef.com/view/LOOK_FIERCE. Accessed 12 January 2012.

'Tyra's Message' (2009) TZONE Foundation, http://tzonefoundation.org/tyras-message/. Accessed 20 March 2014.

'TZONE Camps at Scripps' (2011) *Scripps College Media Relations*, http://media.scrippscollege.edu/feature-stories/tzone-camps-at-scripps. Accessed 20 March 2014.

'TZONE Celebrity Supporters and Events' (n.d) Look to the Stars, http://www.looktothestars.org/charity/450-tzone. Accessed 9 January 2015.

'TZONE Network' (2009) TZONE Foundation, http://tzonefoundation.org/tzone-network/. Accessed 6 April 2012.

'TZONE Story' (2009) TZONE Foundation, http://tzonefoundation.org/tzone-story/. Accessed 20 March 2014.

Weber, D. (2009) *Makeover TV: Selfhood, Citizenship, and Celebrity*, Durham: Duke University Press.

Chapter 5

Celebrating Development Through Sport: Right to Play and Basketball Without Borders

Rob Millington

This chapter explores the intersection of celebrity, aid and international development by focusing on the emergence of two historically unique yet interrelated socio-political phenomena – the rise of celebrity involvement in international aid, and the proliferation of international aid programs using sport as a tool for development in the global South.[1] The celebrity-as-spokesperson for consumer goods or social causes is not a new concept. The celebrity has long been entrenched as the intermediary between corporations, products and the consumer. Yet, recently, we have seen a shift by which the two social phenomena – the celebrity as commercial entity and the celebrity as social activist – have begun to merge, particularly within the realm of international aid and development, creating what Richey and Ponte (2008) call the 'aid celebrity'. As Richey and Ponte (2008: 716) note, aid celebrities arguably 'embody a new positive, win-win approach to solving poverty and disease. After more than three decades of defeatism in development, aid celebrities are the new totems of possibility'.

The emergence of the aid celebrity within the current socio-political climate is unique for at least three reasons. First, a significant shift has occurred in the number and range of celebrities taking part in philanthropic initiatives. Once largely the purview of the business elite, philanthropy (the private donation of capital wealth to causes) and charity (organizations dedicated to the welfare of others) have expanded to include not only 'celebrities' in the private sector, such as Bill Gates and Warren Buffett, but also celebrities from the realm of popular culture, especially film stars, musicians and sport stars. Second, contemporary celebrity-based aid has increasingly focused on social responsibility within the broader global context of international development; Angelina Jolie's status as Goodwill Ambassador to the UNHCR is perhaps the most obvious example. Third, we have seen an increasing commodification of aid where corporations and their celebrity endorsers have sought to align themselves with philanthropic endeavours, in what Samantha King (2006) calls 'cause-related marketing'. In this consumer-oriented form of aid, the power of capitalism is ostensibly harnessed and re-directed towards social good, where a portion of the proceeds of commercial sales are donated to charitable organizations/causes. Examples of such corporate-led consumer-based initiatives include 'pink ribbon' campaigns for breast cancer (King 2006), 'green' initiatives focusing on environmental issues (Brockington 2009), and campaigns to raise funds for the elimination of HIV and AIDS in Africa, such as Product RED, a brand established by the rock star Bono in 2006 ('Our Story' n.d.).

Over the past decade, sport-based corporations like Nike and the US-based NBA have also sought to align themselves with cause-related marketing, to the extent of creating their own programs. Nike is involved in various anti-war, community development, environmental, global homelessness and HIV-awareness programs ('Sport is Our Passion' 2012). The NBA, in partnership with the Federation International Basketball Association (FIBA) holds sport for development camps in the global South through their social responsibility initiative, Basketball without Borders (BWB) ('Basketball without Borders' 2015).

These corporate sport for development programs articulate with a broader movement in international development where sport is increasingly promoted as a tool of development in an endeavour popularly termed Sport for Development and Peace (SDP).[2] The UN, governments of the global North and South, NGOs, and the private sector have all jumped on the SDP bandwagon. In 2014, more than 130 organizations from these sectors enlisted sport as a means of development ('ISCA Moving People' n.d.). While SDP programs diverge in their implementation of sport as a tool of development and aid, their use of celebrities and celebrity athletes is nearly universal. The more than 100 sport stars – including David Beckham and Maria Sharapova – who have been appointed as UN 'Ambassadors' or 'Spokespersons' exemplify this ('Goodwill Ambassadors' n.d.).

This chapter examines programs that use sport as a tool for development in the global South through a combination of celebrity, aid and international development. I first historicize the 'aid celebrity', exploring both the potential benefits and detriments of celebrity involvement in international aid programs. I then examine the origins of SDP programs and the role of celebrity involvement in them. I conclude with a discursive analysis of two SDP programs employing sport celebrities in the development context: the Canada-based NGO Right to Play (RTP), and the NBA's (in conjunction with FIBA) corporate social responsibility program BWB.[3]

A discursive analysis of documents available on the RTP and NBA websites highlights some of the complex political–economic underpinnings of the intersection of sport, celebrity and development. Discourses do not merely reflect social entities and relations, but rather actively construct them. As Norman Fairclough (1992: 4) writes, any discursive event can be seen as simultaneously 'a piece of text, an instance of discursive practice, and an instance of social practice'; texts simultaneously represent reality, enact social relations and establish identities.

By using RTP and BWB as a case study, I demonstrate the symbolic and material effects of the celebrity's involvement in the development landscape. Within the context of neoliberal globalization, the primacy and feasibility of celebrity sponsored aid as a means to sustainable development is worthy of critique. Given the increasing reach and influence that celebrities have been afforded, and given their adoption of 'socially responsible' agendas in the global South, the question becomes what kind of development is being advocated via celebrity-sanctified aid? While the sport-aid celebrity has potential to draw attention to social issues including international development, their positionality within capitalist enterprises may reduce their effectiveness, constrict understanding of development, or even (symbolically and materially) undermine development efforts by contributing to capitalist paradigms of uneven development.

The Celebrity Allure: Ethical Intervention and the Aid Celebrity

The aid celebrity has emerged, at least conceptually, as a key player for reinvigorating what has been seen as a faltering development landscape. Although 'development' ideology had existed for centuries, the contemporary (and problematic) 'western' understanding of development that marked a break from colonial linkages towards a new era of 'compassionate development' can be traced to 20 January 1949 (Esteva 1992). On that day, in the fourth point of his inauguration speech, US President Harry Truman called for a new worldview where the global South would follow in the footsteps of the US, down a path of industrialization, and into a new world of global capitalism, materialism and consumerism. Truman stated,

> We must embark on a bold new program for making the benefits of our scientific advance and industrial progress available for the improvement and growth of underdeveloped areas. The old Imperialism – exploited for foreign profit – has no place in our plans. What we envisage is a program of development based on the concepts of democratic fair dealing.
> (Truman cited in Esteva 1992: 6)

The discourse framed in 'Point Four', and as a result, much of the discourse of the time, changed the construction of the global South from colonial appendages to 'underdeveloped' areas that required the aid of the North. Prior to Truman's inauguration speech, 'development' in the nineteenth and early twentieth centuries was tied to a political ethos in Europe of colonial domination. As Gustavo Esteva (1992: 17) notes, economization and colonization were synonymous: what Truman had succeeded in doing in his speech was to 'free the economic sphere from the negative connotations it had accumulated for two centuries, delinking development from colonialism'. While international development has had a complex and contentious history since Truman's speech, a central theme throughout has been capitalist growth.

The increasing celebritization and corporatization of development initiatives, exemplified by Product RED and BWB, are some of the latest manifestation in this timeline, where the celebrity and capitalist consumption are seen as means of raising awareness and funds for international aid projects. This new(er) form of compassionate development is heavily influenced by what Heribert Dieter and Rajiv Kumar (2008) call 'development biz' and 'development buzz' in reference to the growing commodification of the development and aid industries, and the increasing popularities of these endeavours. Development biz encompasses the bureaucracies, agencies and NGOs that mark the professionalization of global development. Development buzz comprises rock stars and celebrities.

The celebrity as activist and philanthropic aid worker began to emerge with the civil rights, anti-war and environmental movements of the 1960s and 1970s. Richey and Ponte (2008: 716) argue that the culminating moment in the rise of celebrity-activist was the Bob Geldof-led Band Aid recording of 'Do They Know It's Christmas' in 1984 and the related Live Aid concert a year later – viewed by an estimated international audience of two billion people – that raised almost USD 150 million. Live Aid is largely credited for setting the wheels in motion for the nexus of compassionate aid, the celebrity activist and commercialism, which is typified by fund-raising drives through concerts, television specials and consumer goods.

The successes of celebrity diplomacy in the post-Live Aid era lie not only in the gaps in the structure and agency of global governance, but also in the nature of globalization (Cooper 2008). The nature of globalization itself affords the celebrity opportunities to formulate, sell and target their initiatives to the public, as well as to government officials, and to bring issues like underdevelopment and AIDS to the forefront of public consciousness. In the words of Andrew Cooper (2008: 17), 'Celebrities provide a convenient surrogate for, and a conduit in response to, the traditional bonds that hold society together, performing a mobilizing, interpreting, and, most importantly, mediating function within traditional institutions'.

While celebrities are productive in their ability to fill the gaps in global governance, where they hold perhaps their greatest strength is in raising awareness of, and generating funds for, global aid. The celebrity makes global health issues and development visible to 'Northern' audiences, allowing for participation in international aid through consciousness raising, advocacy, material support (donations) and consumption (both directly through the purchase of products linked to socially responsible initiatives like Product RED, and indirectly through the support of celebrities and corporations as is the case with BWB). Celebrity involvement in the development context marks a significant shift in how development and global aid are presented, one that proposes to show a more meaningful commitment to development and towards mobilizing capitalism for productive means. The celebrity ostensibly brings an air of legitimacy to development and aid endeavours via the celebrity's visibility and recognizability, and influence in popular media and politics.

In many ways, the corporate sponsor and the celebrity have emerged to represent the 'faces of ethical intervention in the world' (Richey and Ponte 2006: 5). Together, they bring attention to humanitarian aid endeavours and encourage the average consumer to participate in them by purchasing products. As the Product RED campaign posits, 'the only sustainable way that [HIV and AIDS in Africa] could be addressed by business was if there was a way to generate revenues for companies, then some of the profit could be channelled to Africans with AIDS' (cited in Richey and Ponte 2006: 7).

In the context of the long and contentious history of international development, the emergence of celebrity and corporate sponsored aid is perhaps not unexpected. What is significant, however, is the extent to which capitalist/consumer-oriented aid, underpinned by the support of celebrities, has begun to take hold. Sport celebrities are also playing an increasingly prominent role in this arena.

Pitfalls and Profits/Prophets: Sport, Capitalism and Development

While it is perhaps obvious (in terms of marketing) that celebrities can and do promote development, the involvement of the sporting celebrity in development programs is potentially problematic for at least three reasons. First, given the ties of the celebrity and sport to commercialism, the neoliberal ideologies to which they are linked may be antithetical to global development. As David Andrews and Steven Jackson (2001: 1) argue, 'the contemporary celebrity is an embodiment of the twinned discourses of late modernity: neo-liberal democracy and consumer capitalism'. The rise of celebrity is inextricably linked to the rise of commercial capitalism and mass mediatization; one cannot be separated from the other (Rojek 2001).

In the same way that soft drinks cannot be unlinked from brand names like Coca-Cola or Pepsi, sporting celebrities cannot be unlinked from professional leagues like the NBA, and numerous corporate brands such as Nike. Just as celebrities urge us to consume Coca-Cola, they now ask us to consume development. Locating capitalism within the celebrity/development/aid paradigm is crucial given that the positionality of the celebrity reflect neoliberal patterns of global capitalism that are part and parcel of an ongoing history of (neo) colonialism and unequal/underdevelopment. Making development issues a marketable commodity through celebrity endorsements and corporate social responsibility programs – for instance, Bono's mantra for Product RED that 'saving lives is sexy' (Richey and Ponte 2008) – proffers a sanitized understanding of development that may obfuscate political, social and structural causes of underdevelopment.

Second, given the highly complex and precarious development context, it is important to consider how well suited the celebrity is for addressing issues of under/unequal development, and how their positionality affects the development landscape. In a book on celebrity diplomacy, Cooper (2008) posits that the largely untrained background of the celebrity compared to the traditional diplomat, elected officials or development practitioners, and given the contentious and complex nature of international development, potentially positions the celebrity to do more harm than good. While celebrities certainly draw attention to international development efforts, the content of the messages they provide may proffer an oversimplification of political issues that fail to account for the complexities of development. Dieter and Kumar (2008: 260) similarly point out, 'Inevitably, development buzz has to keep its message simple, driven by the need for slogans, images, and anger. Unfortunately, although the plight of the bottom billion lends itself to simple moralizing, the answers do not'. This is evident with Product RED, where such an approach 'allows Bono and Product RED to focus on cool, sexy branding rather than on poverty, inequality and disease', which has resulted in 'the marriage of consumption and social causes [as] one and indivisible' (Richey and Ponte 2008: 716; see also Bell and Van den Bulck, Claessens and Panis, in this book).

As Simon Darnell (2007) argues in his work on RTP, the exchange of ideas and feelings between the celebrity and RTP participant is overshadowed by global socio-economic inequalities. Although the sporting hero has traditionally been perceived as epitomizing social ideals, and as embodying values learnt on the playing fields that will readily transfer into everyday life (Lines 2001), the cultural capital and (Northern) experiences of these celebrities may not be transferable to the global South. The star power of the western athlete may attract Northern audiences, but it may have little personal or cultural significance in the development context (Smart 2007: 573).

Finally, the symbolic capital of the celebrity provides stark juxtaposition (in terms of their positionality in the global North and the divide in material wealth emblematic of stratified global economic inequality) to images of the malnourished, impoverished 'Other' that are projected through these campaigns as the recipients of aid. In this regard, there is something unique that sport and the sporting celebrity offer to the analysis of celebrity-based aid. In contrast to images of malnourished children mired in poverty in Africa broadcasted to billions of people in 'Do They Know It's Christmas' in 1984, and Live Aid in 1985 (Richey and Ponte 2008: 716), the images projected through sport celebrities involved in SDP programs show images of happy, healthy, active children participating in sport. Such images offer a counter-narrative to the homogenized and universalized understanding of poverty and underdevelopment in the global South, and mark a significant turn away from the images associated with the marketing of international aid in the 1980s. This is one of the proclaimed benefits of the various celebrity-sponsored SDP initiatives that have emerged since the 1990s.

SDP: Right to Play and Basketball without Borders

Since the early 2000s, the UN has actively promoted sport as a tool of social, economic and political development. The adoption of 2005 as the International Year for Sport and Physical Education by the UN and the creation of the UN Office on SDP (UNOSDP) are illustrative of the celebrated position of sport within the development paradigm. Sport has influenced the development landscape at the level of policy, where the UN has outlined the contribution of sport to all eight Millennium Development Goals and has tied it to Poverty Reduction Strategy Papers (PRSPs) (Sport for Development and Peace International Working Group 2008). Sport has also influenced the development landscape in practice through the proliferation of SDP programs, such as RTP and the Kenyan-based Mathare Youth Sport Organizations, as well as more corporate formations such as BWB, Nike's Let Me Play program and the International Olympic Committee's Olympism in Action program.

The support of sport celebrities has been crucial to the ascension of SDP as a viable development practice through their promotion of and involvement in SDP programs. Indeed, the 'spheres within which sport celebrities operate as cultural and economic agents have broadened beyond the playing field and corporate endorsement' to include international aid initiatives seeking to capitalize on the visibility of athletes (Andrews and Jackson 2001: 7). International development programs have increasingly looked to celebrity endorsers for the values they ostensibly embody, that is, hard work and dedication, and for the global audience to which they have access. On this point, Andrews and Jackson (2001: 8) note, 'only sport has the nation, and sometimes the world, watching the same thing at the same time, and if you have a message, that's a potent messenger'.

Sport celebrities are active in a variety of international aid/development initiatives. NBA athletes Yao Ming and Steve Nash, for example, have worked with the Red Cross and Aid Still Required (a disaster-relief program in Haiti), respectively. Footballers David Beckham and Zinedine Zidane have worked for the United Nations Children's Fund (UNICEF) and the United Nations Development Programme (UNDP), respectively. However, the sport celebrity is most active and visible in international aid initiatives as part of SDP programs.

The NGO RTP and the NBA/FIBA's BWB program are two prominent SDP programs that feature the sport celebrity as development practitioner. RTP grew out of Olympic Aid, which was inaugurated in 1992 under the auspices of the Olympic Organizing Committee in preparation for the 1994 Winter Olympic Games in Lillehammer. The focus of Olympic Aid was to utilize the fame of athletes participating in the games to generate funds for people in 'war-torn countries and areas of distress' ('History: The History of Right to Play' 2013). Under the direction of Johann Olav Koss, the four-time Norwegian gold medalist speed-skater, Olympic Aid raised USD 18 million for building hospitals in Sarajevo, schools in Eritrea, 'mother/child programs' in Guatemala, refugees in Afghanistan and children with disabilities in Lebanon ('Our Story' 2013).

In the late 2000s, Olympic Aid (due to sponsorship conflicts) transitioned to RTP. RTP is an NGO that holds development programs in the global South by using sport celebrities from more than 40 countries to act as 'Athlete Ambassadors' and 'role models' for children around the world, because of their experience with 'the power of sport, and its ability to build essential life skills such as self-esteem, discipline, fair play, respect and teamwork' ('Athletes' 2013). Many of the celebrities participate in local camps by acting as councillors, coaches and educators on issues ranging from AIDS to health and fitness. RTP stresses that these celebrities receive no compensation for their aid. Their work is purely philanthropic. Some famous RTP Athlete Ambassadors include: Canadian hockey player Wayne Gretzky; Congolese basketballer Dikembe Mutombo; US footballer Steve Young; and British soccer player Joe Cole.

Although BWB is not the only corporate sport for development program (Adidas and Nike are also enthusiastic proponents of corporate philanthropy initiatives), BWB proves an interesting case study because of its cross-promotion of its product, the NBA, and development in the global South through NBA celebrities. The program is intended as a form of global outreach in which the global South can benefit from the wealth – economic, intellectual and otherwise – that the NBA has to offer. According to an NBA press release:

> The NBA's global outreach program Basketball without Borders transcends all boundaries by uniting young people from diverse cultural, national and economic backgrounds on four separate continents to learn through the sport of basketball. The program uniquely incorporates basketball instruction and educational programs that create a forum for important social issues such as HIV/AIDS prevention while emphasizing the importance of education and healthy living.
> ('Basketball without Borders Community Outreach' 2006)

The NBA touts BWB as a means to social and economic development in the global South by wedding basketball with education on important social issues and the development of sport-related infrastructure ('Basketball without Borders Mission' 2015). The league claims to be able to contribute to development while promoting their product and corporate agenda in the global South. It runs camps for participants aged 19 and under from across regions in developing countries. Participants are almost exclusively boys. While the NBA began to incorporate young women into their campaign in 2010, their participation remains limited. At each camp, NBA celebrities such as Chris Bosh, Dwight Howard and Dirk Nowitzki (who all attended the 2010 camp in South Africa) are selected to act as camp ambassadors to coach the participants, and provide education on healthy eating, life skills and AIDS. Players are also active in the community, making appearances at local hospitals and at reading and learning centers that the league has helped to build ('Basketball without Borders Mission' 2015).

In the summers of 2011–2014, BWB camps with numerous NBA celebrity ambassadors were held in Johannesburg, South Africa ('Basketball Without Borders, Africa 2013' 2014; 'Basketball without Borders' 2015). Previously, BWB camps have taken place in other developing nations such as Senegal (2010), Mexico (2009), China (Beijing in 2005 and 2009, and Shanghai in 2006 and 2007), Turkey (2002 and 2008) and India (2008) (for a list of all BWB camps see http://bwb.fiba.com/camps). Moreover, multinational corporations such as Reebok and McDonald's have been active in the program, with Reebok providing clothing for campers, and McDonald's (somewhat ironically) providing information about proper nutrition ('Basketball without Borders Makes Inaugural Trip to China' 2005).

The draw of sport celebrities as promotional entities in development efforts is readily apparent. Sport celebrities can aid in raising awareness of issues of global underdevelopment and development programs through their positionality in the cultural milieu. It is also clear that the discourses produced through RTP and the NBA's documents on the BWB program, and popular media coverage of these programs, are intended for an audience located mostly outside of the areas in which they operate, and are constructed such that they increase the marketability/visibility of both RTP and the NBA, and the programs they promote (see righttoplay.com and nba.com). However, it is my contention that the marketing of these efforts to audiences outside of the global South is emblematic of some of the broader concerns with celebrity involvement in the development context. Celebrity marketing may undermine such aid efforts, and the knowledge produced through such marketing may have deleterious consequences for how aid is conceptualized.

Discourses of Development: Celebrity and SDP

Development programs like RTP and BWB can be seen as contact zones (between celebrities and their audiences in the global North and the recipients of aid in the global South) that reproduce hegemonic ideologies surrounding development and underdevelopment. From a Foucauldian perspective, development is itself a discourse that constructs its own reality by producing and reaffirming dominant ideologies governed by a range of dichotomies, such as North/South, developed/developing and white/black (Kiely 1999). It is through discourse that a dominant understanding of development is constructed to make truth claims surrounding what underdevelopment looks like, where it is located and how it can be addressed. Development narratives are often constructed through the developer, whether on a structural level (the economic policies of the International Monetary Fund and the World Bank, for example), or on the ground level (through the discursive constructions of development organizations and practitioners), which holds both symbolic and material consequences for how we approach international aid. Thus, while celebrities do raise awareness regarding development, their experiences and actions form narrative devices that produce knowledge of the subjects of development and also of their surroundings (Kiely 1999: 31). Narrowly defined understandings of development often shape and are shaped by hegemonic power relations, which are formed in historical patterns of unequal distribution of resources. In turn, those relations both produce and arise from notions of superiority regarding the position of the global North in relation to the global South (Darnell 2007).

Development programs like RTP and BWB reproduce hegemonic ideologies surrounding development and underdevelopment in two key ways. The first way is through the celebrity encounter with, and production of, the 'Other' in the global South. The second way in which celebrity involvement in development programs like RTP and BWB can contribute to the hegemony of underdevelopment is through the reproduction of power dynamics between the embodied locations of the global North and global South.

Inherent to development programs like RTP and BWB is the movement of individuals, most often from the global North into the global South, to provide aid to a myriad of social issues. As such, development programs become a contact zone between people from the global North and South, both physically and symbolically, where both developer and recipient are influenced and defined within the development terrain. Discursively, the two sides shape identities in juxtaposition to one another: the celebrity as benevolent aid worker, representative of development and symbol of commercialism; the recipient often framed as the grateful, passive 'Other' (Razack 2005; see also Bell and Van den Bulck, Claessens and Panis, in this book).

Othering is a style of thought based upon the ontological and epistemological distinction made between the global South (the Other) and the global North. In exploring the intersection of identity and space locally and globally, Narda Razack (2005) argues that racialized bodies are viewed differently in Northern and Southern spaces. Razack notes that identities remained tied to colonial linkages as white bodies remained privileged in both Northern and Southern spaces. Yet the hegemony of globalization in the post-colonial order has complicated realities of privilege and oppression, rendering both more covert and subversive. In this regard, development projects – similar to colonial encounters – create a contact zone in which peoples 'come into contact with each other and establish ongoing relations, usually involving conditions of coercion, racial inequality, and intractable conflict' (Razack 2005: 93). Importantly, however, as Mary Louise Pratt (1992) notes, all sides involved in such contact zones are transformed by the contact – albeit within structures of domination – and that both aid worker and aid recipient have agency and power in these interactions. Here, I explore how the discourses produced by celebrities within the contact zones of RTP and BWB influence our understanding of the role of the celebrity in the development context, the means in which development is enacted, and the impact it may have on people in the development context.

While the celebrity has the ability to draw the attention of much of the global North towards issues of poverty, health and development in the global South, the type of attention that is garnered may in reality draw attention to their actions rather than the social and structural realities of underdevelopment. This obfuscation is demonstrated in the following quote from RTP athlete ambassador and two-time Canadian Olympic gold-medalist Catriona Le May Doan:

> It's been absolutely incredible, and truly life changing. The fact of knowing [Right to Play founder] Johann [Koss] from speed-skating, and seeing what he has done with his passion, and what he and his entire team have created, and how it has grown, and then to go into the field, to go to Tanzania and experience that difference first hand, it's changed my life. And at that time, my daughter was just a baby, and to go there and to see these babies in a community that had nothing, and to see them doing the same actions that my baby-girl was doing was absolutely incredible. And it really made an impact on me, and the fact that being a mom, I want to make sure that when she's older, she understands that she's very fortunate to live in Canada.
>
> (Doan 2010)

The celebrity may be just as passionate and committed as other development workers; yet, their involvement in the development context may be as much about marketing and drawing the attention of Northern audiences to these particular programs and the celebrities themselves. Here, Doan demonstrates how the celebrity is also shaped and changed within the contact zone of development through the discursive juxtaposition of her children with those in RTP programs. Such constructions also demonstrate that the attention garnered by audiences outside of the global South may in fact focus on the actions of the celebrity, rather than the issues they attempt to draw attention to. In this regard, the celebrity athlete benefits from this arrangement, as his/her actions are viewed as altruistic (seen here in the framing of Koss), thus augmenting both the sport star's popularity and the support of audiences in the global North. By reaffirming the benevolence of SDP initiatives and celebrities therein, critical analysis of how these programs enact development may be overshadowed. The potential pitfalls of these endeavours, such as the reproduction of hegemonic power relations, unequal economic encounters and neocolonial practices, are ostensibly blocked.

In this way, the role of the celebrity may draw attention away from issues of underdevelopment in the global South, and towards the compassion of particular stakeholders. Richey and Ponte (2006) highlight this point in their work on Product RED by arguing that 'Bono is the totem of "compassionate consumption", steering attention from the causes of poverty, such as the inequities of systems of production and trade, by focusing on the outcome, HIV/AIDS' (Richey and Ponte 2006: 21). Similarly, RTP and BWB materials focus more on the actions of the celebrities than the conditions of poverty, or what the RTP and BWB are doing to address those conditions.

The focus on the celebrity and outcomes rather than on specific development issues is evident in the following quote from cyclist Lance Armstrong, previously located on the RTP website. In the words of Armstrong:

> Sport for development and peace programs are harnessing the power of sport and play to put children on a healthier development path. As my personal experiences have shown, sport has the power to change and heal lives, to build self-esteem, confidence, and leadership and to create extraordinary possibilities.
>
> ('Athlete Quotes' n.d.)

That the actions of Lance Armstrong can have real and measureable effects on the lives of those in RTP's programs is certainly true. However, the narrative produced by these organizations, again largely for an audience outside of the global South, focuses on outcomes such as self-esteem, confidence, and leadership, rather than on the processes or causes of underdevelopment.

RTP and BWB and the celebrities within may argue that perhaps it is not the role of the organizations to address root causes of unequal development, or that this is merely the marketing face of these organizations. Although this may be true, the fact remains that these narratives get taken up in popular media to create an understanding that something tangible is happening in the development context to address underdevelopment. Moreover, given that SDP initiatives and the involvement of celebrities is posited as a new, multilateral and dedicated effort to eradicating poverty and underdevelopment, the narrative devices presented may in fact demonstrate the re-packaging of old development tropes.

The second way in which celebrity involvement in development programs like RTP and BWB can contribute to the hegemony of underdevelopment is through the reproduction of power dynamics between the embodied locations of the global North and global South. Narrative devices produced within RTP and BWB go beyond raising awareness that parts of the global South are in need of development. They actively shape understanding of the reality of development, and who embodies the racialized and spatialized (in the sense that development is something that only occurs in the global South) location of the global South. The discourses produced in the development/aid context positions the global North (via the intervention of aid programs, the celebrity, capitalism) to manage and produce the global South politically, ideological and imaginatively (Said 1978: 3). Celebrity aid in the development context thus has the potential to be marginalizing and patronizing by constructing the global North (and positioning themselves) as the possessors of knowledge and power, which is then imparted to recipients in the global South (Darnell 2007).

In the NBA's documents on BWB, many parts of the global South are portrayed within a restricted framework of poverty and destitution that serves to (re)produce the dominant (stereotyped) vision of the area. In this regard, the celebrity creates a 'regime of truth' (to use a Foucauldian term) over developing countries that reinforce the dichotomization and divide between the global North and South. Jan Nederveen Pieterse (2000: 180) argues, 'development can best be described as an apparatus that links forms of knowledge about the Global South with the deployment of forms of power and intervention, resulting in the mapping and production of Third World societies'. This mapping is reflected in BWB documents where the experiences of NBA athletes in South Africa enact truth claims that articulate with dominant understandings of what underdevelopment 'looks like':

> They witnessed first hand the degradation and squalor that the innocent children of Kliptown are being born into. For a population of over 40,000 there are only 49 working taps. The central points of each community, these same taps are used for washing, cleaning and of course drinking. The lack of basic hygiene was particularly striking; five families, of maybe seven members or more, would share a single toilet. It was evident for all to see, and for anyone that as willing to listen that the residents are desperate for basic development to better the intolerable living conditions that they endure each and every day.
> ('NBA Players See a New World' 2005)

This quotation frames the global South as a dire, impoverished area. The fact that the children of Kliptown are living in overcrowded, unhygienic conditions is worthy of concern and political action, and making these conditions known is certainly important. However, it is unclear how the actions of celebrities in BWB are alleviating poverty. Again, the role of the celebrity in the development context ostensibly focuses on outcomes, for example, increasing self-efficacy and providing education, rather than the root causes of underdevelopment. While the argument can be made that it is outside the celebrities' capacity to do so, the images projected to audiences outside of the global South propose a solution to underdevelopment (see also Van den Bulck, Claessens and Panis, in this book).

The quotation above also highlights how the developer often speaks for the recipients of aid in the global South. Although both the celebrity and recipient of aid hold agency in the contact zones of RTP and BWB, the celebrity may hold the balance of power through their positionality as development actor. These unequal power dynamics become apparent in that the narratives produced regarding development (through RTP and BWB) are from the developers themselves. Rarely do we hear how those who are the subjects of development conceptualize and understand these endeavours. As Darnell (2007) notes in his work on RTP, the development paradigm in which RTP works depends on a professionalized hegemony of development workers, which justifies the intervention of actors from the global North in the global South to promote development. Within this context, discourses of development 'speak for, and presume to understand the experiences of the recipients of aid, which may serve to remove their voice' (Darnell 2007: 570).

Some comments made by an NBA employee about the participants at a BWB camp in South Africa highlight the effective removal of the voice of the recipients of aid. An NBA scout says of the participants,

> They've been unbelievable. They're like sponges. Their attention spans are unbelievable. The more you talk the more they listen. They don't ask a lot of questions because they're not used to instruction [...] They're like kids in a candy store.
> ('Africa 100 Camp: Q&A with Scout Tony Ronzone' 2003)

Here, the participants in the camp are not themselves asked about their experience or understanding of BWB, but are rather framed as appreciative and eager to absorb the knowledge imparted by the celebrity aid worker.

The infantilizing construction of participants in the camp as 'sponges' who are 'not used to instruction', and 'kids in a candy store', reflects the unquestioned appreciation with which they are assumed to accept development, and the construction of the other 'who is seemingly grateful for the material means that provide respite for his/her marginalization' (Darnell 2007: 570). As Arturo Escobar (1995) argues, this is part of an ideological foundation of development, in that the infantilization of the so-called 'third world' is integral to development as means of salvation. Thus, the very idea of BWB is predicated on this infantilization, as without it the global South and these athletes, would not be framed as in need of the intervention of the NBA.

Furthermore, by not referring to any of the programs' participants directly, these comments further reflect how they are objectified and seen through the lens of the NBA as commodities. Rather than speaking to the experiences of the athletes – or better yet, allowing them to speak for themselves – the athletes are objectified and framed from a western viewpoint. Although similar descriptors may be applied to children in a global North sporting context as well, colonial histories of infantilization and paternalism make such tropes all the more problematic.

In the dominant discourse presented by athletes, the image of the receptive, grateful and spoken-for recipients of aid is presented in juxtaposition to the benevolence of the celebrities who are donating their time. This discourse is presented for the audience of North America so as to frame the NBA as deserving of our attention and consumption. This is reflected in the following narrative of former NBA'er Jerome Williams at the South Africa camp in 2005 as he speaks for the experience of the children at the camp while constructing NBA players as compassionate and charitable. In the words of Williams,

> To see that many kids with their attention on you; hanging onto your every word – it's very heartfelt. You want to give them so much but you only have a short amount of time. But I think every NBA player did a great job in terms of uplifting the students. The children got a lot out of it, knowing they have NBA players supporting them.
> ('The Junk Yard Dog Blog' 2005)

This discourse presents NBA athletes as, first, qualified development practitioners who have the campers 'hanging on their every word', and second, as benevolent for donating their time to this cause. Moreover, the idea that the campers 'got a lot out of it *knowing* they have NBA players supporting them' (emphasis added) suggests that the campers benefit from this aid because the support of the celebrity seemingly does more than that provided by others. In reality, this support is fleeting as the celebrities leave the contact zone of BWB to return to North America and their professional sporting career, while underdevelopment persists. What also needs to be questioned is for whom this narrative is being constructed. The narrative of the athletes being touched by the campers, wanting to do so much in such a short period of time, and uplifting the students, may have only a temporary impact on the campers while making a more lasting impression on the North America audience for whom this narrative is presented.

While the discourses produced by RTP present the media face of celebrity philanthropy, one that articulates with and produces dominant understandings of development, it should be noted that these organizations do provide a social good, and can produce counter-narratives to depictions of poverty in the global South. Programs like BWB do draw attention to the condition of the global South as presented (although in a limited fashion) in the discourse surrounding the league. This point is reflected in an interview for the NBA with Amadou Gallo Fall, a native of Senegal who received a basketball scholarship in the US, and later became the Director of Scouting for the NBA's Dallas Mavericks. To cite Fall,

> People are so quick to expand and report on all of the calamities here. Africa, a lot of the time, is synonymous with misery and AIDS and the killings in Rwanda. There's never anything good coming out of here. [The BWB's Africa 100 camp] is something good. If people are able to make the most of this, hopefully it will change the perceptions of Africa […] This is a great opportunity for a cross-cultural exchange.
> (Fall cited in Kim 2003)

Fall is correct in pointing that much of the discourse that has surrounded Africa has focused on disasters and tragedy. However, the 'good' that BWB presents is not without its limitations.

The knowledge production of BWB fails to disrupt the dominant construction of Africa as a region that is in need of the intervention of the global North. In this way, BWB spreads assumptions and constructs a reality from a western perspective that serves to marginalize and other those in the global South. In the words of Wolfgang Sachs (1992: 5), 'Knowledge, however, wields power by directing people's attention; it carves out and highlights a certain reality, casting into oblivion other ways of relating to the world around us'.

Although sport is constructed as a field in which geographical, cultural and economic gaps may be bridged, the discursive framework that is presented by celebrities in RTP and BWB complicates such understandings. In these narratives, sport is the vehicle that allows the donors of aid to speak for the recipients of aid. The BWB and RTP participants are constructed as grateful for the respite that the camp provides, however temporary that respite may be, while the hegemony of the global North and the celebrity is reproduced by the very act of being credited for their generosity and philanthropic acts (Darnell 2007).

Conclusion

This chapter has explored the forces that have permitted the emergence, and perhaps need, for celebrity activism in development projects, by asking two related questions. Firstly, what global, socio-historical and political–economic forces have allowed for the emergence of the sporting celebrity as a harbinger of global development and aid? And, what are the effects of celebrity-sponsored aid in the sport for development context? There has been a proliferation of development programs utilizing sport and celebrities as key components to their organizations. The celebrity has the ability to draw attention to development programs, global poverty, and epidemics such as AIDS. The sporting athlete, moreover, is often heralded as a viable role model through the seemingly universal and integrative social practice of sport (Darnell 2007). Yet, these interrelated processes should not go unchallenged.

I have argued for a more critical understanding of the aid celebrity operating in the development context by undertaking a discursive analysis of two SDP programs, RTP and BWB. While complex issues are at play in RTP and BWB, the themes of 'compassionate' development, neoliberal capitalist ideologies and racialized and spacialized knowledge construction are key. The discourses surrounding the programs as proffered through the celebrity (re)shape our commonsense knowledge of what the global South looks like, who occupies this space and what development is (and is not). While the celebrities may be well intentioned, and consciousness raising is an important facet to any social movement, how such discursive practices shape realities and symbolically and materially contribute to marginalizing and hegemonic relationships should not be taken lightly. The role of the celebrity may, in actuality, do little beyond (temporarily) drawing the attention of North Americans to the plight of the global South, and may fail to address the more systematic and structural issues of underdevelopment. As John Cameron and Anna Haanstra (2008: 1477) argue, 'while representations of people in the global South as helpless victims has proven to be an effective fund-raising tool, it has not only fostered profound misunderstandings of developing countries, but also largely failed to stimulate interest and engagement in development issues among Northern publics'.

It is unclear how the philanthropic interest and engagement of the celebrity-athlete in the global North contribute to sustainable and multilateral development. Although the sporting celebrity forms an immediate connection with Northern audiences through their visibility and emotional connection with their fans, they frequently present an oversimplified and sanitized image of development, often as the result of a need to present straightforward and digestible messages to audiences outside of the development context. While the celebrity acts as a privileged emotional conduit for representing what the global South looks like, and how the intervention of the global North (via the celebrity) can produce tangible aid, their actions in the development context also present a paradox. The rise of the celebrity is the product of the same forces of neoliberal globalization – including globalized media, and the sport-industrial complex – that have in fact contributed to the (re)production of global inequality by unevenly distributing access and associated benefits of globalization into the hands of transnational corporations, international financial institutions and governments of the global North.

How the recipients of aid in the global South conceptualize the actions of the celebrity in the development context, moreover, is largely overlooked. Development through sport programs like RTP and BWB are (to a certain extent) dependent upon the dichotomy that is created through globalization and neocolonial encounters between the empowered and marginalized. These unequal encounters may be (re)produced rather than overcome through sport. The reproduction of racialized bodies, Othering, and white privilege are often reinforced in the development context as the unequal distribution of resources on which development is predicated that constructs a 'grid of intelligibility that produces and constrains racial subjectivity and knowledge' (Darnell 2007: 561). For Maria Eriksson Baaz (2005: 123), in the discourse of development African *subjects* are represented as the passive recipients of aid – the *objects of development* – who have no voice, identity or contributions to make. The global North is constructed in contrast as active subjects, development workers, fund-raisers and world citizens.

Ultimately, the reliance on celebrities to be the face and voice of ethical intervention in the global South serves to reaffirm those in the global South as the (post) colonial Other, that may overlook their agency and voice. Achille Mbembé's (2001) argument regarding the detrimental aspects of celebrity activists in the 'making and unmaking of Africa' is worth quoting at length. On hegemonic constructions of Africa from the global North, Mbembé (2001: 3) writes, 'In the very principle of its constitution, in its language, and in its finalities, narrative about Africa is always a pretext for a comment about something else, some other place, some other people. More precisely, Africa is the mediation that enables the West to accede to his own subconscious and give a public account of its subjectivity'. In these ways, the means in which discursive constructions of development produce knowledge of the global North and South holds material implications for how we understand development, the global North and the global South. The use of sport celebrities in the development context may produce understandings of the global South for Northern audiences that draw on and reproduce (neo)colonial and hegemonic understandings of the region, and that contribute to underdevelopment rather than combatting it.

Notes

1   In this chapter, I use the terminology of 'global South' and 'global North' in place of what has conventionally been called the Third and First Worlds. While this is an attempt to

2   mitigate the problematic connotations of Third World versus First World, the terms are not without contention. First, they are geographically misleading as evidenced, for example, by Australia's geographical location in the global South, but economic and political position in the global North. Second, as with most generalizations, the dichotomization of global South and global North is homogenizing and proposes a neat global division of the 'haves' and 'have-nots', as opposed to a more nuanced and accurate understanding of development as diasporic: there are pockets of development and underdevelopment within any given country, regardless of their position in the global North/South. Despite such limitations, the terms 'global South' and 'global North' are useful in conventionalizing the relations between these two parts of the globe, and in highlighting ongoing historical patterns of (neo)colonialism between the two regions (O'Brien and Williams 2007).

2   The United Nations, Educational, Scientific and Cultural Organization (UNESCO) argues that sport holds a significant role in promoting social integration and economic development, and promotes the ideals of peace, fraternity, solidarity, non-violence, tolerance and justice. Moreover, sport is seen as a tool to strengthen social ties in post-conflict situations, and to promote health and wellness in the face of extreme poverty and epidemic illness, including AIDS (Sport for Development and Peace International Working Group 2008). Sport is also promoted as a catalyst to achieving the Millennium Development Goals when used in conjunction with national PRSPs that provide a framework for the attainment of growth and reduction of poverty. Numerous countries (including Cape Verde, Mozambique, Sierra Leone, Tanzania and Uganda) have integrated sport into their PRSPs (Sport for Development and Peace International Working Group 2008: 9).

3   Emerging in the 2000s from its predecessor Olympic Aid, 'RTP's mission is to use sport and play to educate and empower children and youth to overcome the effects of poverty, conflict and disease in disadvantaged communities' ('Mission, Vision and Values' 2013). RTP currently has programs in over 20 countries, including Benin, Botswana, Burundi, China, Ethiopia, Ghana, Jordan, Kenya, Lebanon, Liberia, Mali, Mozambique, Pakistan, Palestinian Territories (West Bank and Gaza), Peru, Rwanda, South Sudan, Tanzania, Thailand and Uganda.

Since 2001, the NBA's BWB program has been held throughout the globe as part of the league's social responsibility initiative, NBA Cares. Between 50 and 100 of the best young talents (aged 19 and under) from Europe, Asia, South America and Africa are selected to participate in the annual event that occurs in countries as diverse as South Africa, China, Mexico and India. The program is intended as a form of global outreach in which the global South can benefit from the wealth – economic, intellectual and otherwise – that the NBA has to offer by employing NBA athletes (including Dirk Nowitzki, Dwight Howard and Chris Bosh) as camp counsellors, educators and development practitioners.

References

'Africa 100 Camp: Q&A with Scout Tony Ronzone' (2003) NBA Media Ventures, 5 September, http://www.nba.com/global/africa100_ronzone.html. Accessed 10 January 2015.

Andrews, D.L., and Jackson, S.J. (2001) 'Introduction: Sport celebrities, public culture, and private experience', in D.L. Andrews and S.J. Jacks (eds) *Sport Stars: The Cultural Politics of Sporting Celebrity*, New York: Routledge, pp. 1–19.

'Athlete Quotes' (n.d.) Perpetual Motion, http://data.perpetualmotion.org/Multisport/Athletes.htm. Accessed 5 March 2015.

'Athletes' (2014) Right to Play, http://www.righttoplay.com/the-team/Pages/AthletePrograms.aspx. Accessed 21 March 2014.

Baaz, M.E. (2005) *The Paternalism of Partnership: A Postcolonial Reading of Partnership in Development Aid*, New York: Zed Books.

'Basketball without Borders' (2015) NBA Media Ventures, http://www.nba.com/bwb/. Accessed 10 January 2015.

'Basketball without Borders, Africa 2013' (2014) NBA Media Ventures, http://www.nba.com/bwb/africa_2013.html. Accessed 10 January 2015.

'Basketball without Borders Community Outreach' (2006) NBA Media Ventures, 11 April, http://www.nba.com/bwb/comm_outreach2006.html. Accessed 20 March 2014.

'Basketball without Borders Makes Inaugural Trip to China' (2005) NBA Media Ventures, 16 June, http://www.nba.com/bwb/asiarelease2005.html. Accessed 20 March 2014.

'Basketball without Borders Mission' (2015) NBA Media Ventures, http://www.nba.com/bwb/mission.html. Accessed 10 January 2015.

Brockington, D. (2009) *Celebrity and the Environment: Fame, Wealth and Power in Conservation*, London: Zed Books.

Cameron J., and Haanstra, A. (2008) 'Development made sexy: How it happened and what it means', *Third World Quarterly*, 29, 8: 1475–89.

Cooper, A. (2008) *Celebrity Diplomacy*, Boulder: Paradigm Publishers.

Darnell, S. (2007) 'Playing with race: RTP and the production of whiteness in "development through sport"', *Sport in Society*, 10, 4: 560–79.

Dieter, H., and Kumar, K. (2008) 'The downside of celebrity diplomacy: The neglected complexity of development', *Global Governance*, 14: 259–64.

Doan, C.L-M. (2010) 'Athlete's voice', Right to Play TV, 25 February, http://righttoplaytv.com/video/watch/6ts0cB1Wa84BFAS8TSWNYl. Accessed 3 October 2010.

Escobar, A. (1995) *Encountering Development: The Making and Unmaking of the Third World*, Princeton, NJ: Princeton University Press.

Esteva, G. (1992) 'Development', in W. Sachs (ed.) *The Development Dictionary: A Guide to Knowledge as Power*, New Jersey: Zed Books, pp. 6–25.

Everett, M. (1997) 'The ghost in the machine: Agency in "poststructural" critiques of development', *Anthropological Quarterly*, 70, 3: 137–51.

Fairclough, N. (1992) *Discourse and Social Change*, Cambridge, UK: Polity Press.

Fusco, C. (2005) 'Cultural landscapes of purification: Sports spaces and discourses of whiteness', *Sociology of Sport Journal*, 22: 283–310.

Giulianotti, R. (2004) 'Human rights, globalization and sentimental education: The case of sport', *Sport in Society*, 7, 3: 355–69.

'Goodwill Ambassadors' (n.d.) United Nations: Sport for Development and Peace, https://www.un.org/wcm/content/site/sport/home/unplayers/goodwillambassadors. Accessed 20 March 2014.

'History: The history of Right to Play' (2013) Right to Play, http://www.righttoplay.com/International/about-us/Pages/History.aspx. Accessed 20 March 2014.

'ISCA. Moving People' (n.d.) International Sport and Culture Association, http://www.isca-web.org/english/aboutisca. Accessed 10 January 2015.

Kidd, B. (2008) 'A new social movement: Sport for development and peace', *Sport in Society*, 11, 4: 370–80.

Kidd, B., and Donnelly, P. (2000) 'Human rights in sport', *International Review for the Sociology of Sport*, 35, 113: 131–48.

Kiely, R. (1999) 'The last refuge of the noble savage? A critical assessment of post-development theory', *The European Journal of Development Research*, 11, 1: 30–55.

Kim, R. (2003) 'Africa 100: Interview with Amadou Gallo Fall', NBA.com, 2 September, http://www.nba.com/news/fall_interview_030829.html. Accessed 10 January 2015.

King, S. (2006) *Pink Ribbons, Inc.: Breast Cancer and the Politics of Philanthropy*, Minneapolis, MN: University of Minnesota Press.

Lines, G. (2001) 'Villains, fools or heroes? Sport stars as role models for young people', *Leisure Studies*, 20, 285–303.

Mbembé, J.A. (2001) *On the Post-Colony*, Berkeley, CA: University of California Press.

'Mission, Vision and Values' (2010) Right to Play, http://www.righttoplay.com/canada/about-us/Pages/mission.aspx. Accessed 20 March 2014.

'NBA Players See a New World' (2005) NBA Media Ventures, 10 September, http://denvernuggets.org/bwb/NBA_Players_See_a_New_World.html. Accessed 6 March 2012.

O'Brien, R., and Williams, M. (2007) *Global Political Economy: Evoluton and Dynamics*, New York: Palgrave MacMillan.

'Our Story' (n.d) (RED), http://www.red.org/en/about. Accessed 10 January 2015.

'Our Story' (2013) Right to Play, http://www.righttoplay.com/International/about-us/Pages/OurStory.aspx. Accessed 20 March 2014.

Pieterse, J.N. (2000) 'After post-development', *Third World Quarterly*, 21, 2: 175–91.

Pratt, M.L. (1992) *Imperial Eyes: Travel Writing and Transculturation*, New York: Routledge.

Razack, N. (2005) '"Bodies on the move": Spatialized locations, identities, and nationality in international work', *Social Justice*, 32, 4: 87–104.

Richey, L.A., and Ponte, S. (2006) 'Better (RED)™ than dead: "Brand aid", celebrities and the new frontier of development assistance', *Danish Institute for International Studies*, 26: 1–33.

Richey, L.A., and Ponte, S. (2008) 'Better (RED)™ than dead? Celebrities, consumption and international aid', *Third World Quarterly*, 29, 4: 711–29.

Rojek, C. (2001) *Celebrity*, London: Reaktion Books.

Sachs, W. (1992) 'Introduction', in W. Sachs (ed.) *The Development Dictionary: A Guide to Knowledge as Power*, New Jersey: Zed Books, pp. 1–5.

Said, E.W. (1978) *Orientalism*, New York: Pantheon Books.

Said, E.W. (1994) *Culture and Imperialism*, New York: Vintage Books.

Smart, B. (2005) *The Sport Star: Modern Sport and the Cultural Econonmy of Sporting Celebrity*, Thousand Oaks: Sage Publications.

Smart, B. (2007) 'Not playing around: Global capitalism, modern sport and consumer culture', in R. Giulianotti and R. Robertson (eds) *Globalization and Sport*, Malden: Blackwell Publishing and Global Networks Partnership, pp. 6–27.

'Sport is Our Passion' (2012) Nike, www.nikeforbetterworld.com/about. Accessed 28 February 2012.

Sport for Development and Peace International Working Group (2008) *Harnessing the Power of Sport for Development and Peace: Recommendations to Governments*, Toronto, Canada: Right to Play.

'The Junk Yard Dog Blog' (2005) NBA Media Ventures, 12 September, http://www.nba.com/bwb/jyd_blog.html. Accessed 10 January 2015.

Chapter 6

World Relations and Development Issues: Framing Celebrity Philanthropy Documentaries

Hilde Van den Bulck, Nathalie Claessens and Koen Panis

This chapter examines a sample of celebrity philanthropy documentaries to identify different views on international relations, the nature of development problems, and ways to solve them, and analyzes if and how these elements are related to the different philanthropic traditions in the celebrity's country of origin. By means of mediated communication, society discusses ethical, social and political issues through the celebrity construct – itself a mediated interplay between a public, private and 'real' persona. Celebrities – of both global fame and local appeal, from the fields of entertainment and other spheres of life – increasingly engage in philanthropic activities and activism. In the process, they express public views on world problems and relations. According to critics, this celebrity involvement bears witness and further contributes to the spread of neoliberal modernization and cultural imperialist paradigms with regard to global inequality ('the West' versus 'the Rest'), ignoring alternative views of international relations and development based on structural changes, self-reliance and an understanding of development as equal partners (Said 1978, 1995; Bhabha 1994; Escobar 1995; Ponce de Leon 2002; Easterly 2006). To allow a more detailed examination and evaluation of this claim, we provide a comparative framing analysis of testimonials by celebrities coming from different welfare regimes with varying philanthropic traditions to explore if and how these traditions relate to the celebrities' presentations of world relations and developments issues.

Celebrity, Political Persona and Humanitarian Traditions

Chris Rojek (2001: 42) contends that celebrity is a construct, continuously moulded and reconstructed by media and audiences. This process is based on mediated communication – the type of characters that the celebrity plays or the style of music that they perform, media coverage of these and other aspects of their life and the consumption and discussion thereof by fans and wider audiences. The celebrity construct is also a mediated interplay between a public persona or image based on public activities, a private persona based on the private life as it is presented to the world, and glimpses of the perceived real person behind the image – 'off-guard, unkempt, unready' (Holmes 2005: 24) – as captured by paparazzi and appropriated by media and audiences.

Celebrities increasingly engage in philanthropic and humanitarian causes, whether as global superstars, successful entrepreneurs, local television entertainers, sporting personalities or It-girls (young women who, temporarily, attract intense media coverage that is unrelated or disproportional to their professional achievements) (Panis and Van den Bulck 2014: 24). In doing so, they create a political persona, whether from personal conviction and a need for self-fulfilment or from a utilitarian attempt at self-promotion (Street 2004: 434; Cashmore 2006: 221). Prototypical examples of the former type of political persona include musician Bono and actor Martin Sheen whose respective work on poverty alleviation and environmental activism is viewed by audiences as credible and legitimate (Meyer and Gamson 1995: 189; Huddart 2005: 40). An example of the latter type of political persona is socialite Paris Hilton, whose post-prison plans for a humanitarian visit to Rwanda at the invitation of the Playing for Good charity lost credibility by clashing with her public image as a self-promoting rich girl ('Paris Hilton's Rwanda Trip Postponed' 2007). As such, the political persona bridges and interacts with the public and private image of a celebrity, connecting private views and emotions with the celebrity's public performances.

The rapid growth of celebrity engagement in philanthropic and socio-political causes has captured academic attention, with scholars approaching the phenomenon in different ways. Some scholars emphasize political engagement, or what is described as 'celebrity politics' and 'celebrity diplomacy' (West and Orman 2003; Street 2004; 't Hart and Tindall 2009). Others define celebrity engagement in such causes in terms of a more general social commitment, that is, as 'celebrity philanthropy', 'celebrity humanitarianism' and 'celebrity activism' (Wheeler 2002; Thrall et al. 2008; Nickel and Eikenberry 2009). For example, Stephen Huddart (2005: 8) defines a celebrity activist as 'a performer [who] takes a public stand on a social issue, acts as spokesperson for a charity or participates in a benefit performance'. Conversely, scholars such as Patricia Mooney Nickel and Angela Eikenberry (2009: 975) put more emphasis on the self-promotional media hype involved in celebrity 'giving and volunteering, raising money or in other ways supposedly helping those less fortunate' (see also Murray, in this book). This chapter examines the broader issues associated with celebrity engagement in philanthropic and humanitarian endeavours rather than speculating about the personal politics and motivations of individual celebrities per se.

Scholars associate the growing phenomenon of celebrity philanthropy with wider social, cultural and political trends. As consumer culture encroaches on ever more areas of social life, humanitarian organizations are forced to employ marketing techniques (Fain 2008: 1). 'Hard news issues' such as famine and foreign affairs are increasingly approached from a 'soft news angle' following a market-driven media logic (Evans and Hesmondhalgh 2005). Additionally, news reporters tend to focus on well-known, institutionalized humanitarian organizations rather than new and smaller players (Verhulst and Walgrave 2005; Panis and Van den Bulck 2014), further obliging the latter to revert to an eye-catching approach to increase its newsworthiness. At the same time, relationships between citizens and politics are changing as many people lose confidence in traditional party politics and opt for alternative forms of political or social engagement (Van Aelst and Walgrave 2001), often following their favourite celebrity's lead (Van den Bulck and Tambuyzer 2008: 100). All of these trends provide fertile ground for employing celebrities in the promotion of philanthropic and humanitarian causes.

Scholars analyzing the welfare state see the recent exponential growth of celebrity philanthropy as indicative of shifts in welfare regimes affecting different traditions of philanthropic fund-raising and approaches to humanitarian action (Esping-Andersen 1990; Salamon 1995; Powell and Hewitt 2002; Vamstad 2007). Philanthropy was always a significant force in all types of welfare regimes. Even in social democratic welfare states, for example, those in Scandinavia, which are known for their reliance on the public sector funding of social services, philanthropy exists as a substantial funder of international aid, primarily through civil society organizations based on mass membership. In corporatist welfare regimes like Belgium and the Netherlands, philanthropy has a longstanding tradition as part of the funding of welfare organizations, especially those originating in the Protestant and Catholic churches. Yet, with the state under pressure to spend less and perform more, philanthropy as part of the intermediary organizations between citizens and the state is being replaced by a new, individualized philanthropy where large, professional and often multinational organizations collect funding directly from individual donors using modern marketing techniques, mass media and celebrities – the focus of our study. The latter is typical of (neo)liberal welfare regimes with a tradition of private funding, market-based welfare solutions and means-tested public benefits, such as the US. The UK, historically evolved from a social democratic to a liberal regime, has a long tradition of a strong voluntary sector. An important aim of the current study, then, is to analyze if and to what extent the testimonials of celebrity philanthropists bear witness to these different (and shifting) welfare state regimes, or primarily voice neoliberal welfare ideas, as some maintain.

Apart from historical differences in modes of fund-raising, Jan Nederveen Pieterse (1998: 18) distinguishes between a North American and European approach to humanitarian action. The North American tradition focuses on the provision of relief and services with an emphasis on practical remedies rather than causes, and views national governments and large NGOs as the key actors and donors (Weiss 1998). In contrast, the European tradition comprises a critical political economy approach that stresses human rights and citizenship, focusing on causes and determining structures, with local people in grassroots organizations and international organizations as the main actors (Duffield 1998).

The chapter assesses if the views expressed in North American, British, Flemish–Belgian and Dutch celebrity philanthropy documentaries reflect these different histories and approaches to welfare, development, philanthropy and humanitarianism. It further explores if and how celebrity philanthropy breaks through these traditions. Research suggests that celebrities prefer to endorse issues supported by large audiences (Wheeler 2002: 78; Panis and Van den Bulck 2012: 84). Additionally, celebrity philanthropists prefer to focus on philanthropic activities with specific and short-term solutions, for example, building a water pump, because involvement in such activities generates more tangible indications of success than lobbying for broader political change. This would suggest that celebrity philanthropy documentaries are more likely to focus on depoliticized issues, specific problems and short-term solutions, that is, elements that are closer to the North American than the European tradition.

That said, philanthropic documentaries featuring western celebrities as the authorial or authoritative subject are about more than different philanthropic traditions and an individual's search for political commitment, personal fulfillment or public attention; they provide a vehicle for mediated social discussion about views on global relationships as a world of 'us' and 'them', 'the West' and 'the Rest'. Scholars of post-coloniality agree that the meaning of 'us' or 'the West' (the studied celebrities' part of the world) cannot be regarded as an essence or as fixed. Its meaning is constituted only in recognition of its relationship with 'them', the Other or 'the Rest' (Said 1978, 1995; Bhabha 1994; Escobar 1995; Easterly 2006), that is, the part of the world represented by the celebrities' testimonials as signifying practices (Ponce de Leon 2002: 278). Achille Mbembé underscores the historical dimension and constitutive nature of this relationship when he states, 'Africa still constitutes one of the metaphors through which "the West" represents the origins of its own norms, develops a self-image and integrates into the set signifiers asserting what is supposed to be its identity' (cited in Abrahamsson 2003: 195). In other words, the relationship between 'the West' and 'the Rest' is not just a matter of identification but is also about the power to determine what constitutes truth and how to define and act upon a situation. It involves ideologies of civilization versus barbarism, and modernity and development versus primitiveness and backwardness. Different ideas about international humanitarianism and development aid flow from different views of these power relationships (see Sachs 2005; Easterly 2006), and these ideas are embedded in celebrity philanthropy documentaries.

A framing analysis of philanthropic documentaries by western celebrities can help to dissect the constitutive nature of the relationship between 'the West' and 'the Rest' both historically and in the present day. Framing analysis as a method is traditionally associated with political communication studies but increasingly it is also used in celebrity studies (Van den Bulck and Claessens 2013a, 2013b). Framing refers to those aspects of 'reality' that are emphasized and represented in the production of a media text through processes of selection, rejection, modification, etc., and that subsequently provide intended audiences with a context and suggested meaning (Van Gorp 2006: 46). Different cultures construct and give meaning to 'reality' though framing packages using different framing devices, such as choice of words or images, metaphors, symbols, numerical data and stereotypes. They also use different reasoning devices – ways of defining an issue, giving the problem a causal interpretation and morally evaluating it, and then recommending a solution (Goffman 1981; Entman 1991: 7, 52; Pan and Kosicki 1993: 67).

A framing approach was used to analyze 12 philanthropic documentaries with a celebrity as the authoritative and hence grounding spokesperson or 'author' (Huddart 2005: 42), expressing verbal and visual views on international relations, the nature of development problems and the question of how to solve them. Three celebrities were selected from the US and the UK, respectively, that is, liberal welfare regimes with a tradition of private funding, market-based welfare solutions and an established tradition of individualized philanthropy. The six celebrities are: (1) Angelina Jolie, Oscar-winning actor and renowned philanthropist, US (Huang 2005); (2) Jay Z, hip hop artist and entrepreneur, US (Huang 2006); (3) Lindsay

Lohan, actor, pop singer and model, US (Sahota 2010); (4) Bob Geldof, singer-songwriter and famous philanthropy activist, Irish but working in a UK context (Maguire 2005); (5) Sienna Miller, actor, model and fashion designer, UK (Serota 2009); and (6) Robbie Williams, singer-songwriter, UK (UNICEFUK 2010). A further six celebrities were selected from corporatist welfare states such as the Netherlands and Flanders/Belgium, that is, countries with a tradition of intermediary welfare organizations and no established tradition of individualized philanthropic initiatives. The six celebrities here are: (1) Luc Appermont, TV presenter, Flanders (Vroom 2006); (2) Goedele Liekens, TV presenter, magazine publisher and activist, Flanders (Felderhof 2007); (3) Roos Van Acker, radio and TV presenter, Flanders (Neuskens 2009); (4) Sylvana Simons, TV presenter, the Netherlands (Naus and Siezenga 2005); (5) Eric Corton, actor, radio presenter, singer and activist, the Netherlands (Corton 2007); and (6) Erik van der Hoff, singer and TV presenter, the Netherlands (Zwart and Brussaard 2009). Hence, each regional grouping is represented by a gender-balanced selection of celebrities from the fields of entertainment and other spheres of life, possessing global or local fame, and differing histories of philanthropy activism.

All of the 12 celebrity philanthropy documentaries were subjected to the same set of questions. What (development) issues are presented as problems? What are the perceived causes of those problems? Who or what is blamed for their existence? What solutions are proposed and who should implement them? What type of moral evaluation is provided? Who are the key agents of positive social change? What is the role of the celebrity philanthropist? The answers were put together in a matrix to find similarities, patterns and trends, and overall consistencies in answers were combined into a frame package (see Gamson and Modigliani 1989).

Analysis of the 12 celebrity philanthropy documentaries reveals four distinct frames and one sub-frame. These frames are categorized as follows: (1) *The West Saves the Rest: Social Engineering*; (2) *The West Helps Save the Rest through Western Organizations*; (3) *The West Helps the Rest Save Itself through Local Organizations*; and (4) *The (Diverse) Rest will Save Itself from Problems Caused by the West*. The first frame contains a sub-frame called *The West saves the Rest: Social Engineering as the White Man's Burden*.

Framing Celebrity Philanthropy

Frame 1, *The West Saves the Rest: Social Engineering*, focuses on offering solutions to identified specific, short-term problems rather than analyzing their underlying causes. For example, *Eric Corton in de Centraal Afrikaanse Republiek* (dir. Corton 2007) documents the Dutch entertainer and Red Cross Ambassador's visit to the Central African Republic as part of the radio telethon *Serious Request* to examine both its limited supply of clean and safe drinking water, and the responses of international humanitarian organizations (Van den Bulck, Panis and Claessens 2013). As Corton explains, 'Every year, one and a half million children die because of diarrhoea and we want to do something about that'. 'People are sick because they have no water or because they drink polluted water' (Corton 2007). In *Soccer Aid Appeal Video From Haiti* (UNICEFUK 2010), Robbie Williams visits Haiti as a United Nations Children's Fund (UNICEF) Ambassador following the earthquake of January 2010, which killed over 230,000 people and made more than one million homeless. In his words, 'They're homeless and it's wrong and we need to put it right. We need your help' (UNICEFUK 2010). Causes, if mentioned at all, are limited to those of a natural or general socio-economic nature (lack of water, earthquake and lack of infrastructure). At no point is western economic development and the broader issue of unequal economic development implied as a cause or potential part of the problem.

The solutions in Frame 1, like the problems they are aimed at, are presented as being specific, technical and hands-on: building schools, roads and wells, providing toilets or food and distributing medicines. They are usually one-size-fits-all solutions, with no reference to the geographical, climatic, social or cultural specificity of different regions that may require specific actions. Solutions are shown to come from western countries and this is presented as the only option.

Two types of actors typically feature in Frame 1: western individuals and western-based NGOs. Western individuals are expected to provide financial support through donations. 'Just 20 pounds could pay for 10 emergency health kits […] So please call […] or go online […] and give what you can. Thank you' (Williams in UNICEFUK 2010). Western organizations are further given the task of making that money work. To cite Corton (2007), the 'Red Cross can help these people by protecting the natural source and by teaching them how to deal with clean water'. Williams states, 'this is where UNICEF and its partners like Plan come in' (UNICEFUK 2010).

Local people are portrayed mainly as innocent victims of dire circumstances. Their names and stories personalize the documentary narrative, in order to elicit empathy from the audience for the cause that the celebrity is supporting, rather than giving them an active voice. Holding a baby girl and seated next to the child's grandmother, Robbie Williams says to the camera and its target western audience over a dramatic musical score: 'Let's help Grandma Lucette and Marie Michelle and other children like her', 'Marie Michelle got the vital nutrition that she needed thanks to UNICEF and Save the Children' (UNICEFUK 2010). In short, only the western celebrities and experts, either representatives of western organizations or independent experts that accompany the celebrity on their journey of discovery, have the authority to explain the identified problems and the appropriate nature of their solutions.

Frame 1 contains a sub-frame, *The West Saves the Rest: Social Engineering as the White Man's Burden*, which identifies problems, causes, solutions and the role of western countries in a similar manner to the main social engineering frame but adopts a different evaluative tone. The problems identified in this sub-frame are poverty, in general, and failing crops, bad roads, malaria, diarrhoea and HIV and AIDS, in particular. The causes of these problems are defined in general terms as relating to a combination of geographical, climatic and economic factors. However, the solutions to these identified problems are described in straightforward terms as financial, specific and technical, and coming from 'the West'.

An example of this sub-frame is provided in *The Diary of Angelina Jolie and Dr. Jeffrey Sachs in Africa* (dir. Huang 2005). In this documentary, Angelina Jolie, famous for her roles as an Oscar-winning actor and as a Goodwill Ambassador for the Office of the UNHCR, visits a UN Millennium Project in Sauri, Kenya, with the famous development economist Dr. Jeffrey Sachs. The Millennium Project is headed by Sachs and was commissioned by the UN's Secretary-General in 2002 to develop a concrete action plan for the world to achieve the Millennium Development Goals of reversing the poverty, hunger and disease affecting billions of people. Providing a specific solution for the food shortages and diseases affecting people in Kenya, Jolie says that buying fertilizer and mosquito nets is only a seven dollar investment: 'It is ridiculous how simple it is' (Huang 2005). She further attributes the simplicity of these solutions to 'Jeff's vision and leadership' under the auspices of the UN (Huang 2005).

In this sub-frame, 'the West' is presented as having not only the ability, but also a moral duty to intervene in the internal affairs of developing countries. This injunction is presented as an extended or general reproach that encompasses viewing audiences. For example, Jolie says, 'Rich nations have seen fit to look away from extreme poverty', 'I am suddenly conscious that we should all get on our knees and fix this' (Huang 2005). In *Telefacts Zomer: Met Luc Appermont naar Filipijnen* (Vroom 2006), Luc Appermont – a Flemish TV presenter and ambassador for Cunina, a Flemish NGO committed to finding foster parents and help for children in developing countries – travels to the Philippines to visit his foster child Cherry and to discuss the work of Cunina. After his arrival, Appermont similarly concludes, 'Seeing this with my own eyes here in the field, I realise we simply cannot leave it at that' (Vroom 2006). In the *Diary of Jay-Z: Water for Life* (dir. Huang 2006), the US-based hip hop artist visits Angola and South Africa as a UNICEF ambassador to learn about the estimated one billion people worldwide who live in areas of scarce potable water and possible solutions to the problems that affect them in consequence. As with commentary on the identified problems and their solutions by other celebrities included in this sub-frame, Jay Z concludes, 'Together we can do this. You can do this' (Huang 2006). The position of the celebrities is central to this moral evaluation. They express the view that not helping is simply not an option for them and for people in western societies, since all should do their bit for humanity. When visiting a field where a woman is working the land, Angelina Jolie (and Jeffrey Sachs) is shown helping to weed the field, provoking Jolie to comment, 'I guess we just felt guilty standing there talking to her and not helping' (Huang 2005). In the execution of these responsibilities, the celebrities often display neomissionary zeal: 'I'm on a mission' (Jay Z in Huang 2006; see also Bell, in this book).

Philanthropy in the international context is presented in this sub-frame as both essential for the advancement of humanity and a personalized moral imperative. Jolie personalizes and universalizes the problems identified in Kenya by comparing herself with African mothers. As she says, 'If my kid was hungry, asked me for food, to not have anything to give my children for dinner, I cannot imagine how horrible that feeling would be as a parent' (Huang 2005). Noting that even hospitals have inadequate access to clean water, Jolie further states, 'I would be scared to death if my child were in that hospital' (Huang 2005). Jay Z somewhat differently reflects on his life and the considerations of racial and socio-economic disadvantage that inform the lives of African Americans and the narratives of hip hop artists. When compared to the lives of people in Angola, he concludes, 'We're not from the hood, by no means, not even close' (Huang 2006).

Official experts from sponsoring organizations frequently accompany individual celebrities on their personalized journey of discovery, further authorizing and supporting the actions and words of the celebrity. Luc Appermont travels with the founder of Cunina and Flemish nuns doing charitable work with children in the Philippines (Vroom 2006). Jay Z travels with Arunabha Ghosh, former Policy Specialist at the UNDP in New York and co-author of the UNDP's Human Development Report 2006 – *Beyond Scarcity: Power, Poverty and the Global Water Crisis*. Walking with Jay Z to a local school, Ghosh underscores the celebrity's concerns about problems associated with the shortage of potable water in Africa by explaining, 'Even while we walk to the school, three children will have died from diarrhoea' (Huang 2006). Jolie travels with economist and UN advisor Jeffrey Sachs, who she describes as, 'one of the smartest people in the world' (Huang 2005). Sachs states of the problems affecting Kenya and the solutions identified by the Millennium Project in Sauri, 'We have to look at these as pretty practical challenges, let's roll up our sleeves and get the job done' (Huang 2005).

In this sub-frame, the provision of western aid is portrayed as having the explicit consent of people in developing countries. A local woman tells Jolie, 'When you come to our aid, we are very pleased' (Huang 2005). This consent is underscored by visual imagery of local children and women singing and dancing to upbeat music, often together with the celebrities (Huang 2005, 2006; Vroom 2006).

Frame 2, *The West Helps the Rest Save Itself through Western Organizations*, focuses on problems rather than solutions. Identified problems are mainly economic and related to poverty and health. Although these problems are examined in-depth, their contributing causes are presented in an implicit fashion as inherent to the area. However, solutions are portrayed as requiring cooperation between western-based organizations and members of the local community rather than 'mere' interference from 'the West'. For example, in *Erik and Sascha in Afrika* (dir. Zwart and Brussaard 2009), a documentary in which Dutch singer and TV presenter Erik van der Hoff and his 16-year-old daughter Sascha travel to Malawi to stay with a local family and discuss the work of Cordaid Memisa – a Dutch Catholic NGO committed to improving health care in developing countries – we are told that 'the local hospital [in Malawi], supported by Cordaid Memisa pays great attention to healing but also to informing the local community'. We are further told, 'Informing is the first step towards change' (Zwart and Brussaard 2009). Solutions consequently are presented as a combination of material aid and information aimed at changing habits and values, traditions and beliefs, rather than a technical one-size-fits-all.

Solutions to the problems identified in Frame 2 are predominantly presented by celebrities and western experts, although local experts working for western-based organizations sometimes are given a voice and praised. In the documentary *Erik and Sascha in Afrika*, Erik van der Hoff and his daughter give a voice to some members of the local community that they stayed with for two weeks in Malawi in order to learn about their life and everyday problems. A local head nurse in the delivery ward of a hospital is filmed saying, 'It is more than a job. I just want to go on and help where I can' (Zwart and Brussaard 2009). However, in the documentary *Wereldjournaal: Sylvana Simons in Tanzania* (Naus and Siezenga 2005), both the featured celebrity and western experts display a degree of paternalism. Dutch TV presenter Sylvana Simons visits Tanzania and lives with a local family to experience their life and problems as an ambassador for Simavi, a Dutch NGO committed to improving the primary health care of the poorest populations of rural Africa and Asia, with particular concern for water and sanitation. A Dutch expert explains during this documentary, 'the clean toilet is the first step, they must now be taught to use it in an hygienic fashion'. Simons as celebrity spokesperson reiterates, 'people are starting to find it normal to have [a clean toilet]' (Naus and Siezenga 2005).

Local non-experts are presented as hospitable, but they are not given a voice. Instead, by inviting various celebrities as guests into their homes, they serve as a conduit for the story of the celebrity exploring the problems the community faces. As van der Hoff puts it, 'although circumstances are much more primitive than we are accustomed to, our host tries her very best to spoil us' (Zwart and Brussaard 2009). Yet, when Simons informs us that a member of the Tanzanian family that she stayed with had contracted AIDS, it is a Dutch expert rather than a family member that explains the complexity of AIDS in the African context (Naus and Siezenga 2005).

Frame 3, *The West Helps the Rest Save Itself through Local Organizations*, defines problems in a less technical manner and with greater complexity. It focuses less on material issues and more on long-term economic, political and cultural complexities for which there are no quick solutions, such as economic underdevelopment, limited human rights and local community rejection of people living with HIV and AIDS. In the documentary *8 Minutes in the DR Congo* (dir. Serota 2009), Sienna Miller, a UK-based award-winning actress, model and fashion designer, travels to the war-torn Democratic Republic of the Congo in 2009 to document the lives of women living in the midst of treacherous conflict, where every eight minutes a woman is raped. Attention is thus paid to the specific rather than generalist cultural (traditions) and other symbolic aspects of reality that are part of the problem. Similarly, in the documentary *Leefwereld in Beweging: Roos Van Acker* (Neuskens 2009), Flemish radio host and TV presenter Roos Van Acker travels to Burundi to examine the problematic situation of women's rights and the work of the African NGO Association des Femmes Juristes du Bénin (AFJB, supported by 11.11.11). Van Acker is shown learning that complex local issues such as the fact that 'women are not entitled to own land', and 'have no economic independence', are problematic for the situation of Burundi women (Neuskens 2009).

Causes behind the problems are presented as complex, albeit mainly of a local nature. For example, in the BBC3 documentary *Lindsay Lohan's Indian Journey* (dir. Sahota 2010), former child model and now Hollywood actor and 'bad girl' Lindsay Lohan travels to India prior to the nation's hosting of the Commonwealth Games to investigate child trafficking for prostitution and factory labour. After discovering that many children are sent away with traffickers by their own parents, she speaks to parents, trafficked children and a former trafficker in West Bengal to learn about the desperate poverty that fuels the trade in children, even as India's economy is booming, and asks what can be done to stop it. A major part of the problem, according to Lohan, is that 'local residents think there is nothing wrong with children working' (Sahota 2010). Flemish TV presenter and (then) magazine publisher Goedele Liekens travels to Kenya to visit a Masai village and local residents and to learn about the work of the African Medical and Research Foundation (AMREF) (dir. Felderhof 2007). AMREF is an African NGO headquartered in Nairobi, Kenya, aiming for better health for every African by helping to create networks of informed communities that work with empowered health-care providers in strong health-care systems. Confronted with the community's rejection of people living with HIV, Liekens points to complex, local causes, such as sex being a taboo topic, which hinders AIDS prevention and treatment (Felderhof 2007).

Proposed solutions are not strictly of a technical or material nature, but instead focus on the need to change certain values, norms, habits and traditions, starting with those that inform the everyday lives of local people. As Lohan states, 'the hope has to be that raising awareness of these stories will help change attitudes' (Sahota 2010). There is a desire to work long term, going to the root of the matter and creating awareness in the local community. 'This seems to me to be the most fundamental type of development aid. When you want to help children, you need to help their mothers, not the other way around' (Liekens in Felderhof 2007). Closely related to this is the expressed need to create awareness and information through community work and alternative methods such as theatre. There is a strong emphasis on working towards empowerment and self-reliance. In Sienna Miller's words, 'The great progress in this region for the past ten years has been to break the silence and make women feel strong' (Serota 2009). Or as Liekens states, 'Young, single mothers come to an AMREF centre to learn a trade like jewellery making to be able to make a living. At the same time they are invited to discuss and learn about safe sex and the like' (Felderhof 2007).

In Frame 3, the experts are almost all local doctors and representatives of local organizations that are seen as the main facilitators of an awareness-creating process. As Liekens explains, 'African doctors from big cities train their colleagues from local hospitals' (Felderhof 2007). Miller informs viewers, 'One man is really the pioneer for women, his name is doctor Mukwege' (Serota 2009). Lohan states, 'It took a [local] charity to offer […] a realistic alternative' (Sahota 2010). The frame thus presents locals in an active/expert rather than passive/victim manner.

No reference is made to 'the West' as part or cause of the problems identified in Frame 3, except in the documentary featuring Sienna Miller. Miller explains that men fighting with different factions rape women in the Congo repeatedly and brutally, as 'a systematic show of force' (Serota 2009). However, 'the purchase of conflict minerals by western countries continues to fuel the bloodshed' (Serota 2009). The term 'conflict minerals' refers here to minerals such as cassiterite, wolframite, coltan and gold, which are mined in the Congo in conditions of armed conflict and human rights abuses, and pass through various intermediaries to support the ongoing fighting before being purchased by multinational electronics companies for use in the manufacture of mobile phones, laptops and MP3 players. In other words, conflict minerals are components in precisely the kinds of consumer goods that most western individuals use on a daily basis.

Finally, Frame 4, *The (Diverse) Rest Will Save Itself from Problems Caused by the West*, is distinctive and found in only one documentary, *Geldof in Africa: The Luminous Continent* (dir. Maguire 2005), making it a counter-frame. This documentary, which follows the Irish-born singer and activist Bob Geldof's journey to Somaliland, focuses explicitly on the causes of problems and presents 'the West' as part of the problem rather than the solution. Starting from Africa's geographical circumstances, which are defined as conditions given from nature rather than problems per se, the 'problems' affecting the region are portrayed as resulting chiefly from the imposition of western ideas and actions, which destabilized once well-functioning political, economic and cultural answers to natural circumstances.

Bob Geldof, an established activist for poverty alleviation in Africa through the 1985 multivenue Live Aid concerts for Ethiopian famine relief, emphasizes the politics of colonialism and globalization (Maguire 2005). Geldof notes, 'Today, climate, geography and environment still influence Africa but modern men imposed another limitation: modern people's politics and political geography'. He points to the western colonizers' notion of the nation state as destabilizing old clan and tribal hierarchies and the unwillingness of the UN and other states to recognize Somaliland. Other aspects of African life depicted as being damaged by western interference include traditional lifestyles in general, destroyed by the exoticism of western 'tourists who come to stare at these exotic people and their beautiful land', and traditional Masai cattle-rearing practices, destroyed by the import of sick cattle by Italian traders, among others (Maguire 2005).

In Frame 4, 'the Rest' rather than 'the West' is presented as knowing what is best for the region, with solutions being portrayed as coming from within Africa (its rich natural and cultural resources) to resolve problems caused by 'the West', as opposed to the more conventional focus on certain problems as inherent to Africa. According to Geldof, 'Somaliland is successful because it combines old clan traditions with the modern needs of the nation state, thus creating a new model African country' (Maguire 2005). As he puts it, the 'Masai are an extraordinarily successful people who have learned to live apart from but alongside the modern state, obeying its laws when they move outside their lands and living by their own codes inside them' (Maguire 2005). Finally, Geldof does not talk with or about international or local development or aid organizations. Instead, he converses with local experts such as elderly clan chiefs about their views on politics and a local doctor about combining western and traditional medicine.

Throughout the documentary, Geldof stresses the positive aspects of what he calls the 'luminous continent': 'The first thing you notice is the light. Light everywhere. Brightness.

Everywhere' (Maguire 2005). This positive imagery is contrasted to the historical depiction of Africa as the 'dark continent' in European colonial literature, and thus from writers living under the 'gloomy Northern skies of Europe'. Against the western view of Africa as an object, Geldof emphasizes the continent's diversity in terms of geography, climate, languages, culture, fauna and flora. As he concludes, 'There are other Africas' (Maguire 2005).

Conclusion

To a certain extent, philanthropic documentaries with a celebrity as the authoritative or grounding spokesperson reflect different philanthropic traditions. Frame 1 and its sub-frame, *The West Saves the Rest: Social Engineering* and *The West Saves the Rest: Social Engineering as the White Man's Burden*, bear the stamp of the US, liberal philanthropic tradition with its stress on individual financial contributions and on technical, material and practical one-size-fits-all solutions that 'the West' can, will and must provide. William Easterly (2006: 6) refers to this as the 'utopian social engineering' of 'Planners'. 'A Planner thinks he already knows the answer: he thinks of poverty as a technical engineering problem that his answers will solve'. *The Diary of Angelina Jolie and Dr. Jeffrey Sachs in Africa* (Huang 2005) provides a striking example of this viewpoint. As economist Jeffrey Sachs tells the watching audience about the solutions provided to the identified problems of a village in Kenya: 'What happened in this village can happen in the next village and the next village and the next village. It can happen all over Africa' (Huang 2005). Jolie further concludes, 'It is possible to end poverty. I am really convinced of it now that I have seen it' (Huang 2005).

Frames 2 and 3, *The West Helps Save the Rest Through Western Organizations* and *The West Helps the Rest Save Itself Through Local Organizations*, bear the somewhat different stamp of the European, corporatist tradition. There is no direct appeal for individual contributions in these frames. Emphasis is placed on the work of western or local organizations and issues relating to cultural and human rights, rather than material social engineering. These examples refute the notion that celebrities as philanthropists are only interested in focusing on specific problems and short-term solutions (e.g. Wheeler 2002; Fain 2008).

The assumption that a documentary's frame reflects the country of origin of the celebrity, though, was only partly confirmed: US stars Jolie and Jay Z seem representative of their US background (Frame 1) as are van der Hoff, Simons, Van Acker and Liekens for the corporatist approach. Yet, other examples such as the Appermont and Lohan documentaries complicate this smooth fit, suggesting other elements are at play, including the production context and the specifics of the celebrity.

Above and beyond the differences, celebrity philanthropy documentaries reveal a number of issues associated with celebrity philanthropy in general, as identified by scholars such as Sharon Fain (2008) and Nickel and Eikenberry (2009). First, apart from the Geldof documentary, there is no discussion of the role of western state governments, even though such governments were the main suppliers of development aid in traditional corporatist welfare states. Likewise, there is limited discussion of the role of philanthropy per se, even though it is questionable whether philanthropic endeavours can compensate for the role once performed by the now crumbling European welfare state (Salamon 1995). Second, with the exception of Frame 4, *The (Diverse) Rest Will Save Itself from Problems Caused by the West*, there is an absence of discussion of the historical role of western development in creating problems for what are now developing countries. This has the effect of presenting international aid and philanthropy in benevolent terms as a 'gift' rather than as an arguably belated return of appropriated resources (Nickel and Eikenberry 2009: 975). Third, celebrity philanthropy documentaries contribute to the objectification of the poor (Fain 2008: 1) by portraying western celebrities as 'saviours' and vehicles to create emotional affiliation with suffering non-western victims. Many of these documentaries present images of celebrities crying over the plight of children and women (Neuskens 2009; Vroom 2006; Sahota 2010). These women and children are displayed, in turn, as weak, innocent and inactive victims, for the most part staring silently into a camera lens (Huang 2005; Huang 2006; Vroom 2006; Felderhof 2007; Neuskens 2009; Serota 2009; Sahota 2010; UNICEFUK 2010).

The mutually constitutive relationship between 'the West' and 'the Rest' reverberates in celebrity philanthropy documentaries via the dichotomies of developed versus backwardness and modernity versus tradition (see also Bell and Millington, in this book). In Frames 1–3, the distinction between the developed West and the 'backwardness' of developing countries is articulated in relation to material and tangible issues. The Jay Z documentary opens with images of western children playing with water abundantly available and contrasts them with images of people in Africa, the Indian subcontinent and elsewhere walking for miles to get limited amounts of clean water (Huang 2006). Sascha van der Hoff (Zwart and Brussaard 2009) exclaims upon entering the home of a Malawian woman, '[At home] even our toilet is bigger than this house!' Contrasting imagery also underscores the perceived inevitable hardship that comes with backwardness. Angelina Jolie has blisters on her hands after five minutes of working alongside Jeffrey Sachs to help a local woman in Sauri weed a field (Huang 2005), while Jay Z (Huang 2006) and Corton (2007) both struggle to carry a bucket of water that they took away from local children to help them by carrying it for them.

In Frame 3, *The West Helps the Rest Save Itself through Local Organizations*, the dichotomy of developed versus backwardness is extended to highlight the apparent failure of developing countries to conform to western standards of good government and good governance (De Maria 2005). Unlike western societies, developing countries are presented as lacking an established knowledge of what is 'right' and 'wrong'. As Lohan puts it, 'People [in India] have only recently understood how harmful it [child trafficking] can be' (Sahota 2010). In Frame 3, developing countries either lack the capacity to develop in a politically appropriate way, as demonstrated by the existence of governmental corruption, or else they lack a democratic, central government and the appropriate legal frameworks required to deal with violations of women's rights and the exploitation of child labour (Serota 2009; Neuskens 2009; Sahota 2010). The highlighting of such issues refutes the idea that celebrity involvement automatically leads to a depoliticization of development issues (Meyer and

Gamson 1995; Nickel and Eikenberry 2009: 977; see also Allatson, Jeffreys and Marshall, in this book). However, the way in which these issues are highlighted simultaneously confirms the Enlightenment notion of 'the Rest' as a blank slate, which lacks any meaningful history or institutions of its own and upon which 'the West can inscribe its superior ideals' (Easterly 2006: 23).

The mutually constitutive relationship between 'the West' and 'the Rest' also reverberates in celebrity philanthropy documentaries via the dichotomy of modernity versus tradition. In all but Frame 4, the counter-frame epitomized by the Geldof documentary (Maguire 2005), western modernity is presented as providing the solutions to the perceived problems of developing countries, problems that are seen to stand in the way of their necessary modernization. Conversely, local traditions, cultural habits, ways of thinking and folklore are often evaluated in a negative fashion and as responsible for identified problems. In the first three frames, *The West Saves the Rest* and *The West Helps the Rest Save Itself through Western Organizations* or *Local Organizations*, local traditions are explicitly presented as in need of eradication. For example, 'The mentality of those men, they are just damn bastards' (Neuskens 2009).

In Frame 4, *The (Diverse) Rest Will Save Itself from Problems Caused by the West*, and in one documentary (Felderhof 2007) in *The West Helps the Rest Save Itself through Local Organizations*, the tradition/modernity dichotomy is reversed in part to value the primitive and traditional as potentially valuable bases for positive social change. As Liekens, a famous Flemish TV presenter and activist, states,

> What is it with Africa? There is something special about the sounds, the smells, the way people look [...] And the rhythm, yes, the rhythm of Africa appeals to our primitive rhythm, to our heart, to the sounds in the womb, back to the primitive feeling, when you felt really good.
>
> (Felderhof 2007)

These words are set against a visual background of colourfully dressed Tanzanian women sitting relaxed under a tree.

Taken as a whole, however, the dichotomous frameworks underpinning celebrity philanthropy documentaries serve to promote a normative ideology of civilization as something that 'the West' has and 'the Rest' lacks (see Bell and Millington, in this book). Celebrities in philanthropic documentaries literally embody this assumption as they are portrayed as transitioning from civilization to non-civilization. The Jolie shown walking around Sauri with no make-up and carrying her own backpack differs markedly from the glamorous Jolie of Hollywood films (Huang 2005). When meeting Indian locals, Lohan exchanges the designer sunglasses she had worn in the car journey for a scarf wrapped around her head in the style of local women (Sahota 2010). In the Appermont documentary, a voiceover states shortly after his arrival, 'Luc has exchanged his suit for a tropical shirt' (Vroom 2006). When Simons arrives in a Tanzanian village, an off-screen voice says, 'Sylvana arrives into a different world' (Naus and Siezenga 2005). Celebrities as embodied signifiers of international developmental aid thus not only endorse certain solutions to perceived problems but also the ideology of civilization that acts as legitimization for western intervention, obliterating any notion of philanthropy and humanitarian intervention as a form of *Realpolitik* (Escobar 1995: 22; Nederveen Pieterse 1998; Easterly 2006).

Acknowledgements

This study is part of a wider research project looking into celebrity activism and its impact on civil society. It is supported by funding from the Fonds Wetenschappelijk Onderzoek Vlaanderen (The Flemish Fund for Scientific Research) and the University of Antwerp's Bijzonder Onderzoeksfonds – Nieuwe Onderzoeksinitiatieven (Special Research Funds – New Research Initiatives).

References

Abrahamsson, R. (2003) 'African studies and the post-colonial challenge', *African Affairs*, 102: 189–210.

Bhabha, H.K. (1994) *The Location of Culture*, London: Routledge.

Cashmore, E. (2006) *Celebrity/Culture*, New York: Routledge.

Corton, E. (dir.) (2007) *Eric Corton in de Centraal Afrikaanse Republiek* [Eric Corton in the Central African Republic], http://seriousrequest.3fm.nl/page/07_textpage/07_eric_corton. Accessed 6 October 2010.

De Maria, W. (2005) 'The new war on African "corruption": Just another neo-colonial adventure?', paper presented at *4th International Critical Management Studies Conference*, Cambridge University, England, 4–6 July.

Duffield, M. (1998) 'Containing systemic crisis: The regionalisation of welfare and security policy', in J. Nederveen Pieterse (ed.) *World Orders in the Making: Humanitarian Intervention and Beyond*, Basingstoke: MacMillan, pp. 80–110.

Easterly, W. (2006) *The White Man's Burden: Why the West's Efforts To Aid the Rest Have Done So Much Ill and So Little Good*, Oxford, UK: Oxford University Press.

Entman, R.M. (1991) 'Framing US coverage of international news: Contrasts in narratives of the KAL and Iran air incidents', *Journal of Communication*, 41, 4: 6–27.

Escobar, A. (1995) *Encountering Development: The Making and Unmaking of the Third World*, Princeton, NJ: Princeton University Press.

Esping-Andersen, G. (1990) *The Three Worlds of Welfare Capitalism*, Cambridge, UK: Polity Press.

Evans, J., and Hesmondhalgh, D. (2005) *Understanding Media: Inside Celebrity*, Maidenhead: Open University Press.

Fain, S. (2008) 'Celebrities, poverty and the mediapolis: A case study of the ONE Campaign', paper presented at the *Media and Humanity Conference*, London School of Economics, England, 21–23 September.

Felderhof, R. (dir.) (2007) *Felderhof Ontmoet – Goedele Liekens en Hans Dorrestijn* [Felderhof Meets Goedele Liekens and Hans Dorrestijn], television documentary, NCRV, NED2, 4 November.

Gamson, W.A., and Modigliani, A. (1989) 'Media discourse and public opinion on nuclear power: A constructionist approach', *American Journal of Sociology*, 95, 1: 1–37.

Goffman, E.A. (1981) 'A reply to Denzin and Keller', *Contemporary Sociology*, 10: 60–8.

Holmes, S. (2005) '"Off-guard, unkempt, unready?" Deconstructing contemporary celebrity in *Heat* magazine', *Journal of Media and Cultural Studies*, 19, 1: 21–38.

Huang, A. (dir.) (2005) *The Diary of Angelina Jolie and Dr. Jeffrey Sachs in Africa*, television documentary, Diary, MTV networks, 14 September, https://www.youtube.com/watch?v=uUHf_kOUM74, https://www.youtube.com/watch?v=OpCnikxLfkE. Accessed 10 January 2015.

Huang, A. (dir.) (2006) *Diary of Jay-Z: Water for Life*, television documentary, Diary, MTV Networks, 24 November, https://www.youtube.com/watch?v=VLCu9JR8Dxs. Accessed 10 January 2015.

Huddart, S. (2005) *Do We Need Another Hero? Understanding Celebrities' Roles in Advancing Social Causes*, Montreal: McGill University.

Maguire, J. (dir.) (2005) *Geldof in Africa: The Luminous Continent*, television documentary, BBC1, 20 June.

Meyer, D.S., and Gamson, J. (1995) 'The challenge of cultural elites: Celebrities and social movements', *Sociological Inquiry*, 65: 181–206.

Naus, T., and Siezenga, A. (eds) (2005) *Wereldjournaal: Sylvana Simons in Tanzania* [World News: Sylvana Simons in Tanzania], television documentary, EO, NED1, 8 December.

Nederveen Pieterse, J. (1998) *World Orders in the Making: Humanitarian Intervention and Beyond*, Basingstoke: MacMillan Press.

Neuskens, K. (ed.) (2009) *Leefwereld in Beweging: Roos Van Acker* [World in Motion: Roos Van Acker], television documentary, SBS, VijfTV, 14 September.

Nickel, P.M., and Eikenberry, A.M. (2009) 'A critique of the discourse of marketized philanthropy', *American Behavioral Scientist*, 52, 7: 974–89.

Pan, Z., and Kosicki, G.M. (1993) 'Framing analysis: An approach to news discourse', *Political Communication*, 10, 1: 55–75.

Panis, K., and Van den Bulck, H. (2012) 'Celebrities' quest for a better world: Understanding Flemish public perceptions of celebrities' societal engagement', *Javnost – The Public*, 19, 3: 75–92.

Panis, K., and Van den Bulck, H. (2014) 'In the footsteps of Bob and Angelina: Celebrities' diverse societal engagement and its ability to attract media coverage', *Communications: The European Journal of Communication Research*, 39, 1: 23–42.

'Paris Hilton's Rwanda Trip Postponed' (2007) *Reuters*, 26 October, http://uk.reuters.com/article/2007/10/26/uk-hilton-idUKN2532366720071026. Accessed 10 January 2015.

Ponce de Leon, C.L. (2002) *Self-Exposure: Human-Interest Journalism and the Emergence of the Celebrity in America, 1890–1940*, Chapel Hill: University of North Carolina Press.

Powell, M., and Hewitt, M. (2002) *Welfare State and Welfare Change*, Buckingham: Open University Press.

Rojek, C. (2001) *Celebrity*, London: Reaktion Books.

Sachs, J. (2005) *The End of Poverty: Economic Possibilities for Our Time*, New York: Penguin.

Sahota, M. (dir.) (2010) *Lindsay Lohan's Indian Journey*, television documentary, BBC, BBC3, 1 April, https://www.youtube.com/watch?v=qC6f6BEIeHM. Accessed 20 March 2014.

Said, E.W. (1978) *Orientalism*, London: Vintage.

Said, E.W. (1995) *Culture and Imperialism*, London: Vintage.

Salamon, L.M. (1995) *Partners in Public Service: Government-Nonprofit Relations in the Modern Welfare State*, Baltimore: Johns Hopkins University Press.

Serota, D. (dir.) (2009) *8 Minutes in the DR Congo*, documentary, http://vimeo.com/12967446. Accessed 20 March 2014.

Street, J. (2004) 'Celebrity politicians: Popular culture and political representation', *British Journal of Politics and International Relations*, 6, 4: 435–52.

't Hart, P., and Tindall, K. (2009) 'Leadership by the famous: Celebrity as political capital', in J. Kane, H. Patapan and P. 't Hart (eds) *Dispersed Leadership in Democracies*, Oxford, UK: Oxford University Press, pp. 255–78.

Thrall, A.T., Lollio-Fakhreddine, J., Berent, J., Donnelly, L., Herrin, W., Pacquette, Z., Wenglinski, R., and Wyatt, A. (2008) 'Star power: Celebrity advocacy and the evolution of the public sphere', *The International Journal of Press/Politics*, 13, 4: 362–85.

UNICEFUK (2010) *Soccer Aid Appeal Video from Haiti*, television documentary, ITV1, 6 June, https://www.youtube.com/watch?v=Tk5nOrSGcm4. Accessed 20 March 2014

Vamstad, J. (2007) *Governing Welfare – The Third Sector and the Challenges to the Swedish Welfare State*, Östersund: Mittuniversitetets Avhandlingsserie.

Van Aelst, P., and Walgrave, S. (2001) 'Who is that (wo)man in the street? From the normalisation of protest to the normalisation of the protester', *European Journal of Political Research*, 39: 461–86.

Van den Bulck, H., and Claessens, N. (2013a) 'Guess who Tiger is having sex with now? Celebrity sex and the framing of the moral high ground', *Celebrity Studies*, 4, 1: 46–57.

Van den Bulck, H., and Claessens, N. (2013b) 'Celebrity suicide and the search for the moral high ground: Comparing frames in media and audience discussions of the death of a Flemish celebrity', *Critical Studies in Media Communication*, 30, 1: 69–84.

Van den Bulck, H., Panis, K., and Claessens, N. (2013) 'Putting the "fun" in fundraising: The Serious Request and Music For Life radio telethons, media, and citizenship', in K. Howley (ed.) *Media Interventions*, New York: Peter Lang, pp. 109–26.

Van den Bulck, H., and Tambuyzer, S. (2008) *De Celebritysupermarkt* [The Celebrity Supermarket], Berchem: EPO.

Van Gorp, B. (2006) 'Een constructivistische kijk op het concept framing' [A constructivist view of the concept of framing], *Tijdschrift voor Communicatiewetenschap*, 34, 3: 246–56.

Verhulst, J., and Walgrave, S. (2005) 'Gezien worden of gezien zijn? Over oude en nieuwe sociale bewegingen in de Vlaamse pers' [Being seen or being sapped? On old and new social movements in the Flemish press], *Mens en Maatschappij*, 80, 4: 305–27.

Vroom, A. (ed.) (2006) *Telefacts Zomer: Met Luc Appermont naar Filipijnen* [Telefacts Summer: Luc Appermont to the Philippines], television documentary, VTM, 20 July.

Weiss, T.G. (1998) 'Humanitarian action in war zones: Recent experience and future research', in J. Nederveen Pieterse (ed.) *World Orders in the Making: Humanitarian Intervention and Beyond*, Basingstoke: MacMillan, pp. 24–81.

Wheeler, R.T. (2002) *The Connected Celebrity and Nonprofit Advertising*, doctoral dissertation, Lagune Hills, CA: Case Western Reserve University.

West, D.M. and Orman, J. (2003) *Celebrity Politics*, New Jersey: Prentice Hall.

Zwart, C., and Brussaard, D. (dir.) (2009) *Erik and Sascha in Afrika* [Erik and Sascha in Africa], television documentary, SBS, Net5, 25 October.

Chapter 7

Raising Africa? Celebrity and the Rhetoric of the White Saviour

Katherine M. Bell

The 'White Saviour' has long been a vehicle for celebrities in Hollywood film. From *Lawrence of Arabia* (dir. Lean 1962) to *Blood Diamond* (dir. Zwick 2006), from the Indiana Jones franchise that began in 1981 with *Raiders of the Lost Ark* (dir. Spielberg 1981) to *Lara Croft: Tomb Raider* (dir. West 2001), actors perform roles as heroes who save the day against all odds and thwart dark and ominous adversaries (Shohat 1991; Shome 1996; Dyer 1997). Pop stars take on characters and 'exotic' identities as well, from the heroic, virginal and steadfast, to the sexy, bad and 'ethnic', as with Madonna's Geisha, Evita or Indian Summer personas (Fouz-Hernández and Jarman-Ivens 2004). And with increasing visibility, the famous perform real-life hero roles as philanthropists who endorse and fund a variety of social causes around the so-called 'developing' world. This chapter explores how the celebrity philanthropist is constructed as redeemer of distant Others and how this philanthropic role mingles with a celebrity's onstage personas to create the White Saviour, a powerful brand of contemporary cultural authority.

Africa has become a particular focus of the celebrity gaze in recent years, a development that I take up here by looking at three iconic celebrities: popular music stars Bono and Madonna and actor Angelina Jolie. These and other well-known people deploy their fame in/on the African continent in a complex admixture of spectacle and branding, using a range of philanthropic models. Bono's Product RED campaign raises money to fight HIV and AIDS in eight African countries. It is a cause-related marketing effort that partners with iconic brands to sell designated products; companies give a percentage of sales towards the cause ('Our Story' n.d.). Madonna started Raising Malawi in 2006 to 'bring an end to the extreme poverty and hardship endured by Malawi's one million orphans and vulnerable children' ('About Raising Malawi' 2009–2015). Jolie's work as a UN Goodwill Ambassador highlights the issue of displaced people around the world, including in Africa ('Angelina Jolie Visits "Dire" Refugee Settlement on Kenyan Border with Somalia' 2010). Unlike Bono, both Jolie and Madonna have also adopted children from African countries, a fact that gives them gendered high-profile roles as famous mothers of needy children.

Mediatized celebrity philanthropy is, after all, about harnessing spectacle. Stars deliver media attention to social causes, often where government will is lacking. Celebrity can cut through the inertia of bureaucracy and governmental politicking, using social, symbolic and economic capital to draw affluent consumers and influential people to the social ills that define Africa in the western mind. Bono is seen cajoling recalcitrant world leaders into making aid commitments. He has been photographed at the shoulder (or the knee) of presidents, prime ministers and popes. Bono, Madonna and Jolie all have the ear of powerful people.

Yet, celebrity philanthropy in 'distant' locales, including in Africa, is fraught with ideological tensions given that no aid happens outside of the colonial legacy and post-colonial machinations that have left their mark on the continent. As publicity generated by famous people highlights the dire social and political inequities of our time, celebrity philanthropy in Africa generates a cultural authority that recentres whiteness, and, in turn, burnishes the celebrity brand. It does this recentring by exoticizing non-specific representations of African countries and peoples, and by creating narratives of near-divine greatness about the celebrity.

The chapter explores the discursive power evinced by Bono, Jolie and Madonna as key figures in contemporary African celebrity aid and diplomacy work. I analyze Madonna's charity, Raising Malawi, and a 90-minute film called *I Am Because We Are* (dir. Rissman 2009), which she produced and narrated in connection with her charity. I look at Jolie's work as a Goodwill Ambassador for the United Nations High Commissioner for Refugees (UNHCR), primarily through a feature-length CNN interview she did with journalist Anderson Cooper in June 2006, titled 'Angelina Jolie: Her mission and motherhood' (Cooper 2006; Bell 2013). I also examine Bono's Product RED campaign website and a 30-minute campaign film called *The Lazarus Effect* (dir. Bangs 2010). These examples demonstrate two particular discourses of speaking *for*, namely a narrative of religious salvation that is prominent in publicity of celebrity philanthropy and a related privileging of celebrity motherhood in the cases of Jolie and Madonna. A critical reading of these cases reveals the ways in which the celebrity gaze on Africa produces material benefits as it maintains a normative discursive space of whiteness. The cases also show the ways in which fame, as a production of 'ideal' race, class and gender helps reproduce the conditions of global capitalism through the media.

This chapter is a call to examine how celebrities are part of a 'discursive formation', everyday discourses that reproduce material life (Foucault 1972). In these examples, the discourses include neocolonial stereotypes of African peoples as passive and helpless. Thomas Nakayama and Robert Krizek (1995) remind us that it is important to examine racial representations from the centres of power as well as from the margins, to decentre whiteness in order to make it visible. This analysis does not negate celebrities' desire to bring their fame to bear on global problems of human deprivation. They do make on-the-ground interventions in the spiral of poverty, illness and repression. Yet, as they speak *for* Africa and *for* themselves, they employ a rhetoric of human communality that works in tension with their (perhaps unintentional) representation of Africans as Other.

Celebrity As a Form of Cultural Authority: Speaking *for* Africa

I represent a lot of [African] people who have no voice at all. In the world's order of things they are the people that count least [...] They haven't asked me to represent them.

It's clearly cheeky but I hope they're glad I do and in God's order of things they're most important.

(Bono cited in Iley 2005)

Celebrity forms a triad with the media/culture industries and the public or audience, and each of the three is produced and enhanced by the others. It is thus not surprising that some people who have success in the entertainment industries would want to 'be a megaphone' for activists and workers engaged on the ground in troubled parts of the world, as George Clooney called it in an interview with CNN's Larry King (2010). They have ready access to both media publicity and to the halls of power. To quote Clooney again, 'My job is to show up, because cameras follow me. That is the best way to spend my celebrity credit card' (Diehl 2010). In short, A-list entertainment celebrities have social and economic capital, and many of them use it to highlight the dire social problems of our day.

Entertainment celebrity, as Clooney's remark suggests, is ultimately a commercial transaction. Individual stars are both brands and products, and they must remain salient in the public mind like other brands (see also Murray, in this book). Their celebrity must be constantly reproduced through their creative production and via their public/private lives. They do charity work, they endorse commercial products, they marry and divorce and they rear children. Increasingly they mete out tidbits about themselves via social media sites such as Twitter. All of these activities service the brand, feeding a parasocial relationship with fans (for a more nuanced discussion see Turner 2014: 102–8). We feel we have a kind of relationship with famous people because of the publicity about them (Dyer 1986). Moreover, their branded personas generate a form of authority in the context of their relationship to fans and the culture industry. This authority gives them media credibility to speak on behalf of distant others.

Because entertainment celebrities derive their authority through their status as pop culture icons, their creative production works in tandem with their philanthropy and aspects of their 'private' lives to produce their personas (Marshall 2010). We come to know them, or the public version of them, by way of both onstage and offstage performances. Both aspects convey ideas and beliefs. Through celebrities we see the public and private realms of life cross, especially given that fans are as interested in what famous people do in life as in what they do on stage or screen (Dyer 1986: 8). This crossing of public and private is part of what generates their authority to speak on behalf of others.

Cultural production, as a site where ideologies are produced, maintained, challenged and transformed, has always been imbued with racialized, gendered, classed and nationalistic meanings. At the height of the British imperial project from the eighteenth to twentieth centuries, all socio-economic classes connected to nation through popular culture and it was instrumental in maintaining empire in Britain (MacKenzie 1986; Richards 2001). 'Every aspect of popular culture contrived to instill pride in the British imperial achievement', says music historian Jeffrey Richards (2001). From novels to stage plays to music halls, and later in feature films, popular culture was 'about gallant imperial heroes showing the flag and quelling the rebellious natives in far-off dominions' (Richards 2001: 2). Music was replete with jingoistic refrains. Postcards, magazine illustrations, advertising and commercial packaging were all geared to the nationalistic project of empire (see also McClintock 1995).

Richards (2001: 525) writes that popular culture had an instrumental role in the colonial zeitgeist to 'reinforce the components of the ideological cluster that constituted British imperialism in its heyday: patriotism, monarchism, hero-worship, Protestantism, racialism and chivalry'. Today, pop culture's role in shaping contemporary values is not diminished, although it is embedded in a somewhat reconfigured 'ideological cluster' of global capitalism. Components of the twenty-first-century cluster include patriotism, celebrity-worship, individualism, consumption and a post-racial colourblindness that obscures the racialized power dynamics at play. Now, with burgeoning media interest in celebrities' private lives, its meanings are equally embedded in the offstage 'real' lives of entertainment celebrities as in their creative roles.

For the three celebrities discussed here, their creative production intermingles seamlessly with their charity work and the public performance of their private lives. Their words and actions are read as representations of their personal views as expressed through traditional mass media and online in social media (Marshall 2010). The ideologies embedded in their creative work reach their fan bases more inferentially than does their philanthropy and self-promotion; yet, the two streams of publicity feed each other and infuse their public personae. Jolie's films, with strong female heroes, are an aspect of her off-screen role as a philanthropist. The same can be said for Bono as front man in an iconic male rock band, and for Madonna with the ever-changing characters of her stage performances and recordings.

Cooper (2008: 116) suggests, for example, that Jolie's 'ability to mix art and real life' gives her a unique credibility. Her work as a star in adventure films, often in 'exotic' locales, bolsters her power as a celebrity ambassador. In fact, Jolie (2003) says her interest in the plight of refugees grew out of shooting on location in Cambodia. Likewise, her philanthropy burnishes her appeal as an actor. Reputation is a powerful factor for better and for worse. Jolie's decision with her partner, Brad Pitt, to give birth to their first biological child, Shiloh, in Namibia generated a measure of negative media coverage. Some media viewed it as a crass juxtaposition between their wealth and the privation in the country (O'Neill 2006). However, they have largely blunted such criticism through their philanthropic work. They have strategically managed publicity to positive effect, as with Jolie's feature interview with CNN's Cooper (2006) that I take up below.

Madonna's foray into Malawi has been more contentious (Grigoriadis 2011). She has been criticized for adopting Malawian children and for her promotion of an African school curriculum with links to a religious group, loosely based on Jewish Kabbalah teachings popular with US celebrities. In his book, *Celebrity Diplomacy*, Cooper (2008: 116) calls her charity work 'crude ventures into Africa'. Biographer Andrew Morton (2001) characterized Madonna as egocentric. Such critiques are not unconnected to Madonna's many pop personas dating back to her early Material Girl image in the 1980s, which some read as aggressively sexual, and others as campy and appropriative (Fouz-Hernández and Jarman-Ivens 2004).

Natalie Clarke (2007: 20) of the UK's *Daily Mail*, for example, suggested Madonna's Malawi project was yet another reinvention 'as Mother Madonna, a leather-booted hybrid of Mother Teresa and Angelina Jolie'. Yet, despite such gendered criticism, Madonna's cultural authority and material resources remain strong. She deploys them in the Raising Malawi charity and in the feature-length documentary, with high production values, that I discuss below.

Bono also mixes his life and celebrity with commerce and philanthropy in such a way that at times they are indistinguishable. While Madonna and Jolie have attracted considerable media coverage for adopting children, Bono's role as the father of four children has received limited media coverage, reportedly because his wife wants their children to have 'private lives' (Russell 2011). However, Bono promotes his wife's fashion label, Edun, a high-end purveyor of 'sustainable' clothing that promotes trade with Africa. He and his wife, Ali Hewson, appeared in 2010 as part of the luxury brand Louis Vuitton's 'Core Values' advertising campaign, wearing the Edun clothing line, in which Vuitton had a 49 per cent stake, and carrying Vuitton bags for the African-themed photo shoot by iconic photographer Annie Liebowitz (4womenCZ 2010; Brockington 2014: 100). The ad featured the couple disembarking from a small plane in the middle of the African savannah. They both spoke of such work as activism and as part of the mission to increase trade with Africa, though the ad campaign had no obvious charitable component.

These artists follow a long colonial tradition of speaking for the Other that tends to make the nameless, faceless Third-World Other a blank recipient of their goodwill (see Millington and Van den Bulck, Claessens and Panis, in this book). For example, Bono made the remark above about speaking 'for people who have no voice at all' upon the 2005 launch of the Product RED campaign. RED is a cause-related marketing effort in which major brands such as Apple, The Gap and Starbucks, and more recently Coca-Cola and Bed Bath & Beyond donate a portion of their profits from designated products. The money goes towards AIDS prevention and treatment through an international agency called The Global Fund, which distributes it in 'qualifying' countries, among them Ghana, Swaziland and Zambia. In saying '[t]hey haven't asked me to represent them. It's clearly cheeky but I hope they're glad I do' (Iley 2005), Bono activates his cultural authority and signals the presumption behind his efforts. He shows an awareness of the power and privilege that he has explicitly used to put the issues of poverty, developing-world debt and AIDS on the public agenda.

By speaking for the Other, Bono continues a long western tradition of creating an 'undifferentiated subject', as Gayatri Spivak (1988) describes the First World practice of conflating and mapping its desires and interests onto the subaltern. So-called First World representation presumes to speak for a generalized subaltern subject, with no distinctions from within. Such representation ventriloquizes the subaltern, produces a universal subject that matters only in relation to its capacity to serve the ventriloquist. As Spivak (1988: 289) puts it, 'This benevolent first-world appropriation and reinscription of the Third World as an Other is the founding characteristic of much third-worldism'. In other words, Bono's speaking *for* does not, indeed cannot, acknowledge a differentiated post-colonial subject. To speak *for* is to maintain the order of things.

The examples discussed here constitute an ideological stance that defines a common good, valued in visitors' terms (Spivak and Harasym 1990; Ogundipe-Leslie 2001). The voices of the non-African celebrities stifle African perspectives on the desired direction of economic and social life. This is how critical scholar Molara Ogundipe-Leslie (2001: 135) explains it, 'The African person is that person who does not have a "self," who gets represented or spoken for by others. At the creative level, travellers and settlers in Africa become the spokespersons for the indigenous peoples'. White celebrities are among the visitors with a uniquely privileged authority to designate what they see to be a collective need. They can 'claim to speak for the communality of humanity' (Dyer 1997: 2). And with the media's fixation on fame and exotic locales as a backdrop for issues, the story invariably becomes about the celebrity's good deeds in a faraway land (Richey and Ponte 2011; Bell 2013).

Celebrity largesse can ultimately take the form of a 'cure' without a thoroughgoing diagnosis. African peoples become 'victims' of poverty or disease, problems that apparently sprang without history, from hapless circumstance, poor choices or rotten luck. Such characterization obscures the ongoing legacy of colonialism, including the substitution of colonial rule for institutions such as the World Bank and International Monetary Fund (Altman 1999; Barnett and Whiteside 2002; Mbaku 2008; Patterson and Kieh 2008; Moyo 2009). Further, there is little space in an ahistorical philanthropy for the specificities of individual African nations and cultures. African problems become generalized and its peoples homogenized. Abstraction is what *invents* Africa in the western mind, as an amorphous locale that is at once exotic, sick, culturally rich, financially poor, diverse and yet non-specific.

The Product RED campaign is an example of this sort of 'cure' without the diagnosis that would be afforded by a contextualized view of poverty and AIDS (Jungar and Salo 2008: 94). The campaign obliterates the colonial history and the context of the HIV and AIDS crisis from the picture it paints in order to create an aesthetic space for affluent consumers to buy their favourite brands, guilt-free. The campaign has said RED wanted to eschew the pictures of despair common to many charity projects (Perry 2008: 288–9). Rather, the funding model hails western consumers as activists, using celebrities to encourage people to choose RED products for all the fashionable things they want or need anyway. RED hinges on the mass purchase of consumer goods, which ultimately makes it a contributor to the global economic conditions that are part of the AIDS epidemic (Bell 2011; Richey and Ponte 2011). The configuration of global capital requires cheap material and human resources, and Africa is home to both. With the corporate relationships upon which RED is founded requiring a fashionable message, we get a stylized Africa that is branded through product designs, campaign promotion and through people as symbols of the power of RED to restore health.

Bono, the personality at the centre of the campaign, deploys his brand to attract other celebrities, corporations and consumer to the cause. Moreover, Brand Bono is valuable. Product RED states that it had raised more than USD 250 million by the start of 2014, helping 40 million people to receive testing, treatment and counselling for HIV and AIDS

('The (RED) idea' n.d.). The campaign was spearheading a drive to 'eliminate AIDS' in Africa by 2015. The RED case, then, well exemplifies the tensions and contradictions within the celebrity gaze on Africa.

As these stars speak on behalf of distant Others in both an activist sense and through their creative output, they represent a contradiction between the desire to alleviate global problems of human privation and discourses that serve to reinforce the dire inequities of globalization. I explore two such discourses below: the frequent theme of divine salvation in celebrity campaigns and in media coverage about them, and a specific dominant ideal of motherhood that Jolie and Madonna, and other female celebrities, model publicly. Both of these themes – divine salvation and 'ideal' motherhood – figure prominently in media publicity surrounding famous philanthropists more broadly, and they speak powerfully about how race, gender and class are constituted globally.

Such publicity reconstitutes these three stars' personas, brands and cultural authority as it offers individualized solutions for complex structural problems. Mass-mediated celebrity philanthropy helps stars ascend from the 'crudely commercial to the sanctified, quasi-religious realm of altruism and charity, while revealing or constructing an added dimension of personality: of compassion and caring', as Jo Littler (2008: 239) puts it. Celebrity philanthropy is a mechanism through which stars speak for themselves as they speak for Others, where they claim authoritative voice regarding the problems of Africa and accumulate more cultural authority along the way.

Ubuntu: The Mission to 'Raise' Africa

When it comes to Africa, celebrities express their message of hope and salvation through a rhetoric of one-world communality. *Ubuntu*: 'I am because we are', as Madonna's film repeats the Zulu phrase (dir. Rissman 2009), *umuntu ngumuntu ngabantu*: 'a person is a person through other persons'.[1] All three of the celebrities discussed in this chapter invoke a version of this South African Zulu-inspired philosophy to explain their motivations for getting involved. This message of human oneness is very compelling. On her website, Madonna's mission is explained similarly: 'We are all inextricably connected. That is why we strive to raise Malawi' ('Why Malawi?' 2009–2015). At the same time, there is a powerful neocolonial echo in the deployment of this theme of communality, one that resonates through much celebrity philanthropy.

Christianity was the 'civilizing' instrument of the colonizing powers in Africa. It is historically entwined with the growth of capitalism and the exploitation of the continent's human and natural resources. The colonial zeitgeist of moral superiority was the mandate for bringing both ideologies of capitalism and Christianity to the so-called 'dark places of the earth' in the nineteenth century (Burton 1994: 40). This is not to say that celebrities operating in Africa are necessarily on an overtly religious mission as was the case under colonial expansion. Yet, the language of their campaigns contains strong religious themes that gesture to an earlier imperialism that asserted the duality of white and divine salvation.

Product RED's signature slogan, for example, is the 'Lazarus Effect', a Biblical reference to Jesus's divine powers to undo death. We hear repeatedly that 'two pills a day' will make the difference between life and death for someone living with HIV. The drugs can and do save the lives of people who are sick, and they are having an impact in many African countries. In the Gospel of John, Jesus demonstrates his divinity by bringing his friend and follower, Lazarus, back from the dead. This story is the basis for numerous RED campaign ads, and inspired the 30-minute RED documentary *The Lazarus Effect* (dir. Bangs 2010) that aired on the US television network HBO on 24 May 2010.

Likewise, the name of Madonna's charity, Raising Malawi, has a missionary ethos. She started it after she reportedly received a call from a local businesswoman in the city of Lilongwe. Victoria Keelan asked her to use her considerable means to help the country cope with the dire circumstances of its many children orphaned by AIDS. Madonna, in her feature-length documentary *I Am Because We Are* (dir. Rissman 2009), confessed that she did not know where Malawi was located. That was the start of the pop star's philanthropic journey to and in Malawi, an experience she describes in the film as doing as much to 'save' her as she is doing to help the country.

Madonna's charity introduced into Malawi a school curriculum linked to the Kabbalah Centre, based in Los Angeles, where she is a member. The centre is popular among some Hollywood elites, Demi Moore, Ashton Kutcher and Rosanne Barr among them, and is based loosely upon the secretive Hasidic mystical tradition in Judaism (Ryan and Christiensen 2011). Judaism is virtually non-existent in Malawi. The organization, Spirituality (later changed to Success) for Kids, or SFK, denies any links to Kabbalah, saying that it teaches personal responsibility and self-determination (dir. Rissman 2009).[2]

The Kabbalah-based program described in the film contains a powerful message that individual strength and perseverance will help Malawi transcend a culture of victimhood. The SFK program emphasizes individual cause and effect as an ethical orientation. 'We are all in control of the world around us', Madonna says in the film, citing herself as an example:

For so many years I played the victim card. When you tap into that consciousness, it keeps you from moving ahead. You get into a cycle of self-destructive behavior. If I could think of a phrase that summed up Spirituality for Kids it's more like 'You're somebody. Believe in yourself. You're not the sum total of your surroundings. You can change your destiny.' And more than anything that's what these kids need.

(dir. Rissman 2009)

Here, Madonna asserts that salvation comes from within, that victimhood is a state of mind and that to suggest otherwise is to abrogate personal responsibility. She invokes a variation of the term 'race card', which became an axiom in the US in 1990s, when former football star, actor and broadcaster O.J. Simpson was on trial for the murder of his former wife,

Nicole Brown. The term had a pejorative meaning that suggested Simpson accused police of racism simply as a smokescreen to obscure the damning evidence of the case. Here, Madonna's use of the term invokes the same meaning that victimhood is something people use to unfairly blame others. She implies that no matter the circumstances of our misfortunes, we must never look for causes outside ourselves.

At the same time, Madonna places her own trials alongside those of people who have no secure access to life's basic necessities. She equates her life after the death of her mother when she was six years old to the lives of children orphaned by AIDS. By personalizing her story, she is recentred in the documentary. Her truth – that we must all pull ourselves up individually – is put forward as a universal solution. This message is a key feature of the American Dream mythology, where individual rights and responsibilities are paramount, where all have the potential to achieve equally and where success comes from hard work. The American Dream is an ideological mainstay of contemporary celebrity in the US (Sternheimer 2011). Fame in that country is frequently viewed as a result of individual genius and hard work even when, as mentioned earlier, it may be bound up in a powerfully complex relationship with the culture industries and audiences (see also Murray, in this book).

The American Dream myth as deployed in the Madonna film is racially charged, though she never mentions race. Her message of individuality is post-racial in that it asserts a level playing field for attaining material security. Post-race, also sometimes referred to as 'colorblind racism' (Bonilla-Silva 2003), is an ideology that asserts that the structural inequalities of race are largely in the past. Thus, socio-economic success is within the grasp of all (Joseph 2009: 239). Post-racial politics assume that the social and civil advances of the twentieth century have largely eradicated historical structural inequalities. The view that race and, in this case, the legacy of British colonial rule, is a distant memory negates the historical inequalities that remain a part of Malawi's ongoing life as a country in a global economy.

The SFK segment of Madonna's film, with its emphasis on individual attitude and hard work, as an example of post-racial ideology, comes at the beginning of a crescendo in the documentary story arc. It appears as a message of hope after extensive documentation of the struggles of numerous individuals living with HIV and their families. The segment is situated just before the script circles back to its overarching message of communality and after a segment that implies causality for current conditions in the fact that people turn to 'backward' ways such as witchcraft as well as to alcohol to escape the grind of poverty.

The film then segues to an upbeat ending, stating that Malawians are finally shedding their worn-out ways and taking responsibility. They are 'more eager to tackle their own problems' as former US President Bill Clinton says in the film, and they want outsiders to 'empower' them. This juxtaposition repeats well-worn narratives of Africa as a primitive place that can be brought into modern times given First World help. Such help includes cultivating a western sense of individuality as a solution to large structural problems.

The philosophy of SFK exemplifies a profoundly contradictory rhetoric regarding Africa. On the one hand, there is *ubuntu*: 'I am not defined without you', as former Malawi finance minister Mathews Chikaonda says in the film (dir. Rissman 2009). On the other hand, we alone must change our own destiny. Personal responsibility is an attractive ethic, particularly when combined with a message of communality. In a sense, universality is fetishized in the use of the borrowed Zulu *ubuntu* concept, and retooled in the language of individualism. This discursive move has the impact of applying a hegemonic US ideological response – individualism – to the specificities of life in Malawi. As an outside solution, it may be attractive to the home audience of potential donors to tout individual responsibility. However, it posits a deeply US value as a universal non-ideological truth (see also Millington, in this book).

Clinton and Madonna repeat the message of oneness while continuing to portray the people of Africa as Other. Clinton says, *ubuntu* signifies 'that what we have in common is more important than our interesting differences'. Those differences and similarities are defined and valued primarily in the so-called First World, by people like him. They reinforce the superiority of the First World in its own eyes, (Ogundipe-Leslie 2001; Spivak and Harasym 1990). Edward Said (2003) has called this *flexible positional* superiority, where western solutions and desires remain at the forefront of interactions with the formerly colonized Other. Indeed, as Said (2003) says, the hegemonic western persona is created in juxtaposition to the Other and the other is essential for dominant identity formation as well.

The 'interesting differences', between 'us' and 'them', as Clinton calls them, are visualized in both the Madonna and Bono films using similar imagery. We hear in both documentaries that Africans have a gloriously untrammelled take on life, and that the developed world must preserve that worldview. People, particularly women, dance and sing in African garb in both films. The scenes are shot without explanation or context about the meanings or significance of the dance. Both films are shot largely in rural areas, presenting a particular image of Africa, including portrayals of 'tribal' people with 'weird' rites of passage. As Ogundipe-Leslie (2001) reminds us, the idea of African woman in the western mind connotes someone who is impoverished, uneducated, primitive and rural. Few of these representations depict the educated, urban or middle classes in African countries, though they are surely essential contributors to the societies' economic and social aspirations.

Ultimately, the celebritized 'traveller' gets to define the quintessence of Africa's diverse peoples. Clinton has the definitive word on the nature of African-ness in Madonna's film:

> People ask me 'Why do you love it so much there?' And I always say it's because they have the highest percentage of people, I believe, anywhere on earth who wake up every day with a song in their heart. They sing through their pain and their need and the madness of people around them. It's almost like an ingrained wisdom of more than 100,000 years.
> (Clinton in dir. Rissman 2009)

As a former US President and head of the William J. Clinton Foundation philanthropic organization ('About Us' n.d.), he is deemed a foremost expert in the film.

Jolie claims a similar expertise in her interview with Cooper (2006). She waxes poetic in describing the Democratic Republic of the Congo, saying 'The Congo is lush, and it's amazing, and [...] all the people, and they're so different. And they're passionate. And they're tough. And they're vibrant. And they're ready to live' (Cooper 2006). Jolie, like Clinton, is deemed to have the authority to pronounce about the general disposition of the people of the Congo. She does it with a sense of great admiration, which makes her remark appear as an optimistic gesture. Yet, such a sweeping pronouncement positions her exoticizing perspective as authoritative and superior (for a different reading see Marshall, in this book).

In her film, Madonna says, 'Being in Africa has made me realize that suffering is subjective. There is an enormous amount of suffering here that is really tangible [...] And yet they have an appreciation and a joy and a gratitude that we could never understand' (dir. Rissman 2009). She presents such comments, as with images of people singing and dancing, and standing in line for food, as evidence of magnificence and resilience as seen through the eyes of the White Saviour.

Jolie, Madonna, Clinton and others express their views about the African continent with great respect, but their characterizations define the Other in a way that minimizes the structural inequalities of race, gender and class, and the uneven impact of globalization. The rhetoric of one-world communality, of 'raising' another, is the discursive space of the White Saviour in all of its 'functional invisibility' (Nakayama and Krizek 1995: 297). For the White Saviour to exist, it must have the Other, in this case Africans, as a singular timeless human monoculture that bears little resemblance to 'us'.

There are moments where Bono's film does decentre whiteness. *The Lazarus Effect* (dir. Bangs 2010) offers a look at on-the-ground AIDS treatment from the perspective of Zambian health-care professionals and patients. It tells of how local workers are distributing medication and promoting openness and HIV testing through the work of Constance Mudenda, who runs three clinics, and Dr. Mannesseh Phiri, a pioneer in the use of antiretroviral therapy. The film is partly about local empowerment and the ground-level effort to destigmatize people living with HIV; the quoting of local professionals is a powerful way of doing so.

I Am Because We Are (dir. Rissman 2009) likewise provides a glimpse at colonial life in Malawi. That history includes direct rule starting in the 1880s and 1890s, when the British established the area as Nyasaland, and when they later established the Federation of Rhodesia and Nyasaland in the early 1950s, against local will. The film includes footage of Lord Perth, a former British colonial minister, admitting that Nyasaland was not a priority: 'I'm afraid its priority slipped although we genuinely were going to do things for them. We kept on finding that other things cropped up, which to us seemed more important' (dir. Rissman 2009). Such references to the colonial project are rare in celebrity work.

Madonna also discusses the problems that generations of grinding poverty have brought to Malawi. She aims to contextualize those conditions within the broader problems of the so-called developed world by pointing to the barbarism of war, environmental disaster, religious and political strife in the US and elsewhere. The film moves through a collage of images of western religious zealotry, clearcutting, gambling, a stock exchange, garbage dumps, flag burning and other violence as evidence that 'modernization equals no humanity', as Madonna says. It attempts to frame local traditional practices in the context of harsh and violent practices globally. It is a move that helps contextualize aspects of life in the country that are often dismissed as backward.

The film ultimately circles back to a we/they 'dichotomy', as Madonna herself calls it:

> You get caught up in this dichotomy where you think 'If they could only understand what I understand then they could fix everything.' Then I look at the way they live and I think 'Oh God, they have illnesses and they have cultural traditions that seem antithetical to life but they're happy. And you could drive down a street in Beverly Hills and [...] and you don't see that kind of joy'.
>
> (Madonna in dir. Rissman 2009)

This characterization suggests that while poverty is primitive, it is where true joy flourishes. It is an invocation of the notion that 'money can't buy happiness' in the face of consumption-dependent modern celebrity.

These manifestations of the White Saviour narrative are sometimes overshadowed by the material impact of fund-raising projects such as Product RED and Raising Malawi. Yet, their racialized 'post-race' stance serves to maintain a neocolonial footprint on the continent and also posits individualistic responses to deep structural problems. The universalizing representations that flow from the cultural authority of celebrity ventriloquize the Other, to return to Spivak (1988), and define the African subject's needs in the context of so-called First World ideologies such as the American Dream.

Below I examine motherhood, a related post-identity narrative that is evident in contemporary philanthropy. Celebrities' deployment of their roles as mothers creates a strong brand of cultural authority that also has an inseverable link to the colonial past.

Mother Africa: Speaking *for* Motherhood

> Next we'll adopt [...] We don't know which country but we're looking at different countries. And it's going to be the balance of what would be best for Mad and for Z right now. You know, another boy, another girl, which country, which race, would fit best with the kids.
>
> (Angelina Jolie in Cooper 2006)

Angelina Jolie made the above remark during a feature interview with CNN's Anderson Cooper in 2006. It contains a bold assumption that she has her pick of children from around the globe. She and her partner, Brad Pitt, can select the gender, race and circumstances of her family to ensure that the adopted members of the Jolie-Pitt clan are good matches with the others. She can essentially shop the world for children, as this statement would have it.

The couple went on to adopt a three-year-old boy named Pax from Vietnam in 2007. Her expression of privileged motherhood in this comment is wrapped up with her social location as a wealthy, famous woman who travels through the world almost without restriction.

The privilege of her whiteness inheres in its invisibility. Its status is essentially that of non-race in that it appears to have a normative essence. 'Thus the experiences and communication patterns of whites are taken as the norm from which Others are marked', as Nakayama and Krizek say (1995: 293). It is partly Jolie's normative invisibility as a white person, even though she is far from invisible as a famous actor, which gives her power. Her identity as someone seemingly without race is partly what enables her to make such a remark without challenge. Anderson Cooper never questions the presumption behind it; Jolie is seemingly a universal subject (Bell 2013).

As such, Jolie embodies a particular kind of twenty-first-century celebrity motherhood that is at once hip and edgy, doting and playful. She is a former Goth turned 'working mom'. The actor once wore a vial of then-husband Billy Bob Thornton's blood around her neck. These days, she cultivates a cleaned-up image on and off-screen and her child-rearing is very public. She and Pitt are frequently photographed with their six children in tow, which serves as a strategy for managing the intense media gaze that follows the Jolie-Pitt brand.

The CNN feature interview introduced her as 'the most famous mother in the world' (Cooper 2006). She and Pitt have three biological children and three children adopted from the so-called Third World, from Cambodia (Maddox), Ethiopia (Zahara) and Vietnam (Pax). Their biological daughter, Shiloh, was born in Namibia in 2006 amid the aforementioned media spectacle and criticism about the resources the small country was required to expend on ensuring the privacy and security of the famous couple. After Pax's adoption, Jolie gave birth to twins in 2008 in Nice, France. The interview was recorded just four days after Shiloh's birth.

Madonna has four children, two of whom are adopted from Malawi. She has used her media access to blend her motherhood with her philanthropy, and to defend herself as an adoptive mother against some of the critiques ('Kristy Wark Interview with Madonna' 2006; 'Alina Cho Interview with Madonna' 2009). She has been criticized in the media over the adoptions, particularly because her child David is not an orphan. His biological father is living in Malawi, although without the means to care for his child, according to media reports. Her second adoptive child, Mercy, has family as well (McDougall 2011). As with Jolie and Pitt, Madonna is frequently photographed with her children; in Africa, on the red carpet, and elsewhere.

Both celebrities – and others such as Sandra Bullock and Mariska Hargitay who adopted African American children – are models for idealized motherhood. 'Proper' motherhood in the western mind is affluent, hip and largely white (Hill Collins 2006). It is also highly commoditized. This sort of motherhood is a lifestyle and an aspect of contemporary popular culture. The media derive valuable content from their fixation on the celebrity 'baby bump' and on the accouterments of child-rearing, from strollers to children's designer clothes. Stars such as Jolie and Madonna model this idealized, wealthy version of motherhood that is seen to be glamorous and consumptive, and is largely unattainable for most women.

Such idealizations characterize what Susan Douglas and Meredith Michaels (2004) call the 'new momism'. They do it all. Jolie, in particular, has a thriving career and presents herself as a devoted and present mother. She is in control of her destiny and motherhood makes her a go-to expert on Africa because its children are in need. In a sense, she has a diplomatic passport to pronounce on all things related to women and children, to speak for those perceived to be voiceless. She claims the privilege of white femininity and its presumption to speak for motherhood.

As this discussion suggests, motherhood is a loaded concept in terms of power relations. It is pregnant with politically charged ideals of purity, race, class and belonging. There are 'real' mothers, legitimized as best suited for reproducing the US population and the 'alleged values of the U.S. nation-state', Patricia Hill Collins says (2006: 55). They are represented in all kinds of media as authentic, sincere, honest and reliable, but also as affluent, heterosexual, married, white and 'American'. People of other races, classes and positions are commonly framed against this ideal as inherently less fit. Those ideals, as Hill Collins (2006) notes, can have direct material consequences for access to resources.

Motherhood has deep roots in the imperial project as well (Burton 1994). African women remain, 'at the heart of the discursive storms around voice and voicelessness', when it comes to their lives as spouses and mothers, as scholar and activist Ogundipe-Leslie argues (2001: 135). In the colonial era of the eighteenth and nineteenth century, white motherhood was juxtaposed with non-white motherhood. By drawing distinctions from their colonial counterparts, white European women could leverage their own aspirations and struggles (Mama 1997). Inequalities of race, class and gender worked together 'generating a repressive imperial ideology' that acted in and on European life (Mama 1997: 49). In fact, the First Wave feminist campaign for women's suffrage was built upon the argument that British women were moral and civilized creatures, and to deny them the vote was to cast them as no better than the 'primitive' women of the colonies who were subject to the brutality of their husbands and to backward cultural norms (Burton 1994).

The historical ideal of colonial women as civilized mothers and keepers of the race, tasked with teaching colonized women about child-rearing, is a trope that lives on in the contemporary western milieu of celebritized parenting. Both Jolie's and Madonna's lives are intimately entwined with the politics of African motherhood and its vast imperial legacy. Even in the RED campaign, Bono deploys famous celebrity mothers such as Christie Turlington and Elle MacPherson as 'ambassadors' to the women and children in designated RED countries (Bell 2011). Their presence has discursive power to represent African motherhood as primitive and unreliable. Their gestures – plucking chosen babies from a harsh existence to live in luxury, being photographed amid a sea of black faces, touching, holding, feeding and playing with children – are highly individualistic acts that reflect and construct their authority.

There is a particular self-referentiality in the mission of these celebrities. They frequently speak as mothers in their media interviews, as Jolie does in the interview with Cooper (2006). Jolie's quote about choosing the birth country of her next adopted child displays a sense of ownership in that she has the run of the so-called Third World and a mandate to be the mother of its children. Behind her comment about choosing her next child is a tacit assertion that her philanthropy serves her parental desires, and vice versa. The CNN interview title itself, 'Angelina Jolie: Her mission and motherhood', makes this symbiotic link between motherhood and missionary zeal, suggesting that her mission in Africa includes being a mother of its children.

When Cooper (2006) asks Jolie about AIDS, it is in the context of the couple's fear that their adopted daughter Zahara would be HIV-positive (she was not). Jolie's discussion of the refugee conditions she has witnessed is tinged with an air of *there but for the grace of God go I*. It can be read as an expression of humility and grace, but it is also self-referential to compare one's privilege to the suffering of others. She tells Cooper (2006) that she reminds herself of what the refugees endure each time she begins to feel negative about something in her life:

Even just today, I was, you know, breast-feeding, and tired, and thinking, God, I really don't know how I'm going to get myself together to be thinking for this interview. But you think, Jesus, the things these people go through. I owe it to all of them to get myself together, to stop whining about being tired, and get there and get focused.

(Cooper 2006)

This sort of remark, while empathetic, also has the effect of juxtaposing her with, and distancing her from, the Other (for a different reading see Marshall, in this book).

Madonna takes up the White Saviour stance directly through the name of her charity, Raising Malawi. It suggests a mission to lift up a poor nation, and to raise its people. The characterization of Africans as childlike, in need of rearing and salvation, is a discourse that dates back at least to the slave trade. People were infantilized visually and in multiple forms of publicity directed at the citizens of colonizing countries (Burton 1994; McClintock 1995; Hall 1997). The name of Madonna's charity is an echo of this imperial past.

I Am Because We Are (dir. Rissman 2009), produced as part of a major publicity effort for the charity in 2009, conveys a strong image of Madonna as mother to both African children and in a larger sense of its peoples. The film opens with scenes of Madonna walking through a village, flanked by a group of people, holding the hand of a young boy. The shot zooms in on the two and eventually on their two hands – black and white. The opening sequence is interspersed with a rapid-fire collage of news headlines about the court case surrounding Madonna's adoption of a young orphan named David Banda, who ultimately became the third of her four children. A Malawian court initially rejected her application to adopt David because his father and other relatives still live in the country. They lacked the means to care for a child. In the film, the singer picks up David's story at the Home of Hope orphanage:

When I returned to Malawi three months later, David's health had deteriorated. He had pneumonia and malaria and God knows what else. There was not medicine for him at Home of Hope, or any means to treat his illnesses. What was I prepared to do? If I was challenging people to open up their minds and their hearts, then I had to be willing to stand at the front of the line. I decided to try and adopt him. The rest is history.

(dir. Rissman 2009)

Madonna never puts her decision to adopt David into a larger context. Malawi has one million orphans and nowhere does she discuss why foreign adoption could be an answer. Nor is it evident why she inserted her personal narrative into the documentary. The choice to include her own adoption story recentres Madonna, a White Saviour who comes in the form of a mother. The narrative, without a broader context about international adoption, stands out as a one-off response to a seemingly intractable problem. Ultimately, Madonna is a traveller, as Ogundipe-Leslie (2001) says, speaking for the parents and children of Malawi and for herself as a mother. She tells her own story, implying that it has wider relevance to the problem of AIDS in Malawi.

Madonna explains neither the controversy about David's case, nor the complexities of international adoption. Headlines that flash through the opening sequence are about the delays she experienced as Malawian courts challenged her right to adopt, but she never takes them up in the film. Thus, she posits adoption of children orphaned by AIDS as a possible universal remedy. Is it a call for other parents to step in and adopt Malawian children? This is not clear. In one study at the University of Liverpool, psychologists suggested that this so-called 'Madonna effect' actually contributed to an increase in international adoptions without a concomitant discussion about the potential repercussions for the children ('New Concerns about International Adoption' 2008). The point is that this aspect of the documentary creates a particularly self-referential construction of Madonna as a White Saviour with the cultural authority to speak as an ideal mother about finding solutions for the large number of children in Malawi who have lost either one or both parents to AIDS.

Madonna's film also highlights the personal help and support she gave to two other children. In one case, a child named Luka had his genitals cut off in an attack. She helped him get the surgeries he needed and helped his family get a new home and places in a private school for Luka and his siblings. In another case, she helps a young orphan named Fanizo get into a posh private school. Her intervention is again decontextualized. She does not set it in the context of other aid efforts or programs so it reads as an individual act by a privileged white woman. To say this is not to critique her desire to assist these or other children; rather it is to suggest that her work re-inscribes a legacy of the white mother figure that dates back to the colonial period.

These examples of celebrity motherhood mixing with philanthropy are a discourse of whiteness enabled by the cultural authority of these famous individuals. There is no inherent problem with deploying affective ways of knowing that flow from an aspect of life that has formerly been devalued, namely the private domestic realm of child-rearing. Yet, in Madonna's and Jolie's deft blending of celebrity philanthropy and motherhood, these stars are primarily constructing and maintaining their own brand and asserting their power to define a common good that serves their own needs (see Littler 2008). Their representations help produce Africa as a large, amorphous locale, replete with already-existing stereotypes of childlike primitivism, that needs mothering. The self-referential nature of this publicity around their efforts sets these celebrities up as mother saviours.

Conclusion

Each of these examples demonstrates the complexity of celebrity involvement in Africa. Famous people can make a material difference in the lives of those they encounter because of their roles as privileged travellers in a globalized world. In some ways, celebrity advocacy has become *the* window on Africa for many Euro-North Americans. It brings the media to places of need that would otherwise remain invisible to people who live in wealthy countries. The language of universal good and the material benefits of philanthropy in Africa make it challenging to critique celebrities' actions, and the underlying rhetoric of the White Saviour that operates in the background.

Yet, as we excavate beneath the contradictory discourses of universality and individuality, and the representations of people in Africa in these cases, we unearth the white subject 'as the universal ubiquitous subject of humanity' (Shome 1996: 513). That universal subject *speaks* the 'truth' of Africa, and sanctions individuals in Africa to speak. The universal subject speaks for the mission of 'raising' Africa, and for the parents and children of Africa. The discursive space of whiteness in Africa must surely be examined as an impediment to Africans' long-term efforts to break the cycles established under colonial rule. The cases here are a part of those cycles through the celebrities' highly individualistic, and in some cases piecemeal, responses. This critique is not to suggest that celebrity activism and philanthropy relating to distant locales can only ever be self-serving for the celebrity or disempowering for those who might be helped by their philanthropic efforts; it is aimed at theorizing the discursive as the material.

The analysis presented here is meant to be part of a conversation that challenges us to think about how celebrity charity work is a double-edged sword. The same celebritized power that can force difficult social problems and political positions to the fore can be part of a rhetoric that shores up the status quo; in this case, a timeworn portrayal of Africa as a place of singular primitive beauty and heartbreakingly intractable problems. Celebrity is a fact of contemporary life that is a deep well of raw power, as the publicity and fund-raising of these and other campaigns suggest. The question becomes how it is deployed or, rather, how it might be deployed in the service of progressive discourses that do not universalize or generalize the Other, and that do not model one-off, self-referential solutions to enormously complex structural problems.

Notes

1   The phrase *ubuntu* has also been appropriated as the commercial brand of a computer operating system, http://www.ubuntu.com/. Accessed 10 January 2015.

2   The son of the Kabbalah Centre's founder, Michael Berg, founded the Raising Malawi charity with Madonna. Madonna severed its connection with the Centre after a scandal over charitable donations that were been unaccounted for, and there is a US federal tax investigation of the Kabbalah organization. Madonna abruptly cancelled plans for a school, similar to one built in South Africa by Oprah Winfrey, in spring of 2011, barely breaking ground, and fired its director. There were extensive media reports about questionable spending practices by those hired to oversee the school project and about the Kabbalah links (Barrett 2011; McDougall 2011). Madonna temporarily suspended the charity, hired a philanthropic oversight organization and changed her options by funding numerous existing schools and programs rather than the original large school project (McDougall 2011).

Acknowledgements

I would like to thank Elaine Jeffreys for her feedback on this chapter. I would also like to thank Crispin Thurlow, Ralina Joseph, Manoucheka Celeste and Rebecca Clark for their very helpful feedback on early drafts of the paper.

References

4womenCZ (2010) *Bono a Ali & Louis Vuitton v Africe* [Bono and Ali and Louis Vuitton in Africa], online video, 16 September. http://www.youtube.com/watch?v=QbkQ2cJ925E. Accessed 10 January 2015.

'About Raising Malawi' (2009–2015) Raising Malawi, http://www.raisingmalawi.org/pages/about. Accessed 10 January 2015.

'About Us' (n.d.) Clinton Foundation, http://www.clintonfoundation.org/about. Accessed 10 January 2015.

'Alina Cho Interview with Madonna' (2009) *American Morning*, television program, 20 December, US: Cable News Network.

Altman, D. (1999) 'Globalization, political economy, and HIV/AIDS', *Theory and Society*, 28: 559–84.

'Angelina Jolie Visits "Dire" Refugee Settlement on Kenyan Border with Somalia' (2010) United Nations High Commissioner for Refugees, 12 September, http://www.unhcr.org/4aac232a9.html. Accessed 10 January 2015.

Bangs, L. (dir.) (2010) *The Lazarus Effect*, film documentary, US: (RED), Home Box Office.

Barnett, T., and Whiteside, A. (2002) *AIDS in the Twenty-first Century: Disease and Globalization*, Basingstoke, Hampshire; New York: Palgrave Macmillan.

Barrett, W. (2011) 'Madonna's Malawi disaster', *Newsweek*, 11 April, p. 15.

Bell, K.M. (2011) '"A delicious way to help save lives": Race, commodification and celebrity in Product (RED)', *Journal of International and Intercultural Communication*, 4, 3: 163–80.

Bell, K.M. (2013) 'Affective expertise: The journalism ethics of celebrity sourcing', in S.J.A. Ward (ed.) *Global Media Ethics: Problems and Perspectives*, Boston: Wiley-Blackwell, pp. 214–34.

Bonilla-Silva, E. (2003) *Racism Without Racists: Color-Blind Racism and the Persistence of Racial Inequality in the United States*, Lanham, MD: Rowman and Littlefield.

Brockington, D. (2014) 'The production and construction of celebrity advocacy in international development', *Third World Quarterly*, 35, 1: 88–108.

Burton, A.M. (1994) *Burdens of History: British Feminists, Indian Women, and Imperial Culture, 1865–1915*, Chapel Hill: University of North Carolina.

Clarke, N. (2007) 'Adopt a baby? No, Madonna wants to take over a nation', *Daily Mail*, 21 April, p. 20.

Cooper, A. (2006) 'Angelina Jolie: Her mission and motherhood', *360 Degrees*, CNN, 23 June, http://transcripts.cnn.com/TRANSCRIPTS/0606/23/acd.02.html. Accessed 9 January 2015.

Cooper, A.F. (2008) *Celebrity Diplomacy*, Boulder: Paradigm Publishers.

Diehl, J. (2010) 'PostPartisan: George Clooney yells "fire!" about Sudan', *Washington Post*, 13 October, http://voices.washingtonpost.com/postpartisan/2010/10/george_clooney_yells_fire.html. Accessed 10 January 2015.

Douglas, S.J., and Michaels, M.W. (2004) *The Mommy Myth: The Idealization of Motherhood and How It Has Undermined Women*, New York: Free Press.

Dyer, R. (1986) *Heavenly Bodies: Film Stars and Society*, New York: St. Martin's Press.

Dyer, R. (1997) *White*, London; New York: Routledge.

Foucault, M. (1972) *The Archaeology of Knowledge*, New York: Pantheon Books.

Fouz-Hernández, S., and Jarman-Ivens, F. (eds) (2004) *Madonna's Drowned Worlds: New Approaches to Her Cultural Transformations, 1983–2003*, Aldershot, Hants; Burlington, VT: Ashgate.

Grigoriadis, V. (2011) 'Our Lady of Malawi', *New York Magazine*, 1 May, http://nymag.com/news/features/madonna-malawi-2011-5/. Accessed 10 January 2015.

Hall, S. (1997) *Representation: Cultural Representations and Signifying Practices*, London; Thousand Oaks, CA: Sage in association with the Open University.

Hill Collins, P. (2006) *From Black Power to Hip Hop: Racism, Nationalism, and Feminism*, Philadelphia: Temple University Press.

Iley, C. (2005) 'Why Africa needs U2'. *London Evening Standard*, 10 June, http://www.standard.co.uk/goingout/music/why-africa-needs-u2-7296226.html. Accessed 24 March 2014.

Joseph, R.L. (2009) '"Tyra Banks is fat": Reading (post)racism and (post)feminism in the new millennium', *Critical Studies in Media Communication*, 26, 3: 237–54.

Jungar, K., and Salo, E. (2008) 'Shop and do good?', *The Journal of Pan African Studies*, 2, 6: 92–102.

King, L. (2010) 'Interview with George Clooney', *Larry King Live*, television program, 16 October, US: Cable News Network.

'Kristy Wark Interview with Madonna' (2006) *Newsnight*, television program, 1 November, UK: British Broadcasting Corporation.

Lean, D. (dir.) (1962) *Lawrence of Arabia*, motion picture, United Kingdom: Horizon Pictures, Columbia Pictures.

Littler, J. (2008) '"I feel your pain": Cosmopolitan charity and the public fashioning of the celebrity soul', *Social Semiotics*, 18, 2: 237–51.

Mackenzie, J.M. (1986) *Imperialism and Popular Culture*, Manchester, UK; Dover, NH: Manchester University Press.

Mama, A. (1997) 'Sheroes and villians: Conceptualizing colonial and contemporary violence against women in Africa', in M.J. Alexander and C.T. Mohanty (eds) *Feminist Genealogies, Colonial Legacies, Democratic Futures*, New York: Routledge, pp. 46–62.

Marshall, P.D. (2010) 'The promotion and presentation of the self: Celebrity as marker of presentational media', *Celebrity Studies*, 1: 35–48.

Mbaku, J.M. (2008) 'Corruption cleanups in Africa: Lessons from public choice theory', *Journal of Asian and African Studies*, 43: 427–56.

McClintock, A. (1995) *Imperial Leather: Race, Gender, and Sexuality in the Colonial Contest*, New York: Routledge.

McDougall, D. (2011) 'Ambition impossible', *Sunday Times* (London), 19 June, p. 24.

Morton, A. (2001) *Madonna*, New York: St. Martin's Press.

Moyo, D. (2009) *Dead Aid: Why Aid Is Not Working and How There Is a Better Way for Africa*, New York: Farrar, Straus and Giroux.

Nakayama, T.K., and Krizek, R.L. (1995) 'Whiteness: A strategic rhetoric', *Quarterly Journal of Speech*, 81, 3: 291–309.

'New Concerns about International Adoption' (2008) *University of Liverpool: Research Intelligence*, 34, http://www.liv.ac.uk/researchintelligence/issue34/adoption.htm. Accessed 24 March 2014.

O'Neill, B. (2006) 'Brad, Angelina and the rise of 'celebrity colonialism', *Spiked*, 30 May, http://www.spiked-online.com/index.php?/site/article/327/. Accessed 24 March 2014.

Ogundipe-Leslie, M. (2001) 'Moving the mountains, making the links', in K.K. Bhavnani (ed.) *Feminism and 'Race'*, Oxford, UK; New York: Oxford University Press, pp. 134–44.

'Our Story' (n.d.) (RED), http://www.red.org/en/about. Accessed 10 January 2015.

Patterson, A.S., and Kieh, G.K. (2008) 'The new globalization and HIV/AIDS in Africa', in G.K. Kieh (ed.) *Africa and the New Globalization*, Aldershot, England; Burlington, VT: Ashgate, pp. 155–76.

Perry, A.T. (2008) *Contagious Communication: The Mediatization, Spacialization and Commercialization of HIV*, Ph.D. thesis, unpublished, University of Washington.

'The (RED) idea' (n.d.) (RED), http://www.red.org/en/. Accessed 10 January 2015.

Richards, J. (2001) *Imperialism and Music: Britain, 1876–1953*, Manchester; New York: Manchester University Press.

Richey, L.A., and Ponte, S. (2011) *Brand Aid: Shopping Well to Save the World*, Minneapolis, MN: University of Minnesota Press.

Rissman, N. (dir.), Madonna (prod.) and Bexley, A. (prod.) (2009) *I Am Because We Are*, motion picture, UK; US: Virgil Films, Semtex Films.

Russell, C. (2011) 'Ali Hewson: It's a wonderful life being Mrs Bono', *Independent.ie*, 27 August, http://www.independent.ie/woman/celeb-news/ali-hewson-its-a-wonderful-life-being-mrs-bono-26765970.html. Accessed 18 August 2014.

Ryan, H. and Christiensen, K. (2011) 'Celebrities gave Kabbalah Centre cachet, and spurred its growth', *Los Angeles Times*, 18 October, http://www.latimes.com/entertainment/la-et-kaballah-founders-story-part-two-htmlstory.html. Accessed 6 March 2015.

Said, E.W. (2003 [1978]) *Orientalism*, London: Penguin.

Shohat, E. (1991) 'Imaging terra incognita: The disciplinary gaze of empire', *Public Culture*, 3, 2: 41–70.

Shome, R. (1996) 'Race and popular cinema: The rhetorical strategies of whiteness in City of Joy', *Communication Quarterly*, 44, 4: 502–18.

Spielberg, S. (dir.) (1981) *Raiders of the Lost Ark*, motion picture, Hollywood, CA: Lucasfilm and Paramount Pictures.

Spivak, G.C. (1988) 'Can the subaltern speak?', in C. Nelson and L. Grossberg (eds) *Marxism and the Interpretation of Culture*, London: MacMillan, pp. 271–315.

Spivak, G.C., and Harasym, S. (1990) *The Post-colonial Critic: Interviews, Strategies, Dialogues*, New York: Routledge.

Sternheimer, K. (2011) *Celebrity Culture and the American Dream: Stardom and Social Mobility*, New York: Routledge.

Turner, G. (2014) *Understanding Celebrity*, second edition, London; Thousand Oaks, CA; New Delhi; Singapore: Sage.

West, S. (dir.) (2001) *Lara Croft: Tomb Raider*, motion picture, Hollywood, CA: Paramount Home Entertainment.

'Why Malawi?' (2009–2015) Raising Malawi, http://www.raisingmalawi.org/pages/why-malawi. Accessed 1 January 2015.

Zwick, E. (dir.) (2006) *Blood Diamond*, motion picture, US: The Bedford Falls, Virtual Studios, Warner Brothers Pictures.

Part 3

India, China and the Americas

Chapter 8

Arundhati Roy versus the State of India: The Politics of Celebrity Philanthropy

Devleena Ghosh

This chapter analyses the nexus of celebrity, political activism and philanthropy associated with the advocacy of Arundhati Roy (b. 1961) in the Indian political and literary scene. Roy, the writer of the Booker Prize-winning novel *The God of Small Things* (1997), is a global literary celebrity and an icon of social activism through her vocal opposition to the state in local, regional and global politics, and her practice of donating substantial prize monies to humanitarian and environmental causes. In particular, after the 9/11 attack in the US, she has been eloquent against US foreign policy directions in the Middle East and elsewhere, having spoken against interventions in Iraq and Afghanistan and against western neoliberal policies in general (Roy 2002, 2003, 2004a, 2004b). Progressive groups, movements and academics, especially in Europe and North America, hold her in admiration, as demonstrated by the numerous awards and prizes that she has received.[1] She is a columnist for *The Guardian* newspaper, has been interviewed by US liberal luminaries such as Howard Zinn and David Barasamian and addressed the World Social Forum in Brazil in 2003 (Barasamian 2001; 'Arundhati Roy with Howard Zinn' 2002; Roy, 2004b). Though her reputation among left-wing activist circles in Europe and North America appears to be assured, her contentious political and social opinions have led to much criticism from all sectors of Indian society, including the communist and socialist left (Guha 2000). In fact, some respected critics have suggested that she stick to writing novels, because her 'vanity and self-indulgence' devalues the work of more serious activists (Guha 2000).

The paradoxical deployment of figures like Roy by state and non-state actors to produce contradictory and ambivalent narratives of history, economy and society for national as well as global consumption is an interesting development in the area of philanthropy, in general, and Indian philanthropy, in particular. As far as philanthropy is concerned, the crucial nature of her contribution lies in her reputation and advocacy; particularly in her opposition to dams, nuclear power and the victimization of minorities and in her support for anti-state insurgencies, such as those in Kashmir and in Chhattisgarh, which put her directly at odds with national modernist discourses of the developmentalist homogeneous state in India. Traditionally, celebrity in India has been harnessed to the national narrative; for example, the actors in early Bombay (now Mumbai) films from *Mother India* (dir. Khan 1957) to *Roti Kapda aur Makaan* (dir. Kumar 1974) became icons through the recounting of post-independence idealism and progress. When Roy leveraged her celebrity against her own nation-state, she changed the lexicon of philanthropic activism in India.

This chapter explores these issues in three stages. It first provides a brief commentary on the status and history of philanthropy in India, especially in the context of religious giving, and discusses the entry of the celebrity into the arena of philanthropy and endorsements in India. It then addresses the criticisms that have been made by scholars and activists of the celebrity interventions of Roy, especially her polemics against the state. In conclusion, it asks whether celebrity philanthropy contains true transformative aspects or whether it compromises the processes of meaning making and re-authoring the social world.

Philanthropy and Celebrity

Philanthropy usually involves the exercise of social conscience in a private capacity. The philanthropist donates part of his/her private resources – time or money – out of altruistic interest to advance social and human welfare and not for direct commercial gain, though in many cases, there may be adjunct advantages such as tax benefits (Newland, Terazas and Munster 2010: 3). Such donations may have personal connections. For example, they may be directed to the donor's ethnic or religious community. However, help to personal family members would not fall within this definition.

In India, philanthropy has, by and large, replaced the word 'charity', which has come to be loaded with connotations of patronage and conservatism, as well as the practice of Christian proselytization in a colonial missionary context (Newland, Terazas and Munster 2010: 4). The words charity and philanthropy have similar roots; both derive from the Latin, charity from *caritas* or loving care, while philanthropy is literally the 'love of man'. A major difference in the modern context is that charity is often seen to focus on the relief of immediate suffering, rather than addressing structural problems or the causes of suffering. In contrast, philanthropy may involve the genuine desire by the wealthy to ameliorate social and political injustice. However, given the unequal power nexus between the giver and the receiver, the motives of the philanthropist may also be mixed (see also Jeffreys, and Marshall, in this book). As Reinhold Niebuhr writes,

> We have previously suggested that philanthropy combines genuine pity with the display of power and that the latter element explains why the powerful are more inclined to be generous than to grant social justice.
>
> (Niebuhr 1932: 127)

Martin Luther King Jr. also focused on the question of social justice in the context of philanthropy when he wrote in *Strength to Love*, 'Philanthropy is commendable, but it must not cause the philanthropist to overlook the circumstances of economic injustice which make philanthropy necessary' (quoted in Martin 1994: 7). Some of the critiques of Roy (as detailed below) have also accused her of having impure motives, seeking personal fame in the guise of championing the oppressed.

Philanthropy in India has become increasingly engaged with social investment and policy reforms. As in Europe and North America, it is also often structured like a business that deals in social investment, thereby indicating its transformative potential (Johnson 2001: 4). The philanthropy sector in India now includes an increasingly diverse array of actors – corporations, NGOs, faith-based groups, entertainment celebrities, and so on. For example, the leading Indian film actor Shah Rukh Khan has lent his celebrity status to anti-poaching initiatives organized by the US-based international wildlife conservation NGO WildAid, in cooperation with India's state authorities and broadcast media ('Shah Rukh Champions the Cause of India's Unsung Heroes – The Forest Guards' 2007). Another Bollywood star, Aamir Khan, is the presenter of a national television series dealing with major problems in India such as female foeticide, domestic violence, alcoholism, and so on ('Aamir Khan the Crusader' 2012).

In any article on celebrity philanthropy, it should be emphasized that giving is by no means limited to the wealthy. Small donations to churches, temples and mosques have historically funded substantial relief for the poor and homeless (Reale 2010). Recent research suggests in fact that the members of the middle income and relatively poor classes are more likely to make charitable donations than the very rich (Piff et al. 2010). This is particularly the case in India with its strongly polyvalent religious culture made up of multiple faiths, in each of which elements of unselfishness or altruism are posited as essential not only for karmic or spiritual gain (*punya*), but also for the psychic and societal benefits. In Hinduism (the majority religion), giving can be constituted as *dana* (giving to one or more individuals) or *utsarga* (donating for the public good) and both these actions contribute the *punya* required to gain salvation (Agarwal 2010: Chapter 2). In Buddhism too, acts of charity accumulate merit (Agarwal 2010). Other major Indian religions such as Islam mandate *zakat* (the giving of a fixed portion of one's wealth) as one of the five pillars of the faith, very similar to the system of tithing in Christianity (Agarwal 2010: Chapters 3 and 4).

In these forms of religious expectations, celebrity has been inconsequential as the purpose of such acts was mainly for spiritual and transcendental gains, rather than publicity, either for the donor or giver. For example, on 27 July 2009, a single anonymous donation of INR 380,000 (USD 7,000) in gold ingots was found at a temple in Indore (Agarwal 2010: 21). Other individual donations to temples are much more insignificant but their cumulative value is immense. The Tirupathi Temple in Andhra Pradesh is estimated to receive INR 9,000 million annually, most of it anonymously (Agarwal 2010: 21).

The entry of celebrity into the sphere of philanthropy makes the act much more mundane; the gain to the celebrity includes the worldly ones of reputation and recognition for good deeds as well as the spiritual merit (see McCracken 1991 on celebrity endorsements). The process of social influence results when the attitudes or causes advocated by the celebrity activist influence significantly the target audience (Kamins 1990). The celebrity is able to maintain such influence because of his/her credibility or attractiveness; however, s/he also possesses symbolic properties that are projected on to the cause that is being endorsed. The target audience of the celebrity activist assumes some of this symbolic capital through the act of solidarity. The message communicated by the celebrity to his/her audience depends for its effectiveness, that is, its credibility and persuasiveness, on her/his 'expertness' and 'trustworthiness', or the celebrity's perceived ability and willingness to make valid assertions on behalf of a product or cause (Dholakia 1977; Sternthal 1978; see also Bell and Murray, in this book).

If expertise and trustworthiness are essential to ensure the credibility of a celebrity (Ohanian 1991), then, Roy achieved both in the initial part of her public career in both the local Indian context and internationally. She changed the lexicon of celebrity philanthropy in India because she was not a Bollywood star but an author who achieved fame in the global literary scene in 1997 with her first novel *The God of Small Things*, for which she received half a million British pounds in advances ('Arundhati Roy' n.d.). Rights to the book were sold in 21 countries. The novel was a runaway success, becoming a best-seller and going on to win the prestigious Booker Prize for fiction in 1997 ('Arundhati Roy' n.d.). Concurrently, she became involved in a number of protest movements: anti-dam and anti-nuclear activism (Roy 1998), and Kashmiri independence (Roy 2011), and she wrote in support of the Maoist insurgency in Chhattisgarh (Roy 2010a), as well as against the death penalties meted out to the perpetrators of various terrorist attacks in India (Roy 2013). Along with her writings and lectures in support of these causes, Roy consistently donated money received as prizes, awards or lecture fees to activist movements. For example, the Booker Prize money and the royalties from her novel went to the Narmada Bachao Andolan, a protest movement against the Sardar Sarovar dam being constructed on the River Narmada ('A Novel Gesture' 1999); and the Sydney Peace Prize of AUD 50,000, which she received in May 2004, was donated to three Aboriginal organizations (NSW Department of Aboriginal Affairs 2004). She has also donated fees received for presenting lectures to various causes, such as the Gujarat earthquake relief organizations (Barasamian 2001).

However, Roy's major symbolic capital lies in her fame, renown and celebrity status as an author, in Noam Chomsky's sense of 'speaking truth to power' not only in her own country but also overseas. As Turner (2004) points out, celebrities must develop a strategy for building and maintaining audience loyalty by forging and safeguarding a symbiotic relationship with the media:

> Celebrity [...] is a genre of representation and a discursive effect; it is a commodity traded by promotions, publicity, and media industries that produce these representations and their effects; and it is a cultural formation that has a social function we can better understand.
>
> (Turner 2004: 9)

In Roy's case, this relationship is ambivalent. Despite her numerous awards, much of the media coverage Roy receives in India is negative; her opponents' characterization of her as naïve, simplistic and anti-Indian is given much publicity (Guha 2000; Parashar 2009).

Writing about celebrities working for environmental causes, Max Boykoff, Mike Goodman and Jo Littler (2010) ask what we should make of these interventions of privileged and over-exposed people speaking for the poor and disenfranchised? Is such intervention effective? Is celebrity 'currency of a kind' as rock singer Bono describes it? Does deploying celebrity really raise awareness of the issues concerned, or does it hijack the subject, obscuring complex political issues?

Boykoff, Goodman and Littler (2010: 4) term such celebrity activity as 'conspicuous redemption' and assert that celebrities now form part of the 'non-nation-state actors', who have increasing influence on various global events. Such high-profile celebrities connect the formal spaces of activist causes and politics operating at multiple scales to those of the spaces of 'everyday' local and global cultures. Other scholars such as Brockington (2009) have commented that celebrity alone does not guarantee success for a cause because the relationships between celebrity, audience and real change are complex. Celebrity endorsement of causes involves the audience in a vicarious involvement; many crucial causes require more vigorous activism and specifically targeted actions at key decision makers (politicians, policy makers, company boards, and so on) (Brockington 2009; see also Van den Bulck, Claessens and Panis, in this book).

In the case of Arundhati Roy, there is no question that her championship of causes has foregrounded them locally in India and, more importantly, in the global arena. However, the effectiveness of her presence and activism in support of various issues has been questioned for displaying naïveté and lack of analytical rigour (Guha 2000; Parashar 2009). In addition, Roy has been criticized for her apparent reluctance to enter into conversations with scholars and activists who disagree with her opinions, including scholars and activists who share progressive political views. For example, in an interview in the journal *Frontline*, Roy responds to historian Ramachandra Guha's criticisms of the 'one-sided' nature of her social activism by saying,

> He's become like a stalker who shows up at my doorstep every other Sunday. Some days he comes alone. Some days he brings his friends and family, they all chant and stamp [...] It's an angry little cottage industry that seems to have sprung up around me. Like a bunch of keening god-squadders, they link hands to keep their courage up and egg each other on – Aunt Slushy the novelist who's hated me for years, Uncle Defence Ministry who loves big dams, Little Miss Muffet who thinks I should watch my mouth. Actually, I've grown quite fond of them and I'll miss them when they're gone.
> ('Arundhati Roy Has Become a Joke: Ram Guha' 2010)

Some of the language used in these critiques, specifically 'shrill' and 'hysterical', have gendered overtones. Such terms are frequently used to trivialize women's voices and actions, imputing emotion and affect as their motivation rather than reason. In spite of this, such criticisms raise important questions about the role and impact of celebrity activists and, consequently, the next section discusses three of the causes that Roy has supported in India, and the nature of criticisms of her support for those causes.

Arundhati Roy Against the State: Critiques and Comments

Arundhati Roy published her first essay on the Sardar Sarovar dam slated for the Narmada River in *Outlook* and *Frontline* magazines in May 1999. This dam, perhaps India's most controversial one, was first envisaged in the 1940s by the country's first Prime Minister, Jawaharlal Nehru, and eventually inaugurated in 1979. It involves the construction of some 3,200 small, medium and large dams on the Narmada River. Those in favour of the dam claim that it will supply water to 30 million people and irrigation to provide food for another 20 million (Sardar Sarovar Narmada Nigam Limited). The anti-dam movement, Narmada Bachao Andolan (Save the Narmada), headed by Medha Patkar, claims that the dams will displace more than 200,000 people, submerge forest farmland, disrupt downstream fisheries, and, in other ways, destroy the fragile ecology of the region. In what was seen as a major victory for the anti-dam activists, the World Bank withdrew from the Narmada project in 1993 ('Narmada Bachao Andolan [NBA] Forces End of World Bank Funding of Sardar Sarovar Dam, India, 1985–1993' n.d.).

This essay was one of Roy's first critiques of the Indian state and she bitterly opposed the Nehruvian paradigm of development through heavy industrialization. Nehru, the first Prime Minister of independent India, is famous for saying that dams were modern India's temples ('Jawaharlal Nehru [1889–1964]: Architect of India's Modern Temples' 2003). Roy, in contrast, subscribes to the arguments mounted by the Narmada Bachao Andolan, especially those against the submerging of villages and the displacement of large numbers of poor people. According to her, 'Big Dams are to a Nation's "Development" what Nuclear Bombs are to its Military Arsenal' (Roy 1999, capitals in original). Roy's article ended with this evocative paragraph, exhorting her audience to join a protest against the submerging of villages:

> This July will bring the last monsoon of the Twentieth Century. The ragged army in the Narmada Valley has declared that it will not move when the waters of the Sardar Sarovar reservoir rise to claim its lands and homes. Whether you love the dam or hate it, whether you want it or you don't, it is in the fitness of things that you understand the price that's being paid for it. That you have the courage to watch while the dues are cleared and the books are squared.
> Our dues. Our books. Not theirs.
> Be there.
>
> (Roy 1999)

In response to this and other pieces written by Roy, Guha (2000), an environmental historian, made a particularly blistering attack on Roy in the newspaper *The Hindu* in 2000. In this, Guha pointed out that the Narmada Bachao Andolan was only one in a series of social movements against large dams and that, in the 1950s and 1960s, many dams that displaced villagers were built in the name of 'national interest' without much protest.

Popular struggles against those displaced by dams began in the 1970s inspired by the work of scholars such as Nirmal Sengupta in the *Economic and Political Weekly* in 1985, which made a strong case for the continuing relevance of indigenous methods of water harvesting (Guha 2000).

According to Guha (2000), the Narmada Bachao Andolan was an effective and vigorous mass popular movement through the 1980s and 1990s, with an exemplary leader (Medha Patkar) and a devoted cadre of workers that included *adivasis* (tribal populations) and peasant farmers as well as students and professionals from the cities. The relative success of the movement was interrupted when the pro-liberalization press turned savagely on the leadership of the Narmada Bachao Andolan movement for hindering the development and growth that would produce jobs and increase basic incomes. Roy's involvement came when the movement needed a champion with a reputation.

Guha (2000) acknowledges Roy's 'courage and commitment', but contends that her advocacy is hyperbolic and self-indulgent, high in emotion and low in analysis, speaking only to the converted. In his words, 'Ms. Roy's tendency to exaggerate and simplify, her Manichean view of the world, and her shrill hectoring tone, have given a bad name to environmental analysis' (Guha 2000). Writing about the people displaced by the big dams, for instance, Roy says, 'True, they're not being annihilated or taken to gas chambers, but I can warrant that the quality of their accommodation is worse than in any concentration camp of the Third Reich' (Roy 1999). A hyperbolic statement such as this negates much of her justified criticism of the impact of the dam on contiguous villages.

Gail Omvedt (1999), another scholar of modern India, wrote in an open letter to Roy that farmers needed both power and water for agriculture. As Omvedt (1999) says of the farmers, 'Their refusal to be victims of development does not mean an opposition to development; they would like a share in it; they would like it to be just and sustainable'. Omvedt adds that the role of NGOs who worked for the acceptance of the principle that those losing their land in the catchment area of dams should get alternative land in the command area and a share of the water of the dam is lost in the blanket no-dam campaign, which is not representative of all stakeholders in the area.

Omvedt and Guha's critique of Roy incorporate the issue of representation of the dispossessed. They contend that the celebrity of Roy highlights a particular point of view, one side of the argument, a romanticized anti-development attitude that does not necessarily lift people out of poverty. Omvedt (1999) remarks that the wages for agricultural and basic manual labour have not changed in real terms for millennia.

Guha himself was an opponent of big dams but he pointed out that the demonization of technology or the comparison of dams to nuclear weapons was unhelpful. It also belittled the work of those attempting compromise, a reduction of submergence of villages while allowing the construction of 'overflow' canals to the water-scarce areas, thus minimizing human suffering without the waste of money already spent on the project. He quotes a progressive legal scholar as saying that Roy's criticism of Supreme Court judges who were hearing a petition brought by the Narmada Bachao Andolan was careless and irresponsible and that the movement should distance itself from her (Guha 2000).

This criticism of Roy as particularly monocular in her views and often tone deaf to other views was reiterated by many critics during the terrorist attacks on Mumbai on 26 November 2008. These attacks consisted of 12 coordinated shooting and bombing incidents across Mumbai by members of the Pakistani Islamist group Laskar-e-Taiba, aided, according to Ajmal Kasab, the only attacker who survived, by the ISI (Inter-Services Intelligence), Pakistan's premier intelligence service. These attacks, which drew widespread global condemnation, killed 164 people and wounded over 300.

In an article in *The Guardian*, Roy (2008) argued that these attacks should be understood in the context of wider issues in the region's history and society, such as widespread poverty, the partition of the subcontinent, the 2002 atrocities against Muslim communities in Gujarat and the ongoing conflict in Kashmir.[2] The article seemed to imply that it was understandable for a group of terrorists to carry out violent attacks because of the state's policies and injustices. Though Roy stated that she believed 'nothing can justify terrorism', the article sought to present the viewpoints of the attackers and was curiously silent about the victims of the attacks. Writing in *The Indian Express*, Tavleen Singh (2008) called Roy's comments 'the latest of her series of hysterical diatribes against India and all things Indian'.

One of Roy's most notorious forays into the realm of public intellectual championing of unpopular causes was an account of her journey with Maoists in the central Indian region of Chhattisgarh, described in 'Walking with the comrades' published in 2010 (Roy 2010a). The Communist Party of India (Maoist) is a far left political party in India that aims to overthrow the government of India through Mao Zedong's concept of 'people's war'. They are active in the forest belt around central India in states such as Chhattisgarh and are often referred to as Naxals or Naxalites in reference to the Naxalbari uprising led by radical Maoists in West Bengal in 1967 (Ramana 2011).

Roy's article makes it clear that the insurgents themselves understood the power of celebrity in both publicizing and aiding their goals. The mode of communication that Roy describes could come straight out of a spy film:

> The terse, typewritten note slipped under my door in a sealed envelope confirmed my appointment with India's Gravest Internal Security Threat. I'd been waiting for months to hear from them. I had to be at the Ma Danteshwari mandir in Dantewada, Chhattisgarh, at any of four given times on two given days. That was to take care of bad weather, punctures, blockades, transport strikes and sheer bad luck. The note said: 'Writer should have camera, tika and coconut. Meeter will have cap, Hindi *Outlook* magazine and bananas. Password: Namashkar Guruji'.
>
> (Roy 2010a)

After accompanying Maoist radicals in their daily activities, Roy (2010a) stated that the Indian Government had 'abdicated its responsibility to the people and launched the offensive against Naxals to aid the corporations with whom it has signed Memorandums of Understanding'.

Roy's description of the Maoists as 'Gandhians with a gun' and 'patriots of a kind', who are fighting to implement the Constitution, while the government is violating it, has alarmed scholars (Roy 2010b). Swati Parashar (2009) of the South Asia Analytical Group comments,

> Her doomsday predictions, her vehement and almost rhetorical rejection of the state and her constant demonizing of the state, her uncritical endorsement of non-state actors and their violent politics, and absolving the people of any responsibility [that] point out some of the dangers of a social conscience unfettered by research.
>
> (Parashar 2009)

Parashar (2009) points out that Roy's analyses of the Maoist insurgency hold merit. The rising gap between rich and poor, severe class and caste injustices, violence against women, *adivasis* and low caste people, the retreat of the state from all welfare and the ruthless advance of the capitalist free market have led to dispossession, immiseration and oppression. In fact, a Government of India Planning Commission Report (2008) entitled *Development Challenges in Extremist Affected Areas* identified the underlying causes of this militant insurgency as 'deprivation, inequality, failure of the state to ensure all segments of society are able to enjoy their basic entitlements and needs, safeguarded by the Constitution and other legislation'. The Commission's recommendations were that programs should be implemented that would have a strong impact on the factors that created these inequities and that 'new initiatives and experiments should be undertaken that can change the system of failure and frustration that dominates and weakens our society' (Government of India Planning Commission 2008: 91).

Most scholars agree that since economic liberalization in 1991, India's political economy has taken a new direction, but has failed to include India's numerous excluded groups. Tribal land, mineral and resource rich has been sold to corporations at the same time as much-needed services dwindled (see Dreze and Sen 2013). The popularity of Maoism was a natural consequence that promises to provide results in a more direct, immediate and localized manner (Chatterjee 2012).

Scholars, such as Devyani Srivastava (n.d.), have agreed with this analysis, pointing out that, since 1991, India has experienced huge economic growth with a 100 per cent increase in per capita income that has not trickled down to the 200 million people still living below the poverty line. The burgeoning of a hyper-consumerist urban culture where shopping malls are built on land acquired by corruption and slum clearances demonstrates the increasing inequity, economic imperialism, government neglect and unchecked corruption. It is not surprising that, in the context of various scams in which politicians make millions and bureaucrats collaborate with corporations to dispossess tribals of their land, these tribals turn to the Maoists for succour and justice.

However, the Maoist insurgency is underscored by the use of violence against ordinary populations who do not support or join them, the large-scale destruction of infrastructure (schools, railway lines and other public utility goods), and extortions from the businesses, kidnappings and summary trial and execution of alleged 'informers'. Dilip Simeon (2010), for example, lists the number of civilian casualties in his article 'Permanent spring':

> On 15 August 2004, the CPI-Maoist shot nine persons in Andhra Pradesh, including a legislator, his son, driver and an employee. On 12 September 2005, its cadre slit the throats of 17 villagers in Giridih. In March 2006, 13 tribals were killed and four injured in a mine blast. The Maoists apologized stating that it was due to a failure in their intelligence.
> (Simeon 2010)

Roy's use of her intellectual celebrity status seldom questions whether anti-state resistance must involve violence that increases people's sufferings. She also ignores other crucial issues, such as the source of the resources and weapons available to the Maoists. There is some evidence to show that foreign intelligence agencies may be supplying sophisticated weapons and training to the Maoists in India (Sharma 2012). In addition, given the amounts of money involved in the supply chain of weapons, the question must be asked as to why is a portion of this money not used to address the starvation and poverty of the people that the Maoists claim to protect? The breakdown of society in the remote areas where the insurgencies occur prevent normal activities such as farming and agriculture. Roy's championing of the poor and the dispossessed do not appear to include the people that Simeon discusses below:

> On 25 February 2006, 25 tribals were killed and 40 injured in a mine triggered by the CPI (Maoist) in Errabore, Dantewada. In July 2006, the CPI (Maoist) attacked a relief camp in the same place, killing 30 tribals, including children. A party spokesperson referred to the children's death as an 'unnecessary loss'. But he continued: 'No people's war can be so clinical so as to have no civilian casualty. It is very tortuous and painful, just as the daily life of the bulk of our population is no less agonizing'.
> (Simeon 2010)

Simeon (2010) argues persuasively that the Maoists have seldom confronted communalism in India that is one of the major causes of violence against ordinary people and that 'people's armies' ultimately become absorbed into the perpetuation of militarism.[3] Suman Banerjee wrote in the 1 November 2003 issue of the *Economic and Political Weekly* that the Naxalites were 'inert' during the past decade in fighting communalism, though *The Milli Gazette* recorded a meeting between Naxalite and Muslim leaders in Andhra Pradesh in 2004 (Khan 2004).

Roy, however, seldom reflects on the question of violence and its ramifications on the people who suffer or inflict it. In a CNN IBN interview, she says that 'my fear is that because of this economic interest the government and establishment actually needs a war. It needs to militarize. For that it needs an enemy [...] you have an army of very poor people being faced down by an army of rich that are corporate-backed' ('What Muslims Were to BJP,

Maoists Are to Congress: Arundhati Roy' 2009). This is counter-intuitive; such insurgencies tie up state resources and reduce profits, especially for those corporations who are involved in extracting the natural resource of the areas where such insurgencies operate. The army and police presence required to pacify such regions is massive and, as Parashar points out (2009), even for a 'militarized' state it is illogical to promote an intra-state insurgency that undermines its legitimacy.

The Maoist's attacks on infrastructure in particular, such as destroying railway tracks, setting railway wagons and stations and public transport buses on fire, and destroying the telecom towers of state-run and private telephone networks, challenge the authority of the state, but more crucially dictate the terms of people's daily lives in Maoist strongholds, and deny facilities and development to those living in the vicinity of the attacks (Ramana 2011: 37). In many cases, the Maoists have better weapons and equipment as well as intelligence than the police and paramilitary forces in India. Most of the police force in India are poorly paid and trained and often unwilling to work in insurgent areas. Many of those killed are not middle class or comfortably situated but young and poor men who are not the privileged agents of the state that Roy describes. The beheading of Francis Induwar in 2009 is an example of a Maoist assassination of an ordinary policeman, the only earning member of his family, rather than a wealthy, powerful class enemy (Mahapatra 2009). Roy remained silent on the death of Induwar while protesting the arrests of Maoist leaders and ideologues like Kobad Ghandy and Chhatradhar Mahato ('Naxalites Behead Cop Taliban Style' 2013).

Roy is justified in her critique of the state and its oppressive role in the causes detailed above; an informed intellectual and democratic discussion of state policy is essential to the democratic functioning of any society. Moreover, the state has responded to those particular issues by military or legislative force rather than dialogue or negotiation. However, Roy uses her celebrity status to forward a politics of despair where the state is only a purveyor of violence. She does not suggest alternatives as to how the state may be fought/critiqued; rather she legitimizes all anti-state violence. And she ignores all evidence that may complicate her rhetoric; for example, the Maoist fetishization of militarism connected to the capture of state power through armed struggle as evinced by the slogan 'Lal Qila par Lal Jhanda' (Red Flag on the Red Fort) (Sundar 2011). The Indian flag that flies above the Red Fort in India's capital city, Delhi, symbolizes the rule of the national government; the overthrowing of this government and taking power is the ultimate goal of the Maoists.

Conclusion

An anti-establishment stance is, in some ways, a logical one for a celebrity of Arundhati Roy's stature. Since the publication of Roy's immensely popular novel, her reputation has been built on her polemical writing. During the second Gulf War and the Allied invasion of Iraq, these pieces were inspirational and revolutionary (Roy 2002, 2003, 2004a). However, Roy's oppositional and contrarian stance now reflects a kind of tunnel vision where the state has no role except that of oppressor and all insurgents are always justified in their actions. Victimhood is used to justify violence but only in the case of anti-state resistance. Her articles in *The Guardian* on the Mumbai attacks in 2008 imply that it is understandable that foreign nationals may commit brutal acts of terror within another state because of its treatment of minorities. This is exactly the kind of US interventions in the Middle East that she has rightly condemned (Roy 2008). The Muslim community in Mumbai implicitly rejected this view, and initially refused to bury the Mumbai attackers in their cemetery. One of their spokespersons said 'People who committed this heinous crime cannot be called Muslim' (Friedman 2009).

Causes for justice have always had their armed manifestations, whether in the independence struggles, resistance to social oppression or rights based movements. However, it is more difficult for these movements to identify the moment when violence outlives its purpose. The Liberation Tigers of Tamil Eelan (LTTE) in Sri Lanka is a case in point. Having refused all negotiated settlements, it was eventually wiped out by the Sri Lankan Government in 2009 ('Sri Lanka's Tamil Tigers "defeated"' 2009). Deaths of civilians in such cases are collateral damage made essential by history, what Albert Camus (1981: 130) termed 'rational murder'.

In this context, other progressive scholars, such as Nandini Sundar (2011), who have spent years studying the Maoist movements in India, point out that the Indian state has an ethical and moral responsibility to provide justice to its most underprivileged, such as its tribal populations. They should be accorded dignity and respect. Sundar writes bitterly about the lack of appreciation for tribal lifestyles, the labelling of tribals as 'pre-political' people who merely need food and jobs to be happy while insurgents in Kashmir are offered political solutions. She quotes the US journalist I.F. Stone about US military views of Vietcong guerrillas, 'What rarely comes through to them are the injured racial feelings, the misery, the rankling slights, the hatred, the devotion, the inspiration and the desperation'. Sundar (2011) calls for simple yet often elusive correctives: apologize to tribal communities for how the country has treated them, and take a genuine interest in helping them provide for their basic needs.

Celebrity endorsement of social movements is therefore always a double-edged sword. It can attract media attention where otherwise the cause is absent in the public sphere. It may also bring adherents who were previously ignorant or uninspired (see Jeffreys, and Marshall, in this book). It can also detract attention from other active interventions on the ground (for example, the activists in Chhattisgarh working to improve indigenous conditions through legal means).

However, the media focus is generally soon diverted to the celebrity and the cause often becomes lost in hyperbole and polemic. Such oppositional, often didactic, highly aestheticized forms of expression hamper progressive discourse or the search for alternatives. Guha (2000) quotes Roy as saying, 'When NATO bombed Yugoslavia, a tiger in the Belgrade Zoo got so terrified that it started eating its own limbs. The people of the Narmada Valley will soon start eating their own limbs' (Guha 2000). These trenchant critiques of the state ignore the fact that in democracies, with nascent civil societies, the state is often the only recourse for ordinary people. This is why non-state groups like the Maoists and the LTTE have run mini-states in their areas of influence. People make up and are imbricated in the state; they do not exist outside of it.

In some contexts, Roy (2008) exhorts people who are the targets of violence or terror to consider the whole context rather than demonizing particular agents, religions or communities, and warns that state action should not use such crises to retaliate against its critics; that is, the state must be 'just'. However, tacit endorsement of radical causes, where resistance to the state is valorized but little alternative for change is indicated, make for limited politics. It lacks transformative aspects – the ability for meaning making and an opportunity to re-author the social world. The aura of exclusiveness and glamour that surrounds the celebrity may render suffering relevant to domestic audiences but it also distances it. Media focus inevitably defaults to the celebrity; the cause is one more source of illumination for the stage on which s/he performs. The market consumes the philanthropic impulse and redistributes it through the culture industry as a depoliticized and profitable version of its once critical impulse (Jameson 1998).

Notes

1 Roy's many awards include: the Lannan Foundation's Cultural Freedom Award in 2002; 'Special recognition' as a Woman of Peace at the Global Exchange Human Rights Awards in San Francisco in 2003; the Sydney Peace Prize in 2004; the Sahitya Akademi Award, a national award from India's Academy of Letters, which she declined to accept, in 2006; and the Norman Mailer Prize for Distinguished Writing in 2011.
2 The violence in Gujarat started on 27 February 2002, when a train carrying Hindu pilgrims caught fire, killing 59 people. In a retaliatory spree by Hindu mobs nearly 2,000 people, mostly Muslims, were slaughtered, tens of thousands were displaced, and countless Muslim homes were destroyed. Kashmir is a territory in the north of the Indian subcontinent that is in current dispute between India and Pakistan. There is a strong Indian army presence in this area to contain various insurgencies, protest movements and the hostile border with Pakistan. The army has been accused of atrocities against citizens.
3 In India, the term 'communalism' implies hatred and violence between communities of different religious denominations, mainly between Hindu and Muslim communities. The partition of the subcontinent before and just after independence in 1947 was accompanied by riots between these communities in which millions of people were killed. Other such riots include the ones following the destruction of the Babri Mosque in Ayodhya in 1992 and the Gujarat riots (mentioned above in Note 2).

References

'Aamir Khan the Crusader' (2012) Mid-Day NDTV, 6 May, http://movies.ndtv.com/television/aamir-khan-the-crusader-624896. Accessed 5 March 2015.

'A Novel Gesture' (1999) *Frontline*, July, 16, 14: 3–16, http://www.frontline.in/navigation/?type=static&page=flonnet&rdurl=fl1614/16140360.htm. Accessed 10 January 2015.

Agarwal, S. (2010) *Daan and Other Giving Traditions in India: The Forgotten Pot of Gold*, New Delhi: AccountAid.

'Arundhati Roy' (n.d.) Biblio.com, http://www.biblio.com/arundhati-roy/author/2907. Accessed 11 September 2013.

'Arundhati Roy Has Become a Joke: Ram Guha' (2010) *Outlook*, 29 October, blogs.outlookindia.com/default.aspx?ddm=10&pid=2371. Accessed 10 January 2015.

'Arundhati Roy with Howard Zinn' (2002) *Lannan*, 18 September, http://www.lannan.org/events/arundhati-roy-with-howard-zinn/. Accessed 10 January 2015.

Barasamian, D. (2001) 'Interview with Arundhati Roy', *The Progressive*, April, http://www.progressive.org/intv0401.html. Accessed 10 January 2015.

Boykoff, M., Goodman, M., and Littler, J. (2010) '"Charismatic megafauna": The growing power of celebrities and pop culture in climate change campaigns', Paper 28, posted at Kings College London, Department of Geography, http://www.kcl.ac.uk/sspp/departments/geography/research/epd/BoykoffetalWP28.pdf. Accessed 10 January 2015.

Brockington, D. (2009) 'Getting development into the news: The role of celebrity in development', *Development@manchester: Cross-Disciplinary Perspectives on Development Research*, 3, December, The University of Manchester, http://www.sed.manchester.ac.uk/idpm/research/publications/dev@man/devman-research-note-200903.pdf. Accessed 10 January 2015.

Camus, A. (1991) *Between Hell and Reason*, Hanover, NH: Wesleyan University Press, http://www.ppu.org.uk/e_publications/camus2.html. Accessed 10 January 2015.

Chatterjee, S. (2012) 'Flaws in India's strategy to counter the Maoist insurgency', *Global Observatory*, 13 August, http://theglobalobservatory.org/analysis/338-flaws-in-indias-strategy-to-counter-the-maoist-insurgency.html. Accessed 10 January 2015.

Dholakia, R.R., and Sternthal, B. (1977) 'Highly credible source, highly persuasive facilitators or persuasive liabilities', *Journal of Consumer Research*, 3: 223–32.

Dreze, J., and A. Sen (2013) *An Uncertain Glory: India and its Contradictions*, Princeton, NJ: Princeton University Press.

Friedman, T. (2009) 'No way, no how, not here', *New York Times*, 17 February, http://www.nytimes.com/2009/02/18/opinion/18friedman.html?_r=0. Accessed 10 January 2015.

Government of India Planning Commission Report (2008) *Development Challenges in Extremist Affected Areas*, April, New Delhi, http://planningcommission.nic.in/reports/publications/rep_dce.pdf. Accessed 10 January 2015.

Guha, R. (2000) 'The Arun Shourie of the left', *The Hindu*, 26 November, http://www.hindu.com/2000/11/26/stories/13260411.htm. Accessed 10 January 2015.

Jameson, F. (1998) *The Cultural Turn: Selected Writings on the Postmodern, 1983–1998*, New York: Verso.

'Jawaharlal Nehru (1889–1964): Architect of India's Modern Temples' (2003) *The Hindu*, 7 July, http://www.hindu.com/thehindu/mp/2003/07/07/stories/2003070700880200.htm. Accessed 10 January 2015.

Johnson, P. (2001) 'Global social investing: A preliminary overview', The Philanthropic Initiative, Boston MA, May, https://www.cbd.int/financial/charity/g-globalsocialinv.pdf. Accessed 10 January 2015.

Kamins, M.A. (1990) 'An investigation into the "match up" hypothesis in celebrity advertising: When beauty may be only skin deep', *Journal of Advertising*, 19, 1: 4–13.

Khan, A. (2004) 'Naxalites and Muslims', *The Milli Gazette*, 16–30 November, http://www.milligazette.com/Archives/2004/16-30Nov04-Print-Edition/163011200481.htm. Accessed 10 January 2015.

Khan, M. (dir.) (1957) *Mother India*, motion picture, India: Mehboob Productions.

Kumar, M. (dir.) (1974) *Roti Kapda Aur Makaan*, motion picture, India: Chandivali Studio, Filmistan Studios, Mohan Studios, R.K. Studios, and Rajkamal Studios.

Kugelman, M. (2011) 'Looking out, looking in: Surveying India's internal and external security challenges', in M. Kugelman (ed.) *India's Contemporary Security Challenges*, Washington, DC: Woodrow Wilson International Centre for Scholars Asia Programme, pp. 29–47.

Mahapatra, D. (2009) 'Francis Induwar not the last victim of the Naxals and Maoists', *The Times of India*, 19 October, http://articles.timesofindia.indiatimes.com/2009-10-19/india/28078582_1_naxals-francis-induwar-orissa. Accessed 10 January 2015.

Martin, M.W. (1994) *Virtuous Giving: Philanthropy, Voluntary Service and Caring*, Bloomington, IN: Indiana University Press.

McCracken, G. (1991) 'Who is the celebrity endorser? Cultural foundations of the endorsements process', *Journal of Consumer Research*, 16: 310–21.

'Narmada Bachao Andolan (NBA) Forces End of World Bank Funding of Sardar Sarovar Dam, India, 1983–1993' (n.d.) Global Non-violent Action Database, http://nvdatabase.swarthmore.edu/content/narmada-bachao-andolan-nba-forces-end-world-bank-funding-sardar-sarovar-dam-india-1985-1993. Accessed 10 January 2015.

'Naxalites Behead Cop Taliban Style' (2013) *Hindustan Times*, 10 September, http://www.hindustantimes.com/News-Feed/India/Naxalites-behead-cop-Taliban-style/Article1-461684.aspx. Accessed 10 January 2015.

Newland, K., Terazas, A., and Munster, R. (2010) 'Philanthropy: Private giving and public policy', Migration Policy Institute, September, http://www.migrationpolicy.org/programs/migrants-migration-and-development. Accessed 10 January 2015.

Niebuhr, R. (1932) *Moral Man and Immoral Society*, Louisville, KY: Westminster John Knox Press.

NSW Department of Aboriginal Affairs (2004) 'Mudgin-gal women share peace prize spotlight', http://www.daa.nsw.gov.au/daanews/2/peaceprizemudgingal.html. Accessed 6 February 2013.

Ohanian, R. (1991) 'The impact of celebrity spokespersons' perceived image on consumers; intention to purchase', *Journal of Advertising Research*, February–March, pp. 46–53.

Omvedt, G. (1999) 'An open letter to Arundhati Roy', Friends of River Narmarda, http://www.narmada.org/debates/gail/gail.open.letter.html. Accessed 10 January 2015.

Parashar, S. (2009) 'A response to Arundhati Roy: "The heart of India is under attack"', Hariharan's MI blog, guest column, Paper 3489, 5 November, http://hariharansmiblog.blogspot.com.au/2009/11/response-to-arundhati-roy-heart-of.html. Accessed 10 January 2015.

Piff, P.K., Kraus, M.W., Cote, S., Cheng, B.H., and Keltner, D. (2010) 'Having less, giving more: The influence of social class on prosocial behaviour', *Journal of Personality and Social Psychology*, 99, 2, August.

Ramana, P. (2011) 'India's Maoist insurgency: Evolution, current trends and responses', in M. Kugelman (ed.) *India's Contemporary Security Challenges*, Washington, DC: Woodrow Wilson International Centre for Scholars Asia Programme, pp. 29–47.

Reale, A. (2010) 'Acts of god(s): The role of religion in disaster risk reduction', *Humanitarian Exchange Magazine*, 48, October, http://www.odihpn.org/humanitarian-exchange-magazine/issue-48/acts-of-gods-the-role-of-religion-in-disaster-risk-reduction. Accessed 10 January 2015.

Roy, A. (1997) *The God of Small Things*, New York: HarperPerennial.

Roy, A. (1998) 'The end of imagination', *Outlook India*, 3 August, http://www.outlookindia.com/article.aspx?205932. Accessed 10 January 2015.

Roy, A. (1999) 'The greater common good', Friends of River Narmada, April, http://www.narmada.org/gcg/gcg.html. Accessed 10 January 2015.

Roy, A. (2002) *The Algebra of Infinite Justice*, London: Flamingo.

Roy, A. (2003) *War Talk*, Cambridge, MA: South End Press.

Roy, A. (2004a) *The Checkbook and the Cruise Missile: Conversations with Arundhati Roy*, interviews by David Barsamian, Cambridge, MA: South End Press.

Roy, A. (2004b) 'Do turkeys enjoy Thanksgiving?', *The Hindu*, 18 January, http://www.hindu.com/2004/01/18/stories/2004011800181400.htm. Accessed 10 January 2015.

Roy, A. (2008) 'The monster in the mirror', *The Guardian*, 13 December, http://www.guardian.co.uk/world/2008/dec/12/mumbai-arundhati-roy. Accessed 10 January 2015.

Roy, A. (2010a) 'Walking with the comrades', *Outlook India*, 29 March, http://www.outlookindia.com/article.aspx?264738-0. Accessed 10 January 2015.

Roy, A. (2010b) 'Naxals are patriots', *Hindustan Times*, 21 November, http://www.hindustantimes.com/News-Feed/Bhubaneshwar/Naxals-are-patriots-Arundhati/Article1-629303.aspx. Accessed 10 January 2015.

Roy, A. (2011) 'The dead begin to speak up in India', *The Guardian*, 30 September, http://www.guardian.co.uk/commentisfree/libertycentral/2011/sep/30/kashmir-india-unmarked-graves. Accessed 10 January 2015.

Roy, A. (2013) 'A perfect day for democracy', *The Hindu*, 10 February, http://www.thehindu.com/opinion/lead/a-perfect-day-for-democracy/article4397705.ece. Accessed 10 January 2015.

Sardar Sarovar Narmada Nigam Limited (2013) 'NARMADA – the lifeline of Gujarat', 23 September, http://www.sardarsarovardam.org/Client/Index.aspx. Accessed 20 March 2014.

'Shah Rukh Champions the Cause of India's Unsung Heroes – The Forest Guards' (2007) WildAid, 13 July, http://www.wildaid.org/news/shah-rukh-champions-cause-india%E2%80%99s-unsung-heroes-forest-guards. Accessed 10 January 2015.

Sharma, D. (2012) 'Maoists building weapons factories in India with help from China', *India Today*, 26 April, http://indiatoday.intoday.in/story/chinese-intelligence-training-and-funding-maoists-in-india/1/186191.html. Accessed 10 January 2015.

Simeon, D. (2010) 'Permanent spring', *Seminar*, 607, March, http://www.india-seminar.com/2010/607/607_dilip_simeon.htm. Accessed 10 January 2015.

Singh, T. (2008) 'The real enemies', *Indian Express*, 21 December, http://www.indianexpress.com/news/the-real-enemies/400963/0. Accessed 11 September 2013.

'Sri Lanka's Tamil Tigers "Defeated"' (2009) *Aljazeera*, 17 May, http://www.aljazeera.com/news/asia/2009/05/2009516125146283478.html. Accessed 10 January 2015.

Srivastava, D. (n.d.) 'Maoist insurgency: The war within', *La Renaissance de l'Inde*, pp. 77–86, http://www.societe-de-strategie.asso.fr/pdf/agir43txt8.pdf. Accessed 10 January 2015.

Sternthal, B., Philips, L.W., and Dholakia, R. (1978) 'The persuasive effect of source credibility: A situational analysis', *Public Opinion Quarterly*, 42, 3: 285–314.

Sundar, N. (2011) 'At war with oneself: Constructing Naxalism as India's biggest security threat', in M. Kugelman (ed.) *India's Contemporary Security Challenges*, Washington, DC: Woodrow Wilson International Centre for Scholars Asia Programme, pp. 46–68.

Turner, G. (2004) *Understanding Celebrity*, London; Thousand Oaks; New Delhi: Sage.

'What Muslims Were to BJP, Maoists Are to Congress: Arundhati Roy' (2009) *The Times of India*, 25 October, http://articles.timesofindia.indiatimes.com/2009-10-25/india/28073656_1_unconditional-talks-arundhati-roy-maoists. Accessed 10 January 2015.

Chapter 9

Celebrity Philanthropy in China and the Zhang Ziyi Scandal

Elaine Jeffreys

This chapter looks at the politics of philanthropy in contemporary China by examining a series of charity scandals involving the internationally acclaimed Chinese actor Zhang Ziyi, and other entertainment celebrities and corporate figures. Zhang Ziyi is one of China's most famous celebrities, being ranked as the second most famous female celebrity in greater China (mainland China, Hong Kong and Taiwan) by *Forbes* magazine in 2014 (Flannery 2014).[1] *Forbes* issued its inaugural list of China's top 100 power-ranking celebrities in 2004, demonstrating the growing importance of the PRC in global cultural markets. As with the US list, China's celebrities are ranked by combining income from salaries and endorsements with the number of times they appear in various media formats.

Zhang Ziyi rose to international fame via her starring role in Ang Lee's martial arts movie *Crouching Tiger, Hidden Dragon* (2000). A global cinematic phenomenon in 2000–2001, *Crouching Tiger* earned more than USD 200 million worldwide, becoming the most commercially successful foreign-language film in US history and the first Chinese-language film to find a broad US audience (Klein 2004: 18). Since then, Zhang has gone on to enjoy critical acclaim for her starring roles in Hollywood films, such as *Memoirs of a Geisha* (dir. Rob Marshall 2005), and in Chinese-language blockbusters, such as *Hero* (dir. Zhang Yimou 2002) and *House of Flying Daggers* (dir. Zhang Yimou 2004). Voted as one of the 'most beautiful people in the world' by many fashion and celebrity magazines, she has appeared as the 'face' of international cosmetics giant, Maybelline, and as an 'ambassador' for OMEGA Watches ('Maybelline' n.d.; 'Zhang Ziyi' 2014).

As an A-list celebrity, Zhang Ziyi has been the focus of both praise and criticism in China. In 2006, Zhang Yiwu, a literature professor at Peking University, famously summed up the political significance of transnational celebrities such as Zhang Ziyi and basketball player Yao Ming for promoting a positive image of modern China internationally, by declaring that they were worth more than '10,000 of the philosopher-sage Confucius' (Xiao 2010). Adding to an impressive list of industry awards, Zhang Ziyi was voted as being among the Top 10 Chinese Celebrities with the Best Public Images at China's annual Huading Awards in May 2010 ('Actress Zhang Ziyi Wins Public Image Awards' 2010; 'Zhang Ziyi' 2010). This award recognizes the public images and social influences of Chinese entertainment celebrities, based on the results of nationwide polls and the decision of a jury panel.

However, Zhang Ziyi has also been the focus of negative publicity, chiefly relating to quasi-sex scandals. She was accused of rising to fame by sleeping with Zhang Yimou, the director of three films in which she played a starring role: *The Road Home* (1999), *Hero* (2002) and *House of Flying Daggers* (2004) (Yuan Lei 2007). She was lambasted in China's media for her role in *Memoirs of a Geisha* (dir. Marshall 2005). The original release of this film in China was cancelled because of strong anti-Japan sentiment flowing from the ongoing failure of the Japanese Government to offer a formal apology for World War II military atrocities. These atrocities included the massacre of an estimated 300,000 people in Nanjing between late 1937 and early 1938, and the abuse of thousands of Chinese women as sex slaves. In this context, Zhang's portrayal of a woman selling her virginity to the highest Japanese bidder was viewed as a national insult (Bezlova 2006; 'China Bans Memoirs of a Geisha' 2006). In 2009, Zhang Ziyi was called 'unpatriotic and shameless' for becoming briefly engaged to an Israeli venture capitalist, and enabling the paparazzi to circulate semi-nude photographs of the couple sunbathing on a beach (Tan 2009; Song, Yin and Guo 2010). More recently, Zhang Ziyi sued a US-based Chinese online news outlet for claiming that she was paid to have sex with numerous top Communist Party officials, including Bo Xilai, a political leader imprisoned in 2012 for corruption and collusion with murder ('Zhang Ziyi Sues US Website over Bo Xilai Link Claims' 2012).

Along with the taint of sexual promiscuity, Zhang Ziyi became the focus of intense public scrutiny in the PRC in 2010 for allegedly defaulting on a pledge to donate CNY 1 million to the Sichuan earthquake disaster-relief funds. The earthquake of 12 May 2008, which measured 7.8 on the Richter Scale, not only killed an estimated 70,000 people and left five million homeless ('Sichuan Earthquake: Facts and Figures' 2009), but also produced a dramatic rise in individual and corporate philanthropy in China. Philanthropic donations in 2008 amounted to a total figure of CNY 100 billion or 0.4 per cent of China's Gross Domestic Product (GDP), exceeding the documented total for the preceding decade (Wang 2008; 'Zhongguo cishan paihangbang fabu "lai juan qiye heimingdan" liuchan' 2009).[2] Zhang's 'failed pledge' led fans and critics to accuse her of charity fraud and bringing shame on philanthropy causes and the Chinese nation, in bilingual blogs and online videos (Alexandra099tianya 2010; Dogonfire2005 2010; MyLara2010 2010; 'Open Letter to Zhang Ziyi about "Fake" Donation' 2010; 'Zhang Ziyi 100 wan meijin de 5.12 dizhen juankuan ta zai nali?' 2010; Zong He 2010). Dubbed 'donation-gate', the associated controversy obliged Zhang Ziyi to hire a team of US-based lawyers, to give an exclusive interview to the state-run *China Daily*, and to engage in renewed philanthropic endeavours, in an effort to clear her name (Zhou 2010a, 2010b).

The chapter first explains how the Zhang Ziyi donation-gate scandal came to public attention and the nature of its development and resolution. It then locates the origins of that controversy in an escalating series of scandals associated with the Sichuan earthquake disaster-relief efforts, underscoring how public distrust of the wealthy and famous poses problems for the development of a philanthropic culture in China. Critics of US-based celebrities often claim that celebrity philanthropy is a cynical marketing exercise designed to improve a star's brand power and an apolitical mode of philanthropy that thrives on adoring fans, not on accountability (Wood 2007; Kapoor 2013; see also Murray, in this book). In contrast, I show that public individuals who engage in mediatized philanthropic activities in the PRC are subject to intense public scrutiny and demands for accountability. Rather than exposing the self-centred egoism and fallibility of modern-day celebrities, the nature of those demands highlights the problems surrounding recent calls to cultivate a philanthropic citizenry in China.

The Zhang Ziyi Celebrity-Philanthropy Scandal

On 12 May 2008, when the Sichuan earthquake took place, Zhang Ziyi was at the Cannes International Film Festival. Upon hearing of that disaster, which triggered an outpouring of nationalist sentiment in China (Watts 2008), Zhang initiated three philanthropic activities to assist the relief effort. First, she announced that she would personally donate CNY 1 million to the disaster-relief funds, citing the traditional Chinese saying, 'When the country is in trouble, everyone must do their duty' ('Zhang Ziyi xuanbujuan 100 wan, cheng "guojia you nan, pifuzuoze"' 2008). Second, she established the Ziyi Zhang Foundation, a not-for-profit charity registered under the laws of California, US, with a bank account for donors to deposit funds for transfer to the Chinese Red Cross Foundation (Care for Children 2010). Finally, Zhang hosted a fund-raising event at Cannes, which journalists claimed had raised between USD 500,000 and USD 7 million ('2008 Sichuan Earthquake Donations by Chinese Celebrities Closely Inspected' 2010).

Zhang Ziyi became the focus of major public scrutiny in January 2010 for allegedly defaulting on her pledge to donate CNY 1 million to the disaster-relief funds and misrepresenting her other philanthropic activities. The ensuing donation-gate scandal followed speculation about another scandal involving Zhang Ziyi and hints of sexual impropriety – the so-called 'black paint incident', a series of events that took place on the evening of 23 December 2009. A group of unidentified men entered the Park Hyatt hotel in Beijing, where Zhang reportedly owns an apartment. They demanded that security guards tell them where the actor resided, claiming that she had seduced a married man and cheated other people of their money by accepting gifts worth more than USD 29 million from him ('Who's Behind the Zhang Ziyi "Black Paint Incident"?' 2009; Zhou 2010b). Shortly after, another group of unidentified men drove up to the hotel and splashed black paint on a giant OMEGA advertisement board featuring Zhang Ziyi. These events were observed by a waiting crowd of paparazzi who had gathered at the Park Hyatt following a tip-off that Hong Kong actor, Maggie Cheung, and her German boyfriend, Ole Scheeren, were getting engaged at a restaurant in the hotel that evening (Huang 2010). The black paint incident sparked speculation in the press about who had orchestrated the incident and why. It also generated debate on Internet sites, initially on Tianya.cn, which is China's biggest blogging forum, about Zhang Ziyi's moral character. This speculation prompted an unspecified number of netizens to start investigating the actor's life, resulting in the discovery of discrepancies relating to her philanthropic activities (Huang 2010).

An article posted on the Tianya bulletin board system in late January 2010 disputed Zhang Ziyi's claim to have raised over CNY 1 million towards the earthquake disaster-relief funds, saying that she had only contributed CNY 840,000 of that money ('Zhang Ziyi 100 wan' 2010). This claim prompted other members of the public to contact the PRC's Ministry of Civil Affairs, the Chinese Red Cross Foundation and other organizations in efforts to verify (or disprove) Zhang's philanthropic track record ('Donation Details Released to End Debate Dogging Zhang Ziyi' 2010). Apart from confirming that Zhang Ziyi had only donated CNY 840,000 to the disaster-relief funds, in two separate payments of CNY 400,000 and 440,000, these investigations revealed that money raised by Zhang at the Cannes International Film Festival amounted to the paltry sum of USD 1,300 – not the more than USD 500,000 that was reported in the media. The Ziyi Zhang Foundation was also called into disrepute through suggestions that its lack of transparency implied that it was merely a front for charity fraud and personal profiteering (Zhou 2010b).

Zhang and her agent, Ji Lingling, had already attempted to quash associated criticisms by issuing a public statement denying online allegations and promising that accounting records would be made available to the public on 3 February 2010 (Song Jianqin 2010; 'Zhang Ziyi jiu dizhen juankuan fa shengming jiang rushi gongbu zhangmumingxi' 2010). However, Zhang's subsequent silence on the issue, and Ji's failure to provide the relevant records by the specified date, simply added to mounting public criticism of her 'fake philanthropy' (Schwankert 2010). Ji's ultimately bungled attempt to 'clear the record' added more fuel to the controversy. On 5 February, he issued a statement to Sina.com, one of China's most popular web portals, stating that Zhang Ziyi had contributed the promised CNY 1 million in cash to the disaster-relief funds. On 8 February, Ji retracted this statement by making a public apology to the effect that Zhang had just contributed another CNY 160,000 to the Chinese Red Cross Foundation after discovering that her management team had been careless. As a result, they had failed to pay the third and final sum required to meet the original pledge of CNY 1 million (Li 2010; 'Q&A: Zhang Ziyi' 2010).

Zhang Ziyi's perceived failure to respond adequately to public criticisms of her philanthropic activities sparked widespread debate on interactive media forums. Apart from posts on the Tianya.cn blog, which had received over half a million hits and 90,000 replies by early February (Zong He 2010), online videos were posted in both English and Chinese on YouTube demanding that Zhang account for her actions (e.g. Alexandra099tianya 2010; Dogonfire2005 2010; MyLara2010 2010). An open letter was also posted in Chinese on the People's Daily website on 1 March 2010, asking Zhang to answer a series of questions about her donations and to make her philanthropic records available to the public. That letter informed the actor that Chinese 'netizens-cum-detectives' would ensure that she could no longer 'hide' behind the laws of other countries and take advantage of the 'tolerance' of the Chinese people (Pan Yuan 2010). Zhang Ziyi's international celebrity status is reflected in the bilingual nature of these activities, which, unsurprisingly, attracted further comment in broadcast and social media (Pan Yuan 2010; Zong He 2010).

Faced with mounting criticisms of her 'fake philanthropy', Zhang Ziyi gave an exclusive interview to *China Daily*, a state-run English-language newspaper, on 12 March 2010. In that interview, the transcript of which was posted on the *China Daily*'s website in both English and Chinese, Zhang affirmed that she had donated CNY 1 million from her personal finances to the Chinese Red Cross Foundation for the Sichuan earthquake disaster-relief funds (Zhou 2010b). Following two initial payments amounting to CNY 840,000, she made up the shortfall of CNY 160,000 on 8 February 2010. Zhang attributed the delay to her failure to follow-up on instructions that she had given to her staff and denied accusations of fraud and embezzlement. Regarding confusion about the amount of money raised in Cannes, Zhang stated that she had only raised USD 1,300 in cash because of the hasty nature of that fund-raising event. Although only USD 39,000 of pledges amounting to a total of USD 400,000 had been honoured, she was still negotiating a project with potential donors, whose names she was unable to reveal for privacy reasons (Zhou 2010b). Responding to accusations of embezzlement, and inadvertently offering another example of her ineffective philanthropic efforts, Zhang Ziyi noted that a full-page advertisement paid for by the *Hollywood Reporter*, in which the editor-in-chief and Zhang had appealed for funds for the relief of the Sichuan earthquake, had not induced anyone to contribute to her Foundation ('Q&A: Zhang Ziyi' 2010). Zhang vowed to make up for any shortfall if contributions pledged towards the building of a children's centre in Sichuan Province were unforthcoming. Zhang further insisted that she had never tried to enhance her public image by intimating that she had raised between USD 1 and 7 million – those figures had been arbitrarily cited by journalists (Li 2010; 'Q&A: Zhang Ziyi' 2010; Zhou 2010b).

Zhang maintained that she had kept silent about the controversy for two months because she had hired a legal team in the US to investigate the issues raised by China's netizens, and that investigation had taken longer than anticipated ('Q&A: Zhang Ziyi' 2010). However, she was now in a position to confirm that there had never been anything untoward about the running of the Ziyi Zhang Foundation – it is a not-for-profit organization, handled by a professional accountant in a transparent and legal manner. Monies pledged to that Foundation through Zhang's fund-raising efforts in Cannes and elsewhere were earmarked for the building of a children's centre in Deyang City, Sichuan Province, under the auspices of the UK-based international charity Care for Children. As relevant government authorities had only approved that project in November 2009, the building of the centre had not started and hence Care for Children had not received any funding from the Ziyi Zhang Foundation. Funds would be transferred once the building work began, which according to subsequent press releases took place on 1 June 2010 ('Zhang Ziyi to Use Funds from Cannes Charity Drive to Build Children's Shelter' 2010).

Zhang Ziyi concluded the interview by saying that the donation-gate scandal had taught her five things about philanthropy and celebrity. First, effective philanthropy requires more than personal passion: it needs a professional team with the right approach. Second, celebrities have a duty to engage in philanthropic work because they have a public profile, not because they want to boost their image. Third, this necessitates a mediatized approach to generating philanthropy, rather than a low-key or anonymous approach, which she would otherwise prefer. Fourth, the act of giving back through philanthropy is important to someone whose achievements are the result of time and money invested by the Chinese nation and the Chinese people. Finally, and responding to additional questions about the links between the donation-gate scandal and the black paint incident, Zhang stated that the public has a right to know about the private lives of celebrities, within ethical limits. However, members of the public should understand that celebrities are ordinary people and not moral exemplars, even though their domestic and international standing as representatives of China requires them to conduct themselves as perfectly as possible.

In short, Zhang Ziyi affirmed that she had a social obligation, both as a celebrity and as a patriot, to engage in high-profile philanthropic activities, and she vowed to respond to public exposure of her inexperience by righting her errors. In June 2010, Zhang Ziyi made good on that claim by appearing in the earthquake-affected area of Deyang City to announce that work had begun on the construction of a centre for orphans and vagrant children. Zhang further revealed that funding for the centre came from the proceeds of her 2008 fund-raising drive in Cannes, indicating that the pledged sum of USD 400,000 to the Ziyi Zhang Foundation had been honoured. Reportedly choking back her tears, the actor expressed relief that after two years of hard work, the project had finally begun ('Zhang Ziyi to Use Funds from Cannes Charity Drive to Build Children's Shelter' 2010).

While some netizens maintained that their actions had obliged the actor to fulfil her promises by exposing her cynical efforts to 'cash in' on the wave of patriotic sentiment that accompanied the Sichuan earthquake ('Open Letter to Zhang Ziyi about "Fake" Donation' 2010), the available evidence suggests a more complicated story. Contrary to the accusations levelled against her, Zhang's involvement in the Deyang project was confirmed in a press release by the Care for Children organization as early as 8 February 2010 (Care for Children 2010). That involvement contributed to the jury's decision to recognize Zhang's efforts at the Huading Awards in May ('Actress Zhang Ziyi Wins Public Image Awards' 2010). This award arguably demonstrates Zhang's masterful manipulation of the public from the start to the end of the donation-gate scandal. However, a more plausible explanation for that scandal is the one Zhang provided in her interview with the *China Daily* (Zhou 2010b). She had neither the experience nor the professional team required to manage the issues and delays imposed by the lack of a developed institutional framework for philanthropy in China.

In any case, the 'fall-out' from the donation-gate scandal indicates that it offers more than a tale of personal redemption. Concerned netizens promptly proceeded to question the disaster-relief efforts of a wide range of Chinese entertainment stars. Actor Li Bingbing was accused of only donating CNY 500 out of a pledged contribution of CNY 300,000. Singer Hu Yanbing allegedly donated a mere CNY 50 of a publicized CNY 50,000. Zhao Wei, a movie star, reportedly only gave CNY 20,000 of a CNY 100,000 pledge and actor Liu Xiaoqing was criticized for donating CNY 4,300 rather than CNY 100,000 as promised ('2008 Sichuan Earthquake Donations by Chinese Celebrities Closely Inspected' 2010). As suggested by the escalating nature of such allegations on interactive media forums, celebrity philanthropy in China *is* a political affair.

The Politics of Philanthropy in Reform-Era China

'Philanthropy' and 'celebrity' in the contemporary sense of those words did not exist in mainland China until after the PRC Government abandoned socialist, centralized economic planning in favour of market-based reforms in December 1978. After the PRC was founded in 1949, revolutionary hostility ensured that the foundations of pre-1949 elite philanthropy were removed by default – rural gentry, urban capitalists, opposition political figures and religious and cultural elites, became the targets of land redistribution campaigns and mass-mobilization campaigns against counter-revolutionary, capitalist and imperialist behaviours (Zhou and Zeng 2006). Nationalization of industry and the curtailing of the monetary economy subsequently prevented private enterprise and significant private wealth accumulation throughout the Maoist period (1949–1976). Citizens of 'new China' were provided with rudimentary services, including food, employment, housing, education and health care, through state-run work units and rural agricultural collectives. At the same time, China's state-controlled media communicated Party-state ideology and promoted revolutionary role models to generate support for a continued series of mass campaigns, and to create a collective socialist citizenry. Mao-era concepts of citizenship were based on the understanding that state workers were 'the masters of the state' and, as such, they collectively owned the nationalized assets of the formerly private industrial and commercial sectors (Zang 2008: 61–2). Private entrepreneurs and entertainment celebrities have emerged in reform-era China along with the development of a market economy and an increasingly commercialized media (Goodman 2008; Edwards and Jeffreys 2010).

Economic reform since 1979 has produced remarkable improvements in the living standards, education, health and life expectancy of nearly all of China's citizens, while generating a growing divide between the haves and the have-nots. A popular index of inequality is the Gini coefficient, which ranges from 0 (perfect equality) to 1. In 1978, China had a Gini Coefficient of 0.22, making it one of the most egalitarian nations in the world: everyone was poor. In January 2013, the PRC's National Bureau of Statistics released figures about China's Gini coefficient from 2003 to 2012. These figures indicated that China's Gini coefficient had peaked at 0.491 in 2008, but still stood at 0.474 in 2012, making the PRC one of the most unequal nations in the world (Yao and Wang 2013). Some sectors of the population have seized the opportunities created by the commercial expansion of the economy to become newly rich and famous, while other sectors of the population face new forms of social exclusion and systemic disadvantage due to the withdrawal of former state provisions. Hence, China in the early decades of the new millennium faces social problems that resurrect Andrew Carnegie's (1889: 657) famous contention regarding the philanthropic responsibilities of an emerging stratum of self-made entrepreneurs. 'What is the proper mode of administering wealth after the laws upon which civilization is founded [competition and private property] have thrown it into the hands of the few?'

However, the economic and ideological legacies of state socialism continue to influence reform-era China as reflected in public distrust of the rich and famous, and the newness of the PRC's philanthropic culture. 'Hatred of the wealthy' (*chouhen furen*) is a documented phenomenon in China today because 'ordinary people' tend to assume that those who have become newly rich along with the partial privatization of the economy are 'immoral', having obtained their wealth through corruption or the 'theft' of formerly communal assets (Zang 2008: 55–60). Even where personal wealth is arguably the result of talent and good fortune, rich people are still viewed as morally suspect for spending their surplus money in acts of conspicuous consumption, rather than distributing it appropriately to those who are less fortunate. Celebrities such as Zhang Ziyi, for example, are easily opened to criticism as the envied, yet denigrated, idols of hedonistic capitalist consumption when compared with the nostalgically imagined model citizens of an era defined by socialist collectivism and production (Jeffreys and Edwards 2010: 18).

Public distrust of the rich and famous has created problems for the development of elite philanthropy in reform-era China. The following list of events illustrates the newness of philanthropy in general in the PRC. In October 2004, the first government-run public-benefit website, the China Charity Information Center (Juanzhu.gov.cn 2009), was launched by the Ministry of Civil Affairs ('China Launches 1st Official Charity Website' 2004). On 20 November 2005, the first annual China Charity Awards were held at the *China Charity Conference* in Beijing ('First China Charity Awards to be Presented' 2005). The first list of China's top 50 philanthropists was compiled in 2004; and the first list of China's top 50 philanthropic companies was produced in 2005 ('China: Philanthropy Overview' 2006).

On 5 December 2008, President Hu Jintao made PRC history by making philanthropy an integral part of the nation's public policy agenda during a speech to announce the winners of China's fourth annual Charity Awards (Liu Weitao 2008; 'Zongshuji de jiakuai cishanshiye fazhan dongyuanling' 2009). This speech, which the People's Daily described as a mobilization directive, called on Chinese citizens from all walks of life to speed up the development of a philanthropic culture in the PRC, in order to ensure the realization of a 'moderately affluent' (*xiaokang*) and harmonious society by the year 2020. Deng Xiaoping, paramount leader of the PRC between 1978 and 1992, first used the classical term *xiaokang*, which evokes modest prosperity, to describe China's modernization and the goals of economic reform in 1979. Jiang Zemin, PRC President between 1993 and 2003, subsequently revitalized the term in a report that he delivered to the Sixteenth National Congress of the Chinese Communist Party in 2002, titled 'Build a well-off society in an all-round way and create a new situation in building socialism with Chinese characteristics'. In that report, Jiang stated, 'We need to concentrate on building a xiaokang society of a higher standard in an all-round way', which means an estimated per-capita GDP of more than USD 2,000 by the year 2020 ('All about *Xiaokang*' 2002). The Hu Jintao-Wen Jiabao leadership's vision of *xiaokang* socialism continued to evoke sustained economic growth as a means to realize prosperity, but also emphasized the need for that prosperity to be broadly distributed and for economic growth to be balanced with social equality and environmental protection (Jeffreys and Sigley 2009: 11).

In his December speech, Hu Jintao praised the enormous contributions of people in providing relief to the millions of victims of the 2008 Sichuan earthquake, suggesting that the disaster had heralded the birth of a philanthropic citizenry in China (Bao 2009; Wang Zhuoqiong 2008). However, Hu proceeded to qualify his praise for the rapid growth in domestic philanthropy by noting that Chinese philanthropy – in terms of public motivation and the number of philanthropic organizations and donations – lags behind that of developed countries and behind the state of economic development in the PRC. He therefore called on Party members, government departments and business enterprises, as well as 'compassionate' Chinese people, to develop a philanthropic culture in the PRC as quickly as possible, in order to supplement its inadequate social security system (Liu Weitao 2008).

While putting philanthropy 'on the map' in China, the disaster-relief efforts were dogged by scandal from their inception. The Sichuan earthquake of 12 May 2008 immediately generated public condemnations of corporate philanthropy, initially flowing from the circulation of the so-called 'international iron rooster list' (*guoji tiegongji*). In colloquial Chinese, an 'iron rooster' refers to a misanthrope, a bird that will not give up a single feather. Between 14 and 19 May 2008, an SMS was circulated in China that called upon concerned and patriotic citizens to boycott multinational companies, such as Coca-Cola, KFC, McDonald's, Nokia, and Samsung, because of their allegedly 'puny' contributions to the disaster-relief efforts. The SMS called upon concerned citizens to spread the contents of the list and to update it as events unfolded, resulting in widespread debate on interactive media forums such as MSN and QQ ('5.12 Sichuan Wenchuan da dizhen juankuan guoji tiegongji paihangbang' 2008; Hei Ma 2008). Chain letters posted on the Internet and disseminated through mobile phone networks soon translated into civil protests, with an estimated 100 people gathering outside a McDonald's enterprise in Nanchong city, Sichuan Province, to protest the company's perceived lack of genuine philanthropy. Similar protests were waged against KFC in the provinces of Sichuan, Shaanxi, and Shanxi, resulting in the temporary closure of various businesses ('Companies Rush to Show Generosity over China Earthquake' 2008; 'The Story of Donations Gate' 2008).

Public condemnation of multinational companies for their allegedly miserly donations to the disaster-relief efforts quickly translated into praise for local Chinese companies that were seen to have contributed generously. Wanglaoji, a herbal tea soft drink, became famous overnight and reported a significant increase in sales after its parent company, the Jiaduobao Group, donated CNY 100 million at the 18 May 2008 China Central Television Station disaster-relief gala (Fong 2008; McGinnis et al. 2009). This contribution was viewed as providing a concrete demonstration of the company's claim to 'give back' some of its profits by 'zealously' participating in 'public welfare activities and philanthropy' ('Brief Introduction' 2005). A post subsequently placed on the Tianya website called on Chinese consumers to reward the company for its demonstration of 'social responsibility' by buying Wanglaoji products. Netizens also devised and circulated advertising slogans in praise of the company. One slogan stated that 'If you want to donate, you donate CNY 100 million; if you want to drink, you drink Wanglaoji', while other slogans parodied

Coca-Cola advertisements to indicate that Wanglaoji was the better product ('The Story of Donations Gate' 2008).

As it turned out, the perception that multinational companies were busy exploiting business opportunities in China and unwilling to 'give back' chiefly flowed from a lack of transparency and clarity in the reporting of donations, and from the time-delay required to obtain company board and/or shareholder authorization for donations that exceeded the established corporate social responsibility policies of international companies. Many of the 'international iron roosters' had not only made immediate contributions to the disaster-relief efforts, but also sought authorization to increase their original donations. For example, KFC's parent group, the MDGB group, pledged a donation of CNY 3 million immediately after the earthquake. That pledge increased to nearly CNY 16 million on 19 May with an additional contribution of more than CNY 5 million from its employees. Contributions from other multinationals, such as Coca-Cola, McDonald's, Nokia, and Samsung, also increased dramatically in the same period ('China: Multinationals Hear it Online' 2008; 'The Story of Donations Gate' 2008). However, public criticisms of the 'international iron roosters' only abated following concerted efforts by the PRC Government and the US–China Business Council. The PRC's Minister of Commerce convened a press conference to confirm their actual donations on 22 May 2008. Given the limited efficacy of that press release, the US–China Business Council began recording the donations of its member companies on its official website and releasing those figures to the PRC's Ministries of Foreign Affairs and Commerce for dissemination in China's media ('US Company Contributions for Earthquake Relief' 2008).

Nevertheless, accusations of 'donation-stinginess' soon extended to criticisms of two of China's most famous sporting celebrities in the run-up to the 2008 Beijing Olympic Games. Yao Ming, a professional basketball player with the Houston Rockets in the US NBA, was criticized for initially pledging CNY 500,000, which was viewed as insignificant compared to his reported earnings of around CNY 57 million in 2007 (Yao 2008). Liu Xiang – China's first male Olympic gold medal winner in the track and field – was similarly subjected to public criticism for initially pledging, along with his coach, the perceived paltry sum of CNY 500,000.

These criticisms, as with those directed at the 'international iron roosters', proved to be premature or unfounded. The Yao Ming Foundation was established under the auspices of the Giving Back Fund on 10 June 2008 to help raise funds and awareness, in both the PRC and the US, of children's wellness and welfare issues in the earthquake-affected areas. Yao Ming personally contributed an initial start-up fund of USD 2 million to the Foundation, which went on to raise nearly USD 3 million in the US within a year (Cesarone 2009). Liu Xiang went on to contribute a further CNY 2.5 million and personally visited the earthquake-affected areas ('Liu Xiang Teaches Quake Students to Run Hurdles' 2009).

However, by early 2009, China's netizens were calling on government departments and philanthropic organizations to publish earthquake-related 'donation lists', in order to halt the perceived tactic of 'free and dishonest advertising' by companies and celebrities ('Charity's

Best and Worst' 2009). This debate was exacerbated by claims that the China Association of Social Workers, which was responsible for issuing the 2009 'China Philanthropy List', intended to publish a 'name and shame list' of companies that had failed to honour their pledges, one that did not eventuate in practice (Sun Xunbo 2009). Opponents of the publication of such a list pointed out that it was in effect a 'blacklist'. Its publication would not only impugn the brand reputation of certain corporations and celebrities, but also encourage moral blackmail, being based on information that was out-of-date and lacked clarity, and a failure to understand that pledges were often given in stages rather than as a bulk sum (Yao 2008). But, an online survey of netizens' views on NetEase.com, a Chinese web portal dedicated to delivering '"Power to the People" by using the latest Internet technologies to enhance meaningful information sharing and exchange', concluded that nearly 70 per cent supported the 'blacklisting' of companies and celebrities that had failed to honour their pledges. Only 26 per cent of those who responded to the survey opposed the publication of such a list on the basis that it undermined the spirit of philanthropy by turning it into a social obligation (NetEase 1997; Tao Tao 2009).

By 2010, as the Zhang Ziyi scandal attests, the 'naming and shaming' of the rich and the famous on interactive media forums for their allegedly 'fake' philanthropy had begun to focus on China's entertainment stars. While pointing to the democratizing influence of the Internet, by giving a voice to non-elites and providing citizens with an unprecedented degree of participation in China's media, the 'lead-up' to and the 'fall-out' from the Zhang Ziyi scandal highlights a simple fact. The growth of user-generated content, and the rise of the blogger, in particular, does not necessarily contribute to the production of responsible citizens and democratic politics. It also fuels populist denigration of public individuals.

Conclusion

An examination of the Zhang Ziyi scandal and its precursors underscores the politicized nature of wealth, fame and philanthropy in China. It suggests that the economic and social legacies of the Maoist era have created problems for the development of a philanthropic citizenry in China by encouraging an emphasis on philanthropy understood as a social obligation of the wealthy and famous. Celebrities and major corporations in China are expected to 'give back *more*' precisely because they have surplus money and brand power. At the same time, it is assumed that the philanthropic activities of public individuals should be open to public scrutiny because their money and status requires them to accept responsibility for leading positive social change. This remains the case even though the structural problems associated with the undeveloped nature of the PRC's philanthropic sector prevent them from 'doing philanthropy professionally', thereby placing them at risk of public censure. The proliferation of celebrity-philanthropy scandals on interactive media formats further indicates that China's netizens view public criticism as a positive incitement for public individuals to do more and better rather than a potential or actual discouragement.

An evident problem here is that the effective transposition of philanthropy from a desire to assist the public good into an obligation to 'give back' undermines both the principle that people are free to determine how much of their resources they wish to use on 'public endeavours' and the underlying voluntarism of philanthropy. If public individuals are obliged to give back more and publicly, rather than doing so voluntarily based on personal sentiment and a sense of reward, then philanthropy is simply a different and largely unexamined means for ensuring the redistribution of wealth. Alternatively, it places a populist and non-governmental tax on fame and success rather than on surplus capital per se.

Notes

1 *Forbes* extended its China list in 2010 to include celebrities from Taiwan and Hong Kong, as well as mainland China. Zhang Ziyi (at number five) in 2010 was the first-ranked female celebrity ('2010 *Forbes* China Celebrity List' 2010). Obtaining the same ranking in 2014, Zhang Ziyi was the second-ranked female celebrity after Fan Bingbing. The order of the 2014 list was: (1) Fan Bingbing, female actor, mainland China; (2) Andy Lau, male singer/actor, Hong Kong; (3) Jay Chou, male singer, Taiwan; (4) Huang Xiaoming, male actor, mainland China; and (5) Zhang Ziyi, female actor, mainland China.
2 By way of comparison, the total number of donations in the US and the UK in 2006 amounted to 1.7 per cent and 0.73 per cent of GDP, respectively ('International Comparisons of Charitable Giving' 2006).

Acknowledgements

This research was supported under the Australian Research Council's Future Fellowship (FT100100238) funding schemes.

References

'2008 Sichuan Earthquake Donations by Chinese Celebrities Closely Inspected' (2010) Veggie Discourse: Cultures, Movies, Music, Books, and Whatever is Interesting blog, 6 February, http://torisefromashes.blogspot.com/2010/02/2008-sichuan-earthquake-donations-by.html. Accessed 10 January 2015.
'2010 *Forbes* China Celebrity List' (2010) Chinahush, 29 April, http://www.chinahush.com/2010/04/29/2010-forbes-china-celebrity-list/. Accessed 6 March 2015.
'5.12 Sichuan Wenchuan da dizhen juankuan guoji tiegongji paihangbang' [Contributions to Relief Efforts for the Earthquake of 12 May in Wenchuan, Sichuan Province: The International Iron Rooster List] (2008) Baidu.com, http://tieba.baidu.com/f?kz=382700640. Accessed 10 January 2015.

'Actress Zhang Ziyi Wins Public Image Awards' (2010) *China Daily*, 30 May, http://www.chinadaily.net/china/2010-05/30/content_9908909.htm. Accessed 10 January 2015.

Alexandra099tianya (2010) 'Earthquake scandal of Ziyi Zhang, Ziyi Zhang donation-fraud', YouTube, 11 February, http://www.youtube.com/watch?v=jBGhFwq4vm8&feature=related. Accessed 10 January 2015.

'All about *Xiaokang*' (2002) *Xinhua News Agency*, 10 November, http://news.xinhuanet.com/english/2002-11/10/content_624884.htm. Accessed 10 January 2015.

Bao, W. (2009) 'SOEs lead upsurge in charitable donations', *China Daily*, 23 March, http://www.chinadaily.com.cn/bw/2009-03/23/content_7604326.htm. Accessed 29 June 2010.

Bezlova, A. (2006) '*Memoirs of a Geisha* lost in political din', *Inter Press Service (IPS)*, 7 February, http://ipsnews.net/news.asp?idnews=32059. Accessed 10 January 2015.

'Brief Introduction' (2005) Guangzhou Wanglaoji Pharmaceutical Company, http://www.wlj.com.cn/EN/Profile/profile.asp. Accessed 29 June 2010.

Care for Children (2010) 'Ziyi Zhang Foundation makes a significant financial contribution towards Care For Children's ongoing earthquake relief work in Sichuan', *China Retail News*, 8 February, http://www.chinaretailnews.com/2010/02/08/3369-ziyi-zhang-foundation-makes-a-significant-financial-contribution-towards-care-for-childrens-ongoing-earthquake-relief-work-in-sichuan/. Accessed 5 March 2015.

Carnegie, A. (1889) 'Wealth', *North American Review*, 148, 391: 653–64.

Cesarone, J.Z. (2009) 'Yao Ming Foundation raises funds to help rebuild schools in China's quake-ravaged Sichuan', *China View*, 23 May, http://news.xinhuanet.com/english/2009-05/23/content_11421567.htm. Accessed 10 January 2015.

'Charity's Best and Worst' (2009) *China Daily*, 11 April, http://www.chinadaily.com.cn/opinion/2009-04/11/content_7669118.htm. Accessed 29 June 2010.

'China Bans *Memoirs of a Geisha*' (2006) *The Guardian*, 1 February, http://www.guardian.co.uk/film/2006/feb/01/news1. Accessed 10 January 2015.

'China Launches 1st Official Charity Website' (2004) *Xinhua News Agency*, 29 October, www.china.org.cn/english/2004/Oct/110679.htm. Accessed 10 January 2015.

'China: Multinationals Hear it Online' (2008) *Business Week*, 30 May, http://www.businessweek.com/globalbiz/content/may2008/gb20080530_213248.htm. Accessed 10 January 2015.

'China: Philanthropy Overview' (2006) Asia Pacific Philanthropy Consortium, http://www.asianphilanthropy.org. Accessed 29 June 2010.

'Companies Rush to Show Generosity over China Earthquake' (2008) *The China Post*, 4 June, http://www.chinapost.com.tw/business/asia/asia-china/2008/06/04/159516/Companies-rush.htm. Accessed 5 March 2015.

Dogonfire2005 (2010) 'Chinese actress Ziyi Zhang suspected embezzling earthquake relief funds', YouTube, 11 February, http://www.youtube.com/watch?v=rlgs-BhH0Fo&feature=related. Accessed 10 January 2015.

'Donation Details Released to End Debate Dogging Zhang Ziyi' (2010) *Xinhua News Agency*, 1 February, http://english.cri.cn/6666/2010/02/10/1221s549330.htm. Accessed 10 January 2015.

Edwards, L., and Jeffreys, E. (eds) (2010) *Celebrity in China*, Hong Kong: Hong Kong University Press.

'First China Charity Awards to be Presented' (2005) *Xinhua News Agency*, 18 November, http://www.china.org.cn/english/2005/Nov/149243.htm. Accessed 10 January 2015.

Flannery, R. (2014) '2014 Forbes China celebrity list', *Forbes*, 6 May, http://www.forbes.com/sites/russellflannery/2014/05/06/2014-forbes-china-celebrity-list-full-list/. Accessed 10 January 2015.

Fong, C. (2008) 'Recognition for the unknown guru of herbal tea', *Beijing Express*, 3 August, http://thestar.com.my/columnists/story.asp?col=beijingexpress&file=/2008/8/3/ columnists/beijingexpress/21993722&sec=Beijing%20Express. Accessed 29 June 2010.

Goodman, D.S.G. (ed.) (2008) *The New Rich in China: Future Rulers, Present Lives*, Abingdon, Oxon: Routledge.

Hei Ma (2008) 'Sichuan zhenzai juankuan xingdong zhong: Guoji tiegongji mingdan ruxia' [Contributions to the Sichuan earthquake relief efforts: The list of the international iron roosters is as follows], Guba.163.com, http://guba.money.163.com/bbs/sz002230/79299336.html. Accessed 29 June 2010.

Huang, H. (2010) 'Chinese art of revelling in another's pain', *China Daily*, 9 February, http://www.chinadaily.com.cn/cndy/2010-02/09/content_9447615.htm. Accessed 10 January 2015.

'International Comparisons of Charitable Giving' (2006) Charities Aid Foundation, November, http://www.cafonline.org/pdf/International%20Comparisons%20of%20Charitable%20Giving.pdf. Accessed 6 March 2015.

Jeffreys, E., and Edwards, L.P. (2010) 'Celebrity/China', in L.P. Edwards and E. Jeffreys (eds) *Celebrity in China*, Hong Kong: Hong Kong University Press, pp. 1–20.

Jeffreys, E., and Sigley, G. (2009) 'Governmentality, governance and China', in E. Jeffreys (ed.) *China's Governmentalities: Governing Change, Changing Government*, Abingdon, Oxon; New York: Routledge, pp. 1–23.

Kapoor, I. (2013) *Celebrity Humanitarianism: The Ideology of Global Charity*, Abingdon, Oxon: Routledge.

Klein, C. (2004) '*Crouching Tiger, Hidden Dragon*: A diasporic reading', *Cinema Journal*, 43, 4: 18–42.

Lee, A. (dir.) (2000) *Crouching Tiger, Hidden Dragon*, motion picture, Hong Kong: Asia Union Film and Entertainment.

Li, C. (2010) 'Zhang Ziyi fulfills quake donation shortfall', *Shanghai Daily*, 9 February, http://english.cri.cn/6666/2010/02/09/1261s548987.htm. Accessed 10 January 2015.

Liu Weitao (2008) 'Hu Jintao: Fayang rendaozhuyi jingshen reqing canyu cishan huodong' [Hu Jintao: Develop the spirit of humanitarianism, engage in philanthropy enthusiastically], *Renmin Ribao*, 6 December, http://cpc.people.com.cn/GB/64093/64094/8471211.html. Accessed 10 January 2015.

'Liu Xiang Teaches Quake Students to Run Hurdles' (2009) *Xinhua News Agency*, 11 May, http://news.cultural-china.com/20090512105116.html. Accessed 10 January 2015.

Marshall, R. (dir.) (2005) *Memoirs of a Geisha*, motion picture, Los Angeles: Columbia Pictures Corporation.

'Maybelline' (n.d.) Fashion Industry Archive, http://fashionindustryarchive.com/client/Maybelline/. Accessed 6 March 2015.

McGinnis, A., Pellegrin, J., Shum, Y., Teo, J., and Wu, J. (2009) 'The Sichuan earthquake and the changing landscape of CSR in China', *Knowledge@Wharton*, 20 April, http://knowledge.wharton.upenn.edu/article.cfm?articleid=2213. Accessed 10 January 2015.

MyLara2010 (2010) 'Vivi Nevo and Ziyi Zhang are lies', YouTube, 18 February, http://www.youtube.com/watch?v=OChQoOxbk_A. Accessed 10 January 2015.

NetEase (1997) 'Overview: Our mission', 163.com, http://corp.163.com/. Accessed 29 June 2010.

'Open Letter to Zhang Ziyi about "Fake" Donation' (2010) People's Daily, 25 March, http://english.peopledaily.com.cn/90001/90782/90875/6930783.html. Accessed 29 June 2010.

Pan Yuan (2010) 'Wangyou lianming zhi Zhang Ziyi gongkaixin: Wuda yiwen zhizhi pianmu zhajuan' [Netizens send Zhang Ziyi an open letter raising five questions about her 'fake' donations], *Chengdu Shangbao*, 2 March, http://media.people.com.cn/GB/40606 /11051747.html. Accessed 29 June 2010.

'Q&A: Zhang Ziyi' (2010) *China Daily*, 16 March, www.chinadaily.com.cn/china/2010-03/16/content_9594056.htm. Accessed 10 January 2015.

Schwankert, S. (2010) 'Zhang Ziyi begins to address quake scandal – Chinese Red Cross donation made, but questions remain', *Hollywood Reporter*, 9 February, http://www.hollywoodreporter.com/news/zhang-ziyi-begins-address-quake-20432. Accessed 5 March 2015.

'Sichuan Earthquake: Facts and Figures' (2009) International Federation of Red Cross and Red Cross Societies, 7 May, http://www.ifrc.org/Docs/pubs/disasters/sichuan-earthquake/ff070509.pdf. Accessed 29 June 2010.

Song Jianqin (2010) 'Zhang Ziyi shankuan zhijin xialuobuming' [The nature of Zhang Ziyi's donations is still unknown], *Tianfu Zaobao*, 30 January, 14, http://morning.scol.com.cn/new/html/tfzb/20100130/tfzb334529.html. Accessed 9 February 2015.

Song, S., Yin, H., and Guo, Q. (2010) 'Superstar Zhang Ziyi dogged by scandals', People's Daily, 9 February, http://english.people.com.cn/90001/90782/90875/6885230.html#. Accessed 29 June 2010.

Sun Xunbo (2009) 'Wei gongbu juanzeng buduixian "hemingdantixian" kuanrong cishan' [The non-publication of the 'blacklist' of failed pledges epitomizes the philanthropic spirit of benevolence], People.com, 27 April, http://gongyi.people.com.cn/ GB/9200160.html. Accessed 29 June 2010.

Tan, L. (2009) 'Zhang Ziyi sexy beach photo scandal', Chinese-tools.com, 5 January, http://www.chinese-tools.com/china/people/2009-01-05-zhang-ziyi-beach-scandal.html. Accessed 10 January 2015.

Tao Tao (2009) 'Jin qi cheng wangmin renwei baoguang "laijuansiyehemingdan"' [Almost 70 per cent of netizens think a donation blacklist should be published], *Zhongguo Qingnian Bao*, 4 May, http://mnc.people.com.cn/GB/9229806.html. Accessed 10 January 2015.

'The Story of Donations Gate' (2008) *EastSouthWestNorth*, 29 May, www.zonaeuropa.com/20080529_1.htm. Accessed 10 January 2015.

'US Company Contributions for Earthquake Relief' (2008) US–China Business Council, 25 June.

Wang, Z. (2008) 'Quake triggers donation deluge', *China Daily*, 5 December, http://www.chinadaily.com.cn/china/2008-12/05/content_7273896.htm. Accessed 10 January 2015.

Watts, J. (2008) 'Sichuan earthquake: Tragedy brings new mood of unity', *The Guardian*, 10 June, http://www.guardian.co.uk/world/2008/jun/10/chinaearthquake.china. Accessed 10 January 2015.

'Who's Behind the Zhang Ziyi "Black Paint Incident"?' (2009) ChannelNewsAsia.com, 29 December, http://www.channelnewsasia.com/stories/entertainment/view/1027507/1/.html. Accessed 29 June 2010.

Wood, S. (2007) 'Egos without borders: Mapping the new celebrity philanthropy', *Bitch Magazine*, http://bitchmagazine.org/article/egos-without-borders. Accessed 10 January 2015.

Xiao, K. (2010) 'Disasters offer chance for charity to get professional', *Global Times*, 26 April, http://china-wire.org/?p=5087. Accessed 10 January 2015.

Yao, B. (ed.) (2008) 'Do public lists showing quake donations by the rich serve a purpose? No price on love', *Beijing Review*, 25 June, http://www.bjreview.com.cn/forum/txt/2008-06/14/content_127482.htm. Accessed 10 January 2015.

Yao, K., and Wang, A. (2013) 'China lets Gini out of the bottle; wide wealth gap', *Reuters*, 18 January, http://www.reuters.com/article/2013/01/18/us-china-economy-income-gap-idUSBRE90H06L20130118. Accessed 10 January 2015.

Yuan Lei (2007) 'Wang Shuo shuoshuo shuo' [Wang Shuo talks], *Nanfang Zhoumo*, 18 May, http://www.infzm.com/content/591. Accessed 29 June 2010.

Zang, X. (2008) 'Market transition, wealth and status claims', in D.S.G. Goodman (ed.) *The New Rich in China: Future Rulers, Present Lives*, London: Routledge, pp. 53–70.

Zhang Yimou (dir.) (1999) *The Road Home*, motion picture, Hong Kong: Columbia Pictures Film Production Asia.

Zhang Yimou (dir.) (2002) *Yingxiong* [Hero], motion picture, Beijing: Beijing New Picture Film Corporation.

Zhang Yimou (dir.) (2004) *House of Flying Daggers*, motion picture, Beijing: Beijing New Picture Film Corporation.

'Zhang Ziyi' (2014) Wikipedia, http://en.wikipedia.org/wiki/Zhang_Ziyi. Accessed 10 January 2015.

'Zhang Ziyi 100 wan meijin de 5.12 dizhen juankuan ta zai nali?' [Where Is Zhang Ziyi's One Million Dollar Donation to the 12 May Sichuan Earthquake?] (2010) *Tianya Zatan*, 31 January, http://www.tianya.cn/publicforum/content/free/1/1800993.shtml. Accessed 29 June 2010.

'Zhang Ziyi jiu dizhen juankuan fa shengming jiang rushi gongbu zhangmumingxi' [Zhang Ziyi Makes an Announcement about the Earthquake Donations: She Will Reveal All Details] (2010) *Xinjing Bao*, 29 June, http://www.bjnews.com.cn/news/2010/01/29/6571.html. Accessed 9 March 2015.

'Zhang Ziyi Sues US Website over Bo Xilai Link Claims' (2012) *The Straits Times*, 4 October, http://www.straitstimes.com/breaking-news/lifestyle/story/zhang-ziyi-sues-us-website-over-bo-xilai-link-claims-20121004. Accessed 10 January 2015.

'Zhang Ziyi to Use Funds from Cannes Charity Drive to Build Children's Shelter' (2010) ChannelNewsAsia.com, 2 June, http://www.channelnewsasia.com/stories/ entertainment/view/1060575/1/.html. Accessed 29 June 2010.

'Zhang Ziyi xuanbujuan 100 wan, cheng "guojia you nan, pifuzuoze"' [Zhang Ziyi Pledges One Million Saying 'when the country is in trouble, everyone must do their duty'] (2008) Ent. QQ.com, 16 May, http://ent.qq.com/a/20080516/000047.htm. Accessed 29 June 2010.

'Zhongguo cishan paihangbang fabu "lai juan qiye heimingdan" liuchan' [China's Philanthropy List Is Published: The 'Blacklist' of Companies that Failed to Honour Their Pledges Is Aborted] (2009) *Jinghua Shibao*, 25 April, http://news.sohu.com/20090425/n263610850.shtml. Accessed 29 June 2010.

Zhou Qiuguang and Zeng Guilin (2006) *Zhongguo cishan jianshi* [A Short History of Charity in China], Beijing: Renmin Chubanshe.

Zhou, R. (2010a) 'Actress denies charity fraud', *China Daily*, 16 March, http://www.chinadaily.com.cn/china/2010-03/16/content_9593921.htm. Accessed 9 January 2015.

Zhou, R. (2010b) 'Clearing her name', *China Daily*, 16 March, http://www.chinadaily.com.cn/life/2010-03/16/content_9596922.htm. Accessed 9 January 2015.

Zong He (2010) 'Zhang Ziyi shouci huiying "juankuanmen"' [Zhang Ziyi responds to the 'donation-gate scandal' for the first time], *Nanfang Zhoumo*, 16 March, http://www.infzm.com/content/42651. Accessed 29 June 2010.

'Zongshuji de jiakuai cishanshiye fazhan dongyuanling' [General Secretary Issues a Mobilization Order to Speed up the Development of Philanthropic Undertakings] (2009) *Zhongguo Wenming Wang*, 4 February, http://www.ahwenming.com/newsinfo.aspx?ContentID=1194. Accessed 29 June 2010.

Chapter 10

Shakira, Ricky Martin and Celanthropic Latinidad in the Americas

Paul Allatson

The Colombian Shakira (Shakira Isabel Mebarak Ripoll) and the Puerto Rican Ricky Martin (Enrique Martín Morales) are globally famous music stars and, if the US English-language media is a guide, key figures in the popularization of the so-called 1990s Latin Boom in music beyond the Latin(o) American market – Latin(o) American here signifying Latin American and US Latino entities. Outside the realms of popular culture and the global music industries, through which they have sold millions upon millions of recordings, their work as philanthropists is, arguably, less well-known.

Shakira established her Fundación Pies Descalzos (Barefoot Foundation) in Colombia in 2003, out of an antecedent dating from the late 1990s when she was 18. The Foundation's aim, as the official website proclaims, is 'to ensure that every Colombian child can exercise their right to a quality education. Our model targets displaced and vulnerable communities by addressing their unique needs' (Fundación Pies Descalzos 2013). La Fundación Ricky Martin (Ricky Martin Foundation) was launched in 2004 with its first project, The People for Children, which assists children rescued from human trafficking in a number of continents (Martin 2012). Both performers are involved in the Fundación América Latina en Acción Solidaria (ALAS) (Latin America in Solidarity Action Foundation), which Shakira helped establish in 2006. Shakira and Ricky Martin are UNICEF Goodwill Ambassadors. On 5 October 2011, US President Barack Obama appointed Shakira to be part of the White House Initiative on Educational Excellence for Hispanics ('Presidentes Obama y Santos y Shakira hablaron en la Cumbre de las Américas' 2012). For his work against the trafficking in children, Martin was named by the US Department of State as one of the Heroes in Ending Modern-Day Slavery in 2005 (Ricky Martin Foundation official website n.d.).

The artists are pursued relentlessly by the international Spanish- and English-language media industries as sources of regular 'hot copy'. Shakira was ranked by *Forbes* magazine in 2014 at 58 on its list of the 100 most powerful women in the world (Howard 2014). Shakira and Martin are among the top 100 Twitter global users, as calculated by the number of followers, with Shakira appearing in early 2015 at number 15 (well ahead of Bill Gates at 33), and Ricky Martin in the top 90 (Twitter Counter 2015). In March 2014, Shakira's page on Facebook became the most-'liked' page in Facebook history, with nearly 90 million friends ('Shakira Has the Most-"Liked" Page on Facebook' 2014). This social media influence is impressive in matching, and at times surpassing, that of celebrity philanthropists from North America; in March 2014, for example, Angelina Jolie had under 5 million Facebook likes, while Lady Gaga's 'like' count was over 60 million.

Both personalities accord with Matthew Bishop's (2008) definition of the new 'celanthropists': 'celebrities who are adept and professional at using their brand and wealth to play an important role in tackling social issues'. Yet, Bishop also argues that such celanthropy can be explained as a Northern, read US, mode of celebrity philanthropy translocated to or imposed on the global South. As he says of Shakira, 'A pop superstar is trying to take North American philanthropy south, with help from some plutocratic hangers-on, such as Carlos Slim Helú and members of the golden Buffett clan' (Bishop 2008).

In this chapter, however, I eschew the argument that a US mode of celanthropy both overdetermines and explains celanthropic work outside of North America. Indeed, I propose that Shakira and Martin are simultaneously at philanthropic home in the so-called global North (US) and the global South (Colombia and Puerto Rico), and on global levels that dwarf those national locations. With this focus, which accepts a priori that conceptualizations like global North and South are arbitrary and prone to collapse under scrutiny, the chapter adds to scholarship on Latin(o) celebrity in communication, cultural and media studies (Fiol-Matta 2002; Negrón-Muntaner 2004; Sandoval-Sánchez 2003; Fuchs 2007; Valdivia 2008; Beltrán 2009), and to critical interest in celebrity philanthropy as a growing global phenomenon (Cooper 2007; Cottle and Nolan 2007; West 2007; Dieter and Kumar 2008; 't Hart and Tindall 2009; Bishop and Green 2010; Sulek 2010; Tsaliki, Frangonikolopoulos and Huliaras 2011; Colapinto 2012; Kapoor 2013; Brockington 2014; Hassid and Jeffreys 2015). Accordingly, I locate Shakira's and Martin's celebrity philanthropy in a geospatial construct, the Spanish-speaking Americas, without the traditions of philanthropy understood in western capitalist and state terms. I argue that Shakira's and Martin's celebrity *and* philanthropy must be assessed as related historical products of the global mass-media industries in English and Spanish, historical legacies of underdevelopment and US interventions, and transborder community aspirations and formations in the Americas.

The chapter proceeds with an overview of philanthropic-like traditions and new philanthropic enterprises in the Americas, which indicate that while the celanthropy of Shakira and Martin has affinities with North American models, it is also informed by longstanding Latin American charitable and volunteer traditions. I then discuss the artists' philanthropic work in relation to other national and continental legacies, and to a transnational ideal of Latin(o) American identity or sense of latinidad, one enabled by the artists' identificatory connections to their home countries, the continent more broadly and the US itself, commonly cited as the world's second largest Spanish-speaking country. These shifting locations assist the artists in fashioning themselves as embodiments of celanthropic latinidad. Yet, as I demonstrate that self-fashioning also exposes Shakira and Martin and their work to criticisms about celebrity self-interest and apolitical approaches to pressing development issues, as well as about what their particular embrace of latinidad might signify in the US setting. The chapter ends by proposing that, however ambivalent it may be, Shakira's and Martin's pragmatic, yet at times effective, celanthropic latinidad demonstrate how transborder community aspirations in the Americas challenge readings of celebrity and philanthropy as phenomena emanating from the global North only.

Philanthropic Enterprise in Latin(o) America

Scholarship on philanthropy in Latin America and among US Latino communities indicates that a number of philanthropic-like traditions are evident across the Americas ('Latino Philanthropy Literature Review' 2003; Sanborn and Portocarrero 2005; Watson 2008). These traditions include charity work, voluntarism and non-state social welfare support for the poor, as well as religious giving, again largely voluntary, within the Catholic Church apparatus. In addition, *mutualistas* (mutual-aid and self-help associations), clubs and other support organizations were established by specific local communities and immigrant groups from the mid-1800s onwards. Finally, scholars have identified a deeply adhered-to convention among the continent's elites to fund building projects and to donate resources to causes relating to children, education, arts and culture, as well as disaster relief.

The first critical survey of philanthropy in Latin America, *Philanthropy and Social Change in Latin America* (Sanborn and Portocarrero 2005), confirms this generalized assessment in its identification of philanthropic work in seven Latin American countries: Argentina, Brazil, Chile, Colombia, Ecuador, Mexico and Peru. In her overview of the continent, Cynthia Sanborn (2005: 3–29) notes that, notwithstanding the paucity and unreliability of data, three common areas of philanthropic attention are identifiable in the continent: education, health, and arts and culture. For some countries, moreover, community development, active citizenship and human rights are also drivers of philanthropy. Sanborn (2005) points out that the continent's first independent philanthropic foundations, as would be understood in North American terms, date back only to the 1990s, and that they marked a secular shift away from an historical record characterized largely by socio-economic elite contributions to Catholic Church charity initiatives in education and health.

Tom Watson (2008), publisher of the online resource On Philanthropy, provides an overview of Latin American philanthropic trends in the twenty-first century. Some of those trends resist being aligned with North American paradigms given the long historical traditions of voluntarism, often associated with the Catholic Church and Sociedades de Beneficiencia Pública (Secular Societies of Social Benefit), and with Mutual Aid Societies that were formed by immigrants from specific countries, such as China, Italy, Japan and Spain, in the nineteenth and early twentieth centuries. These organizations operated under clear religious or immigrant community rubrics of charity, and focused on providing voluntary funding for social welfare and such services as health and education.

For Watson (2008), the first contemporary philanthropic trend in Latin America is that evangelical Christian and some Muslim actors are now competing with the Catholic Church in funding charitable works, and providing local and national advocacy and support to marginal communities over human rights abuses. A second philanthropic trend is 'Foundation philanthropy', still a weak sector given that tax incentives do not generally encourage Latin America's elite to set up foundations in the way that US-based not-for-profit organizations routinely fund specific services and target philanthropic causes. Given their successes, Shakira and Martin would thus be Latin American leaders in this area. A third trend involves the corporate sector's growing 'social engagement and philanthropic budgets' that suggest a continent-wide move away from mere social responsibility towards corporate support for philanthropic enterprises (Watson 2008). Watson's fourth trend refers to the rise of individual giving as typified by the work of Shakira and Martin, two supercelebrities from among a host of Latin American artists, musicians, actors and sportspeople to have attained international 'star' recognition since the 1990s. For Watson (2008), 'Their visibility and growing wealth has been accompanied by their public commitment to philanthropic efforts, raising the visibility of voluntary commitment to community and establishing philanthropy as a form of societal leadership'. The ALAS Foundation that Shakira helped found, and whose core members include Martin and many of Latin America's leading popular musicians and singers, exemplifies this trend.

By contrast with the scant work on Latin America, most extant studies of Latino philanthropy in the US date from the 1980s and 1990s, and were underwritten by a purported concern with the challenge of galvanizing Latino philanthropy given the lack of philanthropic traditions among US Latino communities as understood in capitalist and US state and philanthropic history terms (Gonzales 1985; Gallegos and O'Neill 1991; Nuiry 1992; Cortes 1995; De la Garza 1997; Campoamor, Diaz and Ramos 1999; Ramos 1999; Ball, Lowe and Phillips 2002). Poverty, socio-economic and political marginalization from the broader US community, the centrality of the family and the power of the Catholic Church in many Latinos' lives were cited as reasons for the absence of Latino philanthropy (Miranda 1999). Yet, the research does reveal a long history of religious giving within the Catholic Church apparatus, as well as the existence of *mutualistas*, clubs and other support organizations, as far back as the mid-1800s (Gonzales 1985). Critics have also noted the transborder links of such organizations with regard to Caribbean- and Mexican-origin Latino communities, and some have identified that a philanthropic drive in remittance flows from the US, most notably in times of natural disaster, but also as a form of binational community building and local infrastructure development (Cervantes 2003; The 2009 Index of Global Philanthropy and Remittances 2009). Yet another study notes a clear rise in US Latino philanthropic foundations from the late 1980s to the early 2000s, and confirms that when Latinos give to charity, their priorities are to causes relating to children, education, arts and culture or to disaster relief in home countries and local communities ('Latino Philanthropy Literature Review' 2003). Again, this is akin to the historically active philanthropy-like traditions across Latin America.

It is thus arguable to a point that the high-profile philanthropic enterprises established by Latino celebrities such as Martin and Shakira are a mass-mediated, transnational evolution of earlier Latin American and Latino philanthropic traditions that now overlap with, and are inflected by, so-called 'North American philanthropy' (Bishop 2008). As Shakira's and Martin's foundations demonstrate, the stars' primary focuses have been on causes related to children's welfare and education. Shakira is explicit on this, 'The benefits are clear, and they help us all: education reduces poverty, decreases violence, and lessens gender inequality. A single year of primary education can mean a 10 to

20 per cent increase in a woman's wages later in life' (Shakira 2013). Martin, too, states that education is central to his philanthropy, 'Education has been our pillar from the outset' (Martin 2012). Both celebrities have contributed to disaster-relief initiatives, for example, fund-raising or providing structural support for the victims of the 2010 Haiti earthquake ('Ricky Martin and Habitat's CEO, Jonathan Reckford, Travel to Haiti in Support of Habitat's Haitian Recovery Efforts' 2010; Gray 2011). They are active in a range of arts and culture enterprises, including the already noted ALAS. Shakira and Martin acknowledge their Catholic backgrounds, the importance of family and their middle-class origins as contextual frames for their philanthropic work (Martin 2010; Cobo 2011). Yet, other transnational legacies and historical links in the Americas also ground and inform the stars' particular approaches to celanthropy.

Continental Legacies and Celanthropic Latinidad

Shakira and Martin are actors in the celanthropic pantheon as understood in the global North; but the same argument can be made of their celanthropy in the global South, in Puerto Rico and Colombia, and the Spanish-speaking world more broadly. It is important here to recall that Puerto Rico is a Caribbean island with the dubious distinction of being the world's longest-running colony, first under Spain, then the US. The latter ruler was responsible for the mass exodus of some half of the island's population to the US mainland under its 'Operation Bootstrap' modernization program in the 1940s and 1950s (Allatson 2007: 152). That exodus made the Puerto Rican diaspora into a distinct Latino historical minority, alongside the more populous Mexican-American/Chicano sector. It also reflected how US rule of the island was overdetermined by Cold War logics and imperatives: Puerto Rico was seen by successive US administrations as a bulwark against communism, and therefore as a geocultural space to be reformed in US-friendly, capitalist ways (Allatson 2007: 152). Shakira comes from Colombia, a country grappling with the unresolved legacies of economic underdevelopment, poverty and racial inequity. Since the 1960s, it has also struggled with armed conflict involving successive federal administrations, left-wing guerrilla and separatist movements, right-wing paramilitary groups, the state's own armed forces, and well-armed drug-trafficking cartels, over which the US has been a shadowy, and at times, sinister influence (Grandin 2006; Yaffe 2011). Moreover, Colombia has been one of the frontline Latin American states in the so-called War on Drugs. That 'War' has been prosecuted by successive US administrations since the 1970s, and has involved enormous military and financial contributions and interventions in attempts to constrain the territorial influence of the drug cartels (Ronderos 2003).

In their public statements and the briefs of the organizations they have founded or been linked to, Martin and Shakira self-consciously appeal to their national origins as keys to understanding their philanthropic work. They also acknowledge the US's role in the persistence of poverty and socio-economic and political power imbalances in Puerto Rico and Colombia, respectively, and the need to address historical legacies of exploitation in the continent more broadly. Martin, for example, used his musical status and popularity to critique US naval use, until 2003, of the Puerto Rican island of Vieques as a missile-testing site. This use was widely regarded in Puerto Rico as symptomatic of the island's fraught colonial relationship with, and dependency on, the US (Falcón 2001; Rojas 2013). He brought the issue to the attention of his fans and wider audiences during acceptance speeches at the 1999 Billboard Awards and at the 2001 MTV Music Awards, where he stated, 'some kids [...] wake up every morning in a little island in the Caribbean called Vieques listening to explosions due to some military exercises' (Rojas 2013: 501). Martin has also supported demands for the release of pro-independence Puerto Rican activists, such as Oscar López Rivera, in US jails on political grounds (Kurshan 2013).

Shakira's philanthropic sense of self is anchored in her native Colombia, and informed by the singer's recognition of the need to address the historical legacies of entrenched socio-economic inequality, and the impact that armed and ideological conflict has had on the country since the 1960s. One of her Foundation's schools in the remote northwestern province of Choco, for example, opened with some 750 pupils in the late 2000s, all the victims of internal population displacement as a result of decades of civil conflict (Mirchandani 2009). Indeed, Colombia continues to lead the world in its numbers of internally displaced people, estimated by the UNHCR at between 4.9 and 5.5 million ('Internally Displaced People Figures' 2015). This means that millions of Colombian children are outside the existing school system, and there is no structural state support for addressing the country's half-century of armed conflict and attendant trauma. Counteracting the combined effects of poverty and displacement drives how Shakira's Fundación Pies Descalzos makes decisions about where to build schools and what to fund. At the school in Choco, the Foundation covers tuition, school supplies and uniforms, and 'their only daily guarantee of a meal' (Mirchandani 2009).

That said, Martin's and Shakira's approaches to celanthropy impel further historicization and contextualization, given they come to an ambivalent junction in the US. In that nationalized space, both Shakira and Martin are 'tropicalized', to use Frances Aparicio and Susana Chávez-Silverman's term, as 'hot Latins' (1997), and yet both also at times self-identify as Latinos. This identity is understood as US-enabled panethnic identifications or latinidades that transcend, but do not negate, identifications based on national origin or historical minority status (Caminero-Santangelo 2007: 1–35).

For instance, on the 2012 re-election of President Obama, who garnered the support of a majority of US Latinos, Martin said,

> As a Latino Puerto Rican U.S. citizen that can vote for the president, it was very beautiful to see minorities getting together for democracy, for freedom, for civil rights. We are part of this country and we move this country as well. We have a voice. And apparently we were very loud.
>
> (quoted in Ramos 2012)

The conjunction of 'Latino Puerto Rican U.S. citizen' here is highly unusual. If it conveys something of a desperate desire to cover many identity bases, it nonetheless does point to Martin's sense of identificatory multiplicity, which can be expanded further to include male, white, middle-class, performing artist, and, since 2010, gay.

As for Shakira, the critic María Elena Cepeda (2010: 63) argues that 'through her music and through her public persona, [Shakira] shapes both in- and out-group notions of what it means to be not only Latina but also *colombiana*'. Cepeda also highlights a suite of identifications, including 'Lebanese-Colombian, Caribbean-Colombian, female, popular performer, and recent U.S. migrant' that indicate how Shakira at once embodies and adds complexity to 'a sense of *Latinidad* and *colombianidad* both within and outside U.S. borders' (2010: 63). To Shakira's multiple subject positions I would add celebrity and philanthropist, for these are identificatory prisms through which she is also 'read' on a global level, beyond her music-star status. The same can be said of Martin as well.

When viewed from the US, the complex panethnic and transnational subject positions occupied by the two artists are significant. They indicate that Shakira and Martin are subject to the highly charged racial-ethnic contours of US identity discourses about national belonging, which have long troped Latinos as somehow alien and/or threatening to the US national imaginary (Allatson 2004). When deployed by anti-immigrant spokespeople, such discourses regard all Latinos as forming a cohesive and coherent grouping. The discourses thus obscure how heterogeneous collective communities – 16 per cent of the total US population, or some 50.5 million people, as at the 2010 Census (Ennis, Ríos-Vargas and Albert 2011) – include diverse peoples and communities with origins across the Americas, and contain significant middle and upper classes, and highly visible, wealthy, educated, media-savvy, politically astute and influential individuals, including the two celebrities at the heart of this chapter.

Shakira and Martin appear to have taken pragmatic advantage of the rise of latinidades in the US since the 1980s to redefine themselves, and therefore their celanthropy function, to use Foucault's conceptualization of an author in a new mass-mediated context, as Latin(o) American artists and spokespeople (Foucault 2007). That is, their primary identifications might be anchored in non-US spaces, but their simultaneous at-homeliness in the US as self-identifying Latin(o)s also enables them to market themselves, however superficially, as literal embodiments of how the differences within and between Latino sectors in that country, and by extension, within and between Latin Americans anywhere, can be overcome. Thus, if their philanthropic work evokes that spearheaded by the likes of numerous super-rich film and music stars in the US, it is also informed by a discourse of latinidad enabled within US borders and activated in Latin America more broadly in what I call a form of celanthropic latinidad.

This celanthropic and identificatory combination has not been without its critics. As the next section details, the artists' celanthropic latinidad is haunted by imperial and capitalist legacies in the Americas, particularly those affecting the US's Latino sectors. Additionally, their celanthropy draws intense media scrutiny, speculation and critique.

Critiques of Celanthropic Latinidad

Clearly, neither Shakira nor Martin are 'typical' Latin(o) Americans, given their wealth and global celebrity status. Moreover, as this section explains, neither artist has been immune to mass-mediated and scholarly interrogation of their identities, their celanthropic work and motives and their private lives. Noting the relocation of many Latin American and Spanish music stars to the US, whose ranks include Shakira and Martin, the Nuyorican cultural critic Alberto Sandoval-Sánchez (2003) has been scathing about what he regards as those 'star' performers' appropriations of an acceptable Latino status. While accepting that such celebrities inevitably contribute to 'the construction and production of U.S. Latino/a identity and the reconnection and recovery of their Latin American roots', their occupation of that identity, he asserts, marginalizes and excludes 'other talented U.S. Latinos/as' (Sandoval-Sánchez 2003: 17–18). Similar observations have been made by Frances Negrón-Muntaner (2004: 268) of Martin, who once famously claimed, 'I am Puerto Rico'. Martin, she states, is so closely associated with Puerto Rico as its purported living embodiment because his US success and attendant 'acceptable' Latino status are predicated on the self-conscious construction of his persona and music as 'modern, technologically advanced, white, and middle-class', as opposed to the island's stereotypical representation as primitive, black and working-class (Negrón-Muntaner 2004: 268). Such criticisms also have in common a sense that Martin, like Shakira, occupies what Cepeda (2010: 63) calls, 'the interstices between the Latin American and the U.S. Latino contained within the rubric of Latinidad'. These celebrities, it would seem, invite scrutiny over their Latin(o) credentials precisely because of their exceptional, interstitial, indeed cosmopolitan, celebrity status.

Sandoval-Sánchez (2003) articulates neatly the political stakes in the critique of Latin American celebrities when articulated from a US Latino perspective. In his words,

> If U.S. Latinos/as are conditioned by the dynamics of domestic colonialism, Ricky must be placed within the context of imperial colonialism. Given that he has crossed over to the English music world, he is seen as a foreigner who has a good command of English, contributing in this way to perpetuate the stereotype of Latinos/as as foreigners and recent immigrants.
>
> (Sandoval-Sánchez 2003: 18)

For Sandoval-Sánchez, who was born in Puerto Rico but has lived for many decades in the US, the white Martin articulates an ideal of Latino privilege that does not relate to the lived experiences of many millions of non-white Latinos in the US. Nor does Martin's well-known support for Puerto Rican independence acknowledge the historical realities of Puerto Rican dependency on the US (2003: 18). As Sandoval-Sánchez (2003: 18) says, Martin's 'ignorance of racism in the U.S. and how Puerto Ricans are seen as people of color distances him from the trials and tribulations of U.S. Latinos/as in respect to their economic and social inequality'. For Sandoval-Sánchez (2003: 17), Shakira too exemplifies the Latin American celebrity who provides an acceptable face to latinidad in the US setting. Moreover, her interstitial location between Latin America and Latin(o) America has also exposed her to accusations of being an apolitical operator and unwilling to take stands on pressing political matters such as opposing Colombia's left-wing guerrilla group FARC (Malcomson 2009), despite the fact that she is on record for appealing to FARC leadership to end their armed struggle (Bishop 2008).

Media criticisms of Martin have also at times been intense, focusing for much of his celebrity career on the disjunction between, on the one hand, his socially progressive public statements and philanthropic activities, and, on the other hand, his highly scrutinized, because 'closeted', private life. Indeed, in his autobiography, Martin himself discusses the personal impact of that disjunction (Martin 2010). His fatherhood of two boys via a not fully understood donor arrangement embroiled him in public debates over celebrity parenthood, but not quite like the debates that dog Madonna and Brad Pitt and Angelina Jolie (Ayers 2011; see also Bell, in this book). His admission of his homosexuality in 2010 and support for LGBTQ people in the Americas (Martin 2010, 251–78) are contrasted with his appearance on the stage of the 2001 inauguration of President George W. Bush, Jr., which sent a message of political and moral conservatism to his fan base, which he now regrets (Martin 2010). After Martin announced his desire to marry his then partner, Carlos González Abella, a Puerto Rican financial analyst and stock broker who shared parenting of Martin's sons, Matteo and Valentino, media speculation across the Spanish-speaking world focused on whether or not Martin would, in fact, take up the Spanish Government's offer of citizenship to enable the couple to marry (Galaz 2011).

As a global celebrity, Shakira, too, has been the target of intense media attention. But, perhaps most telling have been media investigations into ALAS, headquartered in Panama City, which she co-founded. Until April 2014, ALAS's Honorary President was the Colombian Nobel Laureate for Literature, Gabriel García Márquez. The Foundation's website maintains that it aims to 'mobilize Latin-American society towards the implementation of integrated early childhood public policies, so that every child from zero to six years old has access to health plans, education and nutrition' (América Latina en Acción Solidaria [ALAS] 2013). Shakira and Martin are 'activistas' in ALAS, along with dozens of Latin American and Latino music stars. For Scott Malcomson (2009), Shakira's work with ALAS seemed to represent a new philanthropic model: it targeted disadvantage not in 'distant lands' but on the continent in which Shakira and ALAS's roster of supporters lived. Moreover, the range of international and corporate involvement, and ALAS's philanthropic ambition, were unprecedented. In Malcomson's words,

> They have a policy focus—early-childhood nutrition, education and medical care—that is on a scale beyond the reach of private charity. It requires the steady effort of the state. It cannot be addressed by rich countries' check-writing. So the trick is to take pop celebrity,

marry it to big business and permanently alter the way Latin American governments help care for the young and the poor.

(Malcomson 2009)

However, Shakira could not dodge damage to her celanthropic reputation given the Foundation's failure to deliver on its promises. Worse were the allegations of financial mismanagement on the part of her then fiancé, Antonio De la Rúa, son of an ex-President of Argentina and ALAS's Vice-President, and of the executive director of ALAS, Carlos Clemente, who was indicted on corruption charges in Colombia alongside Shakira's then lawyer, José María Michavila (Rodríguez 2009). ALAS's original mission was to fund programs to help needy children. Its stated mission today, however, is to be a social movement that does not fund programs (América Latina en Acción Solidaria [ALAS] 2013). The Foundation's only achievements seem to have been two megaconcerts, held on 17 May 2008: Shakira and others artists performed in Buenos Aires before 180,000 people; in Mexico City, Martin and others performed before an estimated live audience of 200,000 people ('Reunió concierto ALAS a 380 mil personas en México y Argentina' 2008). Neither concert was followed with the promised schools in poor parts of Buenos Aires or Mexico City, despite commitments of USD 200 million from the Mexican Carlos Slim Helú, then the world's richest person, and Howard Buffett, son of the noted US philanthropist Warren Buffett; but both concerts did bolster the celebrity status of the stars involved (Palm 2009; Rodríguez 2009). By 2009, the ALAS enterprise had generated a transnational philanthropy scandal involving five countries: Argentina, Colombia, Costa Rica, Spain and Panama (Palm 2009). Controversies and transnational court cases, in part related to ALAS, continued. De la Rúa sued Shakira for USD 100 million in September 2012 as purported compensation for sacrificing his own career to support Shakira's rise to musical superstardom (Farrés 2013; see also Moreno 2012). Since separating from De la Rúa, Shakira subsequently met and became romantically involved with the Catalan soccer player Gerard Piqué, who plays for Futbol Club Barcelona. This relationship has enabled Shakira to distance herself from the ALAS fall out, given that she, Piqué and their son Milan are now irrevocably part of Spanish and European celebrity discourse. Renewed media interest in Shakira in the US was bolstered by her role as a judge on the US TV music competition, *The Voice*, in 2013 and 2014 (Cruz and Muñoz 2013), which has also helped reinvigorate Shakira's mass-mediated celebrity wellbeing.

The journalistic laying bare of ALAS's financial problems, and the intense media scrutiny of Shakira and Martin's private lives, demonstrates that celanthropy poses potential risks to the celebrities involved in terms of damaged brands and personal reputations (see Jeffreys, in this book). To such media attention is added academic interrogation of their fluid identifications, particularly when moving between the US and the celebrities' homes based in Latin America. That scrutiny and attention, moreover, may distract from and impede assessments of the efficacy of the philanthropic work undertaken by celebrities such as Shakira and Martin, the focus of this chapter's next section.

Celanthropic Latinidad on the Ground

While dealing with intense media scrutiny and journalistic sleuthing for celebrity scandal fodder, Shakira and Martin have claimed to raise public awareness in numerous countries about the global traffic in children, and the importance of early childhood literacy, nutrition and health care as paths out of poverty. This suggests that their celanthropy function rests on their capacities to influence socio-economic change. They do not simply raise international awareness of the issues they care about. They can also request commitments from key political, NGO, corporate and celebrity social actors with the requisite financial and political capital to affect on-the-ground change ('t Hart and Tindall 2009). That approach may reflect how celanthropic latinidad could be signalling a Latin American-modulated mode of philanthropy that conjoins Bishop's (2008) notion of 'Northern' celebrity philanthropy with Latin American traditions among middle and upper classes of helping out, charity and community service.

In this, Shakira and Martin appear to conform to journalist Gibbs' (2005) argument that the philanthropy they practice, nationally and internationally, is characterized by an effective drive to provide a material basis on which the most marginalized denizens of Latin American and other states may gain some socio-economic leverage on the arduous trajectory away from poverty and labour exploitation. Moreover, Shakira and Martin have proved adept at corralling representatives of national governments, including a host of Presidents and Prime Ministers, NGOs, multinational companies, the UN and UNICEF, not to mention millions of their fans, into supporting their philanthropic visions.

For their part, Matthew Bishop and Michael Green (2010: xi) include Shakira as part of the select roster of celebrities who are spearheading the new 'philanthrocapitalism', which they define as a movement among the super-rich 'focused on tackling the world's toughest problems through effective giving'. They also laud her for her 'impressive philanthrocapitalistic brand' ('Did it Work?' 2011). As many journalists have discovered, Shakira's so-called 'brand' has such import that Presidents and other government officials from countries across Latin America, the super-rich in the US and Latin America and even the King of Spain, regularly appear at events she has organized or been involved with in her quest to ensure that children from Colombia and other states will be educated and provided with health care (Bishop 2008; Malcomson 2009). To date, Shakira's Barefoot Foundation has funded eight schools in Colombia (Cobo 2014), and claims to ensure that 5,000-plus children annually receive an education from day care through to primary and secondary levels (Fundación Pies Descalzos 2013). The Foundation has also expanded its operations into Haiti and South Africa, and now claims to be teaching some 30,000 children annually in three countries (Fundación Pies Descalzos 2013).

While the Ricky Martin Foundation has yet to release data on the numbers of children it has assisted, it is clear that the Foundation's Global Awareness initiative is predicated on utilizing celebrities as so-called 'popular educators', raising international awareness of the traffic in children. As a statement on the Foundation website proclaims,

Global Awareness enables us to inform the world of this heinous crime and mobilize people by participating in forums, workshops, media interventions and advocacy efforts. Working in partnership as well as by following a multi-sector alliance model involving civil society, inter-governmental organizations, and the private sector solidifies our mission. To be effective in our goal we advocate for the prevention and protection of this most vulnerable segment of the population against all forms of exploitation.
(Ricky Martin Foundation official website n.d.)

That 'multi-sector alliance model' has seen Martin's Foundation team up with numerous partners. In a short piece Martin (2012) wrote for the Foundation's website, 'Stop the scourge of child trafficking', for example, he names an impressive roster of collaborators on the Foundation's Call and Live project, 'the first regional campaign to combat human trafficking in the Americas': UNICEF, the Habitat for Humanity, Johns Hopkins University's Protection Project, the University of Puerto Rico, Save the Children, RTL Foundation, the InterAmerican Development Bank, the Trafficking In Persons Office, SAP, Doral Bank, Microsoft and the International Organization for Migration. One legal historian, Virginia Garrard (2006: 148), credits the Ricky Martin Foundation with playing a pivotal celanthropic role in not simply raising the facts of contemporary trafficking in and slavery of children to public consciousness in the US and elsewhere, but, more effectively, in keeping the issue on the policy agenda of successive US administrations.

It is useful to end this discussion with the public statements Shakira and Martin made in April and May 2010 about pending legislation in Arizona, the now infamous Support Our Law Enforcement and Safe Neighborhoods Act, or Senate Bill 1070 (SB 1070), which allowed Arizona police to detain anyone in that US state perceived to be an illegal alien. In response to one of the most draconian pieces of anti-immigrant legislation ever proposed in the US – it is now law, although in altered form in response to various legal challenges, and continues to influence legislation in many other US states – the artists again appealed to their status as Latinos in opposing the measure. At the award ceremony for the Billboard Prizes for Latin Music held in Puerto Rico in 2010, Martin declared that Arizona's largely Mexican-origin Latino population was 'not alone', and called for an end to such discriminatory legislation (Note 2010). Shakira travelled to the Arizona capital, Phoenix, to express her critique of legislation that she regarded as contravening 'our civil rights' (Note 2010). Of Shakira's statements since 2010, one Latino journalist concludes, 'The Colombian superstar has hits worldwide, and has used her influence in a variety of ways, including working to influence the [US] immigration debate. She took on SB 1070 as being unfair to families and leaving the vulnerable open to abuse' (Musall 2012). Once again, and notwithstanding critiques from US Latinos about Latin American celebrities appropriating latinidades, those celebrities' public opposition to racially determined anti-immigration legislation in Arizona cannot be dismissed lightly. That opposition indicates that the artists' global celanthropy functions in panethnic Latino solidarity terms meaningful in the US setting, yet resonates transnationally, and meaningfully, beyond that state.

Conclusion

There is no question that when it comes to the celebrity functions of philanthropists, we are embroiled in the messy operations of the global mass-media apparatus that produce celebrities for popular consumption, and the equally messy operations of globalization and its capitalist foundations that underwrite the media apparatus as well (see also Bell; Millington; and Van den Bulck, Claessens and Panis, in this book). Yet, equally it is too neat and simplistic to dismiss the philanthropic work of figures such as Shakira and Martin as only serving the interests of, and benefiting from, the celebrity-generating branches of that apparatus.

More to the point, Shakira's and Martin's celebrity *and* philanthropy are best understood as related historical products of capitalism, the mass media in two global languages at least, and the legacies of underdevelopment and transborder community aspirations in the Americas. An understanding of celebrity philanthropy as formed, critiqued in, and from, the so-called global North is inadequate in grappling with celanthropy that is clearly also anchored in the global South. Perhaps the most important conclusion to be drawn from Shakira's and Martin's celanthropic latinidad, therefore, is that clear-cut distinctions between the so-called global North and South are rendered nonsensical when the celebrities themselves enjoy a privileged homeliness across multiple national, cultural and linguistic borders. Indeed, the artists' pragmatic if controversial embrace of US Latino identification does not simply highlight the transformations of US-based latinidades into new transnational discourses of affiliation. Those transformations indicate the need to question many of the discursive assumptions about celebrity formation and celanthropic enterprise, particularly when conceived as emanating from and operating in the global North and/or in English only.

Acknowledgements

This research was supported under the Australian Research Council's Discovery Projects (DP0985710) funding schemes. I would also like to thank my collaborator Elaine Jeffreys, and the contributors to this collection, for their patience and goodwill.

References

Allatson, P. (2004) *Latino Dreams: Transcultural Traffic and the U.S. National Imaginary*, Amsterdam; New York: Rodopi.

Allatson, P. (2007) *Key Terms in Latino/a Cultural and Literary Studies*, Malden, MA; Oxford, UK: Blackwell.

América Latina en Acción Solidaria (ALAS) (2013) Official website, Spanish-language version, http://www.fundacionalas.org/en, English-language version, http://www.fundacionalas.org/es/. Accessed 17 April 2014.

Aparicio, F.R., and Chávez-Silverman, S. (eds) (1997) *Tropicalizations: Transcultural Representations of Latinidad*, Hanover, NH: University Press of New England.

Ayers, D. (2011) 'Making babies: Cultural response to gay celebrity dads', *The Back Lot*, 3 January, http://www.thebacklot.com/making-babies-cultural-response-to-gay-celebrity-dads/01/2011/. Accessed 10 January 2015.

Ball, E., Lowe, J., and Phillips, E. (eds) (2002) *Abriendo caminos: Strengthening Latino Communities through Giving and Volunteering*, New York: Hispanic Federation.

Beltrán, M.C. (2009) *Latina/o Stars in U.S. Eyes: The Makings and Meanings of TV Stardom*, Urbana; Chicago: University of Illinois Press.

Bishop, M. (2008) 'On the road with Shakira: Making philanthropy contagious', *Intelligent Life Magazine*, Autumn, 16 October, http://moreintelligentlife.com/story/on-the-road-with-shakira. Accessed 11 January 2015.

Bishop, M., and Green, M. (2010) *Philanthrocapitalism: How Giving Can Save the World*, London: A & C Black Publishers.

Brockington, D. (2014) 'The production and construction of celebrity advocacy in international development', *Third World Quarterly*, 35, 1: 88–108.

Caminero-Santangelo, M. (2007) *On Latinidad: U.S. Latino Literature and the Construction of Ethnicity*, Gainesville: University of Florida Press.

Campoamor, D., Diaz, W., and Ramos, H. (1999) *Nuevos Senderos: Reflections on Hispanics and Philanthropy*, Houston, TX: Arte Público Press.

Cepeda, M.E. (2000) 'Mucho loco for Ricky Martin; or the politics of chronology, crossover, and language within the Latin(o) music "boom"', *Popular Music and Society*, 24, 3: 55–71.

Cepeda, M.E. (2010) *Musical ImagiNation: U.S.–Colombian Identity and the Latin Music Boom*, New York: New York University Press.

Cervantes, A. (2003). 'Hometown Associations as catalysts for the development of community foundation: The Zacatecan Case', Center on Philanthropy and Civil Society, May, The Graduate Center, City University of New York.

Cobo, L. (2011) 'Shakira: The Barranquilla bombshell moves easily between the worlds of entertainment and philanthropy', *Poder360º Magazine*, November, http://pages.nxtbook.com/nxtbooks/et/poder1211_v2/offline/et_poder1211_v2.pdf. Accessed 5 March 2015.

Cobo, L. (2014) 'Shakira opens new school in Colombia: "We can change lives"', Latin Notes, *Billboard*, 25 February, http://www.billboard.com/articles/columns/latin-notas/5915715/shakira-opens-new-school-in-colombia-we-can-change-lives. Accessed 11 January 2015.

Colapinto, J. (2012) 'Looking good: The new boom in celebrity philanthropy', *New Yorker*, 26 March, pp. 56–64.

Cooper, A. (2007) *Celebrity Diplomacy*, Boulder; London: Paradigm Publishers.

Cortes, M. (1995) 'Three strategic questions about Latino philanthropy', *New Directions for Philanthropic Fundraising*, 8: 23–40.

Cottle, S., and Nolan, D. (2007) 'Global humanitarianism and the changing aid-media field', *Journalism Studies*, 8, 6: 862–78.

Cruz, F., and Muñoz, P. (2013) 'Shakira presume de hijo en las redes socials' [Shakira shows off her son on social networks], MSN famosos, June 20, http://mujer.es.msn.com/famosos/shakira-y-pique-bebe-milan. Accessed 17 April 2014.

De la Garza, R. (1997) *Latino Subgroups and Their Attitudes Towards Philanthropy: A Comparison Among Them and with Non-Latinos*, Austin, TX: University of Texas at Austin.

'Did it Work?' (2011) Philanthrocapitalism.net, 21 December, http://www.philanthrocapitalism.net/2011/12/did-it-work/. Accessed 1 December 2012.

Dieter, H., and Kumar, K. (2008) 'The downside of celebrity diplomacy: The neglected complexity of development', *Global Governance*, 14: 259–64.

'Discurso de Shakira en la Cumbre de las Américas' [Shakira's Speech at the Summit of the Americas] (2012) Colombianos.us, http://www.colombianos.us/2012/04/el-discurso-de-shakira-en-la-cumbre-de-las-americas/. Accessed 5 March 2015.

Ennis, S., Ríos-Vargas, M., and Albert, G. (2011) 'The Hispanic population: 2010', US Department of Commerce, Economics and Statistics Administration, US Census Bureau, http://www.census.gov/prod/cen2010/briefs/c2010br-04.pdf. Accessed 11 January 2015.

Falcón, A. (2001) 'Liberating Vieques', *The Nation*, 9 July, http://www.thenation.com/article/liberating-vieques#. Accessed 11 January 2015.

Farrés, C. (2013) 'Los Puig "echan" a Fernando de la Rúa y a su hijo Antonio, ex de Shakira' [The Los Puig family reject Fernando de la Rúa and his son Antonio, Shakira's ex], *Economia digital* (España), 28 January, http://www.economiadigital.es/es/notices/2013/01/los_puig_echan_a_fernando_de_la_rua_y_a_su_hijo_antonio_ex_de_shakira_37500.php. Accessed 11 January 2015.

Fiol-Matta, L. (2002) 'Pop Latinidad: Puerto Ricans in the Latin explosion, 1999', *Centro Journal*, 14, 1: 27–51.

Foucault, M. (1977) 'What is an author?', in D.F. Bouchard (ed.) *Language, Counter-Memory, Practice: Selected Essays and Interviews*, Ithaca, NY: Cornell University Press, pp. 113–38.

Fuchs, C. (2007) 'There's my territory: Shakira crossing over', in M. Mendible (ed.) *From Bananas to Buttocks: The Latina Body in Popular Film and Culture*, Austin, TX: University of Texas Press, pp. 167–82.

Fundación Pies Descalzos (2013) Official website, Spanish-language version, http://www.fundacionpiesdescalzos.com/; English-language version, http://www.fundacionpiesdescalzos.com/en/. Accessed 30 January 2014.

Fundación Ricky Martin (2014) Official website, Spanish-language version, http://www.rickymartinfoundation.org/es/; English-language version, http://www.rickymartinfoundation.org/. Accessed 9 January 2015.

Galaz, M. (2011) 'El gobierno concede a Ricky Martin la nacionalidad española para poder casarse' [The government grants Spanish citizenship to Ricky Martin so he can marry], *El País*, 4 November, http://www.elpais.com/articulo/gente/tv/gobierno/concede/Ricky/Martin/nacionalidad/espanola/poder/casarse/elpepugen/20111104elpepuage_3/Tes. Accessed 11 January 2015.

Gallegos, H. E., and O'Neill, M. (eds) (1991) *Hispanics and the Nonprofit Sector*, New York: The Foundation Center.

Garrard, V. (2006) 'Sad stories: Trafficking in children—unique situations requiring new solutions', *Georgia Journal of International and Comparative Law*, 35: 147–73.

Gibbs, N. (2005) 'The good Samaritans', *Time*, 19 December, http://www.time.com/time/magazine/article/0,9171,1142278,00.html. Accessed 9 January 2015.

Gonzales, S.A. (1985) *Hispanic American Voluntary Organizations*, Westport, CT: Greenwood Press.

Grandin, G. (2006) *Empire's Workshop: Latin America, the United States, and the Rise of the New Imperialism*, New York: Metropolitan Books.

Gray, K. (2011) 'Shakira helps rebuild quake-hit Haiti girls school', *Reuters*, 31 March, http://www.reuters.com/article/2011/03/31/us-shakira-haiti-idUSTRE72U7ZF20110331. Accessed 11 January 2015.

Hassid, J., and Jeffreys, E. (2015) 'Doing good or doing nothing? Celebrity, media and philanthropy in China', *Third World Quarterly*, 36, 1: 75–93.

Howard, C. (2014) 'The world's most powerful women 2014', *Forbes*, 28 May, http://www.forbes.com/sites/carolinehoward/2014/05/28/the-worlds-most-powerful-women-2014/. Accessed 11 January 2015.

'Internally Displaced People Figures' (2015) UN HCR, http://www.unhcr.org/pages/49c3646c23.html. Accessed 8 January 2015.

Kapoor, I. (2013) *Celebrity Humanitarianism: The Ideology of Global Charity*, Abingdon, Oxon: Routledge.

Kurshan, N. (2013) 'America's own political prisoners', *Counterpunch*, 16 December, http://www.counterpunch.org/2013/12/16/americas-own-political-prisoners/. Accessed 17 April 2014.

'Latino Philanthropy Literature Review' (2003) Donor Research Project, Center on Philanthropy and Civil Society, City University of New York, http://www.philanthropy.org/programs/literature_reviews/latino_lit_review.pdf. Accessed 9 January 2015.

Malcomson, S. (2009) 'Shakira's children', *New York Times*, 2 June, http://www.nytimes.com/2009/06/07/magazine/07Shakira-t.html?_r=0&ref=magazine&pagewanted=all. Accessed 11 January 2015.

Martin, R. (2010) *Me*, New York: Celebra.

Martin, R. (2012) 'Stop the scourge of child trafficking', Ricky Martin Foundation, 6 June, http://www.rickymartinfoundation.org/. Accessed 11 January 2015.

Miranda, J. (1999) 'Religion, philanthropy, and the Hispanic people in North America', *New Directions for Philanthropic Fundraising*, 24: 59–74.

Mirchandani, R. (2009) 'Pop queen Shakira back to her roots', BBC news, http://news.bbc.co.uk/2/hi/americas/7928271.stm. Accessed 1 January 2012.

Moreno, C. (2012) 'Antonio de la Rúa, Shakira's ex-boyfriend, sues star for $250 million', *Huffington Post*, 6 September, http://www.huffingtonpost.com/2012/09/06/antonio-de-la-rua-sues-shakira_n_1859324.html. Accessed 17 April 2014.

Musall, J. (2012) 'Latino celebrities at vanguard of massive, developing political bloc: What are some past immigration actions by Latino celebrities?', Yahoo! Voices, http://voices.yahoo.com/shared/print.shtml?content_type=article&content_type_id=8013699. Accessed 17 April 2014.

Negrón-Muntaner, F. (2004) *Boricua Pop: Puerto Ricans and the Latinization of American Culture*, New York; London: New York University Press.

Note, J. (2010) 'Shakira, Ricky Martin, Juanes y Paulina Rubio contra la ley de Arizona' [Shakira, Ricky Martin, Juanes y Paulina Rubio against the Arizona law], *Diario Femenino*, 1 May, http://www.diariofemenino.com/actualidad/sociedad/articulos/shakira-ricky-martin-juanes-paulina-rubio-ley-arizona/. Accessed 11 January 2015.

Nuiry, O.E. (1992) 'Give and take', *Hispanic*, April, pp. 18–24.

Palm, M. (2009) 'Directivos de ALAS, en trama de corrupción en España' [ALAS executives in a web of corruption in Spain], *Prensa* (Pánama), 10 March, http://mensual.prensa.com/mensual/contenido/2009/03/10/hoy/panorama/1718112.asp. Accessed 17 April 2014.

'Presidentes Obama y Santos y Shakira hablaron en la Cumbre de las Américas' [President Obama, President Santos and Shakira Spoke at the Summit of the Americas] (2012) Shakira.com, http://www.shakira.com/news/605. Accessed 12 March 2015.

Ramos, H.A.J. (1999) 'Latino philanthropy: Expanding US models of giving and civic participation', *Cultures of Caring: Philanthropy in Diverse American Communities*, Washington, DC: Council on Foundations.

Ramos, Z. (2012) 'Ricky Martin: Puerto Rico needs a "serious" statehood plebiscite', *Huffington Post*, 30 November, http://www.huffingtonpost.com/2012/11/30/ricky-martin-puerto-rico-statehood_n_2220097.html. Accessed 17 April 2014.

'Reunió concierto ALAS a 380 mil personas en México y Argentina' [ALAS Concerts Unite 380 Thousand People in Mexico and Argentina] (2008) Eluniversal.mx, 18 May, http://www.eluniversal.com.mx/notas/507601.html. Accessed 11 January 2015.

'Ricky Martin and Habitat's CEO, Jonathan Reckford, Travel to Haiti in Support of Habitat's Haitian Recovery Efforts' (2010) Habitat for Humanity, 19 January, http://www.habitat.org/newsroom/2010archive/01_19_2010_ricky_martin_recovery_fund.aspx. Accessed 11 January 2015.

Ricky Martin Foundation (n.d.) Official website, http://www.rickymartinfoundation.org/en/. Accessed 11 January 2015.

Rodríguez, G. (2009) 'La última trampa de Antonito' [Little Antonio's latest fraud], *InfoNews: Un mundo, muchas voces* (Argentina), 18 April, http://www.infonews.com/nota.php?id=37253&bienvenido=1. Accessed 11 January 2015.

Rojas, E. (2013) '"Spitting phlegm at the system": The changing voices of anticolonial Puerto Rican protest music', in E. Rojas and L. Michie (eds) *Sounds of Resistance: The Role of Music in Multicultural Activism*, vol. 2, Santa Barbara, CA: Praeger, pp. 491–592.

Ronderos, J.G. (2003) 'The war on drugs and the military: The case of Colombia', in M.E. Beare (ed.) *Critical Reflections on Transnational Organized Crime, Money Laundering and Corruption*, Toronto, Canada: University of Toronto Press, pp. 207–36.

Sanborn, C.A. (2005) 'Philanthropy in Latin America: Historical traditions and current trends', in S. Sanborn and F. Portocarrero (eds) *Philanthropy and Social Change in Latin America*, Cambridge, MA: Harvard University Press, pp. 3–30.

Sanborn, C., and Portocarrero, F. (eds) (2005) *Philanthropy and Social Change in Latin America*, Cambridge, MA: Harvard University Press.

Sandoval-Sánchez, A. (2003) 'Latinos and cultural exchange de-facing mainstream magazine covers: The new faces of Latino/a transnational and transcultural Celebrities', *Encrucijada/Crossroads: An Online Academic Journal*, 1, 1: 13–24.

Shakira (2013) 'My 40 chances: A lifelong commitment to helping others', 40 Chances, 26 June, http://www.40chances.com/blog/shakira-my-40-chances/. Accessed 11 January 2015.

Shakira (n.d.) Official website, English-language version, http://www.shakira.com/index.php; Spanish-language version, http://es.shakira.com/. Accessed 11 January 2015.

'Shakira has the Most-"Liked" Page on Facebook' (2014) ABC News Online, 24 March, http://abcnews.go.com/Entertainment/shakira-page-facebook/story?id=23042406. Accessed 11 January 2015.

Sulek, M. (2010) 'On the modern meaning of philanthropy', *Nonprofit and Voluntary Sector Quarterly*, 39, 2: 193–212.

't Hart, P., and Tindall, K. (2009) 'Leadership by the famous: Celebrity as political capital', in J. Kane, H. Patapan and P. 't Hart (eds) *Dispersed Democratic Leadership: Origins, Dynamics, and Implications*, Oxford, UK: Oxford University Press, pp. 255–78.

The 2009 Index of Global Philanthropy and Remittances (2009) Center for Global Prosperity, Hudson Institute, http://www.hudson.org/content/researchattachments/attachment/979/index_of_global_philanthropy_and_remittances_2009.pdf. Accessed 11 January 2015.

Tsaliki, L., Frangonikolopoulos, C.A., and Huliaras, A. (eds) (2011) *Transnational Celebrity Activism in Global Politics*, Bristol, UK; Chicago, IL: Intellect Press.

Twitter Counter (2015) 'The top 100 users', http://twittercounter.com/pages/100/10. Accessed 11 January 2015.

Valdivia, A.N. (ed.) (2008) *Latina/o Communication Studies Today*, New York: Peter Lang.

Watson, T. (2008) 'Global philanthropy Part 2: Philanthropy in Latin America: Past traditions, future innovations', On Philanthropy, 6 March, http://onphilanthropy.com/2008/global-philanthropy-part-2-philanthropy-in-latin-america-past-traditions-future-innovations/. Accessed 11 January 2015.

West, D.M. (2007) *Angelina, Mia, and Bono: Celebrities and International Development*, Washington, DC: The Brookings Institution.

Yaffe, L. (2011) 'Conflicto armado en Colombia: Análisis de las causas económicas, sociales e institucionales de la oposición violenta' [Armed conflict in Colombia: Analysis of the economic, social and institutional causes of violent opposition], *CS en Ciencias Sociales*, 8: 187–208, http://www.icesi.edu.co/revistas/index.php/revista_cs/article/view/1133/1509. Accessed 11 January 2015.

Chapter 11

Afterword

Paul Allatson and Elaine Jeffreys

In November 2014, 30 years after the first iteration of 'Do They Know It's Christmas' by Band Aid (the supergroup orchestrated by Irish musician Bob Geldof to support famine relief in Ethiopia), a new version of the song was released by Band Aid 30, its aim being to raise funds for the campaign against the Ebola epidemic in West Africa. However, as seems to be the quotidian norm with celebrity philanthropy, Geldof's fund-raising event attracted mixed popular cultural and media reactions that veered from applause and celebration on the one hand, to derision, critique and outrage on the other. The song, it must be said, was a financial success. According to Geldof, it raised some USD 1.7 million in its first few minutes on iTunes alone and sections of the UK press lauded that outcome (Kwong 2014). By contrast, one particularly dismissive take appeared in the UK's *Daily Mail* under the title: 'Do they know it's not the Eighties anymore? As Bob Geldof forms a new Band Aid supergroup, how 30 years have taken their toll on the original line-up' (*Daily Mail* Reporter 2014). The report featured photographs of many participants in Band Aid 30, contrasting them with images of their youthful selves from 1984. The unflattering comparisons suggested that the motley crew of ageing, world-weary but wealthy musicians was no longer up to the task of either music-making or effective philanthropy. More damningly, a host of musicians including the UK-Ghanian rapper Fuse ODG (2014), cited what they interpreted to be the song's pathologized, disease-ridden and poverty-stricken vision of Africa as the reason for their refusal to participate in the event.

Summarizing the mixed reactions to Band Aid 30, the Canadian journalist Matt Kwong (2014) wrote that the resurrected Band Aid model of celebrity philanthropy, while successful from a financial point of view, could also be seen as anachronistic in the digitized, social-mediatized twenty-first century. As Kwong (2014) put it, 'in the age of viral media and [given] a more cynical and sophisticated public, fund-raising strategists say philanthropy is tilting more towards grassroots campaigns and "clicktivism", and away from rock star benefit songs and celebrity-hosted telethons'. Kwong (2014) cited a number of public relations managers who agreed that the gathering of celebrities together for one single fund-raising event or philanthropic cause is now being challenged. That is, we inhabit an epoch in which celebrities and their publicity machines very carefully manage their online and media identities and draw targeted attention to their specific philanthropic campaigns without the need for involvement in such outmoded spectacles as telethons or collaborative songs. The social media realm has also witnessed a shift in expectation among participants in philanthropic and social change campaigns. Participants now post evidence of their involvement with the intention of being acknowledged and recognized – that is, 'liked' and shared – on social media platforms like Facebook, Instagram and Twitter, and in Cloud Funding initiatives. This grassroots-level approach to supporting socio-political and other philanthropic causes contrasts sharply with such past practices as purchasing in a largely unacknowledged manner a record designed and released for the purposes of fund-raising, and which seemed to bring more attention to the celebrity participants than the recipients of the so-called 'Aid'.

As the range of reactions to Bob Geldof's Band Aid 30 recording in support of Ebola victims in West Africa in November 2014 confirmed, celebrity philanthropy generates strongly articulated differences in opinion about its efficacy and the motives of the celebrities who are involved. That trend is recognized by the contributors to this volume for whom the conjunction of celebrity and philanthropy is not simply a growing global phenomenon of importance, but one that also has concrete local manifestations and a range of technologized and mass-mediated effects, consequences and implications. To varying degrees, the contributors in this book also demonstrate that just as there can be no single, untroubled definition of the 'celebrity function', to redeploy Foucault's (2007) conceptualization of an author in the mass-mediated celebrity-industry setting, the same is true of philanthropy. When it comes to celanthropy – what Rojek (2014: 127) calls 'charity projects fronted and, in the public mind, defined by celebrities' – it is clear, as Paul 't Hart and Karen Tindall (2009: 257) note, that 'no grand, one-size-fits-all interpretation is sufficient'.

This truism informs our conviction that the celebrity philanthropy model as understood in the US, and which is commonly identified as being embodied by the celebrity coupling par excellence of Angelina Jolie and Brad Pitt, is not the only model that operates across the globe, or indeed in the North American portions of the global North. Nor should that celebrity coupling be regarded as the template against which celebrity philanthropy anywhere and everywhere is compared, analyzed, judged and deemed to be meaningful, even effective in achieving a range of philanthropic aims. In international terms the Jolie-Pitt duo represents a particularly US-centred (or, at best, transatlantic-centred) celanthropic paradigm, one that in many parts of the world might not even register or compute as being of local note and interest.

The current volume, therefore, can be regarded as an opening gambit in what will hopefully be growing attention to more genuinely transnational critical understandings of celebrity philanthropy and the ways in which it changes shape and has uneven impacts and receptions over historical and geocultural time and place. The book covers some major criticisms of celebrity philanthropy, including that it is a self-serving way of extending the celebrity brand, promotes consumer capitalism and associated inequality, and revives colonialist/orientalist discourses concerning the assumed superiority of the global North vis-à-vis the rest of the world (see Chapters 4–8). Yet, as Jonathan Paul Marshall argues in Chapter 3, criticism of celebrity philanthropy might stem from a desire for tidiness and order in the world that does not acknowledge the complexities of the situation, human motivation, the difficulties of virtue, or unintended effects, and itself does little to fix the situation. Put another way, as Elaine Jeffreys contends in Chapter 2, although supporters

Afterword

frequently overstate the transformative capacity of celebrity philanthropy, critics tend to unify different types of celebrities, philanthropic activities, and even the motivations of individual celebrities and their fans, under the overarching framework of 'bad capitalism and consumer culture at work'. Given the heterogeneity of celebrity and philanthropy, '[f]urther case studies and typologies are required to comprehend the nature and effects of the different kinds of celebrity-mediated philanthropy and activism that exist in the world today' (Stewart 2007: 19). This is particularly important because notwithstanding complaints about the privileged, superficial and racist nature of celebrity philanthropy in the international arena, there are hardly any *empirical* studies of how celebrity-involved or celebrity-inspired philanthropy operates *in practice* in the context of developing countries, what it does for local recipients and how it is viewed and understood by them. Such studies are vital to any informed critique.

Much more, therefore, can be said and thought about celebrity philanthropy. Indeed, it may provide numerous opportunities for people engaged with a range of pressing socio-economic, educational, environmental and cultural causes, and for the champions and detractors of those causes as well. There is a genuine need for nuanced international and comparative research into its growing influence and importance across the globe that moves beyond and thereby challenges North American and/or Anglophone orthodoxy in such fields as celebrity, media, philanthropy and development studies. Noting this need, we conclude the volume here by identifying three additional areas of potential critical interest.

First, given that celebrity itself is constantly changing in response to the inexorable technologization and social mediatization of identities in the twenty-first century, that evolution has as-yet-unforeseen implications for the work of philanthropy as well. Some evidence for this changing environment is provided by the November 2014 reactions to Band Aid 30. The singer Adele apparently eschewed involvement in the celanthropic spectacle, preferring instead to announce her contributions to a range of charitable causes via her own social media accounts (Kwong 2014). Similarly, rapper Fuse ODG (2014) took to an opinion piece in the British newspaper *The Guardian*, backed up by his own social media posts, to explain why he was not going to be involved in Band Aid 30, and how he would contribute in other ways to the efforts to contain the spread of Ebola while not misrepresenting 'West Africa' (see also Kwong 2014).

Second, the transatlantic Jolie-Pitt model is a limited and limiting one when it comes to understanding celebrity philanthropy in genuinely transnational and transcultural terms. One example here will suffice. Since the 2014 collapse of the Argentinian economy, the second in the twenty-first century, an unforeseen celebrity phenomenon has emerged in Argentina that is not as yet replicated anywhere else in the world. This is the eruption into popular cultural and social media attention of photogenic but highly qualified economists now dating the country's music, sport, film and media celebrities and becoming celebrities in their own right, with as yet unknown implications for the evolution of philanthropy and social activism in Argentina and other parts of Latin America ('Celebrity Economists: The Sages of the Pampas' 2014).

Finally, understanding of celebrity philanthropy is constrained by the Anglophone bias of celebrity studies. English currently prevails as a global language, pretty much guaranteeing global celebrity status to numerous stars from Anglophone countries (Ronen et al. 2014). However, *global* celebrity status also depends on direct information flows between other global languages, such as French, Spanish and Chinese, and subsequently indirect communication in localized languages. At the same time, national and transnational celebrity status may equal or even eclipse the scale of global celebrity status in certain communicative frameworks. The international pop star and philanthropist Shakira, for instance, has one of the largest followings on Twitter, with more than 28 million followers at the beginning of 2015 (Twitter Counter 2015). However, Li Bingbing, a renowned actress and philanthropist in China, which happens to be the world's largest media market (Hassid and Jeffreys 2015: 76), but who would have been virtually unknown to Anglophone audiences until her 2014 debut in *Transformers 4* (dir. Bay), has nearly 31 million followers on Weibo – the Chinese-language equivalent of Twitter (http://weibo.com/libingbing). The circulation of celebrity in transnational, but non-western and non-Anglophone settings, underscores the limited nature of praise and criticism of celebrity philanthropy understood as a phenomenon emanating solely from the global North and directed at recipients in the global South.

Here, there are salutary lessons to be drawn from anthropology and subaltern studies about loci of enunciation and the critical presumption to speak for and on behalf of others (Spivak 1998; Mignolo 1995). As Paul Allatson (2004: 14) has argued elsewhere, the need for academic self-reflection on one's own locus of enunciation 'is particularly evident when' critics 'presume to represent, champion, or identify with subaltern subjects without questioning their own authorial relation to the material preconditions of subalternity, or their intellectual complicity in the textual production of subalternity'. With regard to research on celebrity philanthropy, this understanding demands research that actively heeds the viewpoints of the non-global-North recipients of celebrity philanthropic assistance. But that research, as in much ethnographic work, must attend to the subaltern dilemma, by which the first-world intellectual speaks for her/his subjects and constructs the subalternity that concerns herself/himself (Allatson 2004: 40). It also needs to attend to the voices, investments and aspirations of both the fans of celebrity culture and personalities, and the recipients of philanthropic attention alike.

In 1989, the Chicano anthropologist Renato Rosaldo (1989: 12), warned his fellow anthropologists not to structure 'the untidiness of everyday life [events] so that they can be "read" like articles, books, or, as we now say, *texts*' (original emphasis). In the twenty-first century, we would argue that there is a pressing need for a similar critical approach to understanding the messiness of celebrity philanthropy wherever it may be encountered.

References

Allatson, P. (2002) *Latino Dreams: Transcultural Traffic and the U.S. National Imaginary*, Amsterdam; New York: Rodopi.

'Celebrity Economists: The Sages of the Pampas' (2014) *The Economist*, 29 November, http://www.economist.com/news/finance-and-economics/21635016-tango-fame-argentine-economists-tinged-sadness-sages. Accessed 11 January 2015.

Daily Mail Reporter (2014) 'Do they know it's not the Eighties anymore? As Bob Geldof forms a new Band Aid supergroup, how 30 years have taken their toll on the original line-up', *Daily Mail*, 14 November, http://www.dailymail.co.uk/tvshowbiz/article-2833863/As-Bob-Geldof-forms-new-Band-Aid-supergroup-30-years-taken-toll-original-line-up.html. Accessed 6 January 2015.

Foucault, M. (1977) 'What is an author?', in D.F. Bouchard (ed.) *Language, Counter-Memory, Practice: Selected Essays and Interviews*, Ithaca, NY: Cornell University Press, pp. 113–38.

Fuse ODG (2014) 'Why I had to turn down Band Aid', *The Guardian*, 19 November, http://www.theguardian.com/commentisfree/2014/nov/19/turn-down-band-aid-bob-geldof-africa-fuse-odg. Accessed 11 January 2015.

Kwong, M. (2014) 'Band Aid 30 backlash: Celebrity charity model losing lustre', CBC News Canada, 20 November, http://www.cbc.ca/news/world/band-aid-30-backlash-celebrity-charity-model-losing-lustre-1.2840715. Accessed 11 January 2015.

Mignolo, W.D. (1995) *The Darker Side of the Renaissance: Literacy, Territoriality, and Colonization*, Ann Arbor, MI: University of Michigan Press.

Rojek, C. (2014) '"Big citizen" celanthropy and its discontents', *International Journal of Cultural Studies*, 17, 2: 127–41.

Ronen, S., Gonçalves, B., Hua, K.Z., Vespignanib, A., Pinkere, S. and Hidalgoa, C.A. (2014) 'Links that speak: The global language network and its association with global fame', *PNAS*, 111, 52, http://www.pnas.org/content/111/52/E5616.full. Accessed 1 December 2014.

Rosaldo, R. (1989) *Culture and Truth: The Remaking of Social Analysis*, New York: Beacon Press.

Spivak, G.C. (1988) 'Can the subaltern speak?' in C. Nelson and L. Grossberg (eds) *Marxism and the Interpretation of Culture*, London: Macmillan, pp. 271–313.

Stewart, D. (2007) 'Celebrity led humanitarian interventions: Blanket cynicism vs. a framework for success', 29 November, http://www.winstonchurchillbc.org/images/PDF/2008%201st%20Prize%20paper%20-%20Drew%20Stewart.pdf. Accessed 10 October 2010.

't Hart, P. and Tindall, K. (2009) 'Leadership by the famous: Celebrity as political capital', in J. Kane, H. Patapan and P. 't Hart (eds) *Dispersed Democratic Leadership: Origins, Dynamics, and Implications*, Oxford, UK: Oxford University Press, pp. 255–78.

Index

A

Adidas, 91
African Medical and Research Foundation (AMREF), 116
aid celebrity, 85, 87–88. *See also* celebrity philanthropy
Aid Still Required (disaster-relief program in Haiti), 91
AIDS, 91–92, 115–116, 134–135, 137, 141–142. *See also* Product RED campaign
ALAS (Fundación América Latina en Acción Solidaria), 193, 201–202
Allatson, Paul, 216
American Dream myth, 135
American Red Cross, 30–31
America's Next Top Model (television show), 63, 64–65, 67–73, 75–76, 77–78
Andrew, Donna, 45–47
Andrews, David, 89, 90
anti-immigrant legislation, 204
Aparicio, Frances, 198
Appermont, Luc, 111, 113, 114, 118
Argentina, 215
Armstrong, Lance, 95
Association des Femmes Juristes du Bénin (African NGO), 115

B

Baaz, Maria Eriksson, 100
Band Aid (charity supergroup), 29, 87–88, 213–214
Band Aid 30 (charity supergroup), 213–214
Banerjee, Suman, 162
Bankable Enterprises, 63, 64–65
Banks, Tyra
  America's Next Top Model and, 63, 64–65, 67–73, 75–76, 77–78
  career of, 63–66
  TZONE Foundation and, 63, 66, 72–78
Barasamian, David, 153
Barefoot Foundation (Fundación Pies Descalzos), 13, 193, 198, 199, 203
Barr, Rosanne, 134
Basketball without Borders (BWB), 86, 91–92, 93–99
Beckham, David, 86, 91
Beijing Olympic Games (2008), 182
Beverly Hills Choppers, 69
Beyond Scarcity: Power, Poverty and the Global Water Crisis (UNDP), 114
The Big Bang Theory (television series), 69
Bill and Melinda Gates Foundation, 25
Bishop, Matthew, 194, 203
Blood Diamond (dir. Zwick 2006), 127
Bo Xilai, 174
Bono
  The Lazarus Effect and, 128, 134, 136, 137
  as political persona, 108
  poverty in Africa and, 26, 29
  Product RED campaign and, 89, 94–95, 127–129, 131–133, 140
  Time (magazine) and, 21, 25
Boorstin, Daniel, 6, 33

Booth, William, 47
Bosh, Chris, 92
Boykoff, Max, 157
The Brady Bunch (sitcom), 69
Brockington, Dan, 3, 157
Brown, Ashley, 70
Brown, Nicole, 134–135
Buddhism, 155
Buffett, Howard, 202
Buffett, Warren, 25, 85
Bullock, Sandra, 139
Burn, Richard, 46
Bush, George W., Jr., 201

C
Cameron, John, 99
Campbell, Naomi, 28, 64
Camus, Albert, 164
Care for Children (charity), 177–178
Carnegie, Andrew, 23–24, 48, 179
Catholic Church, 35, 195–196
cause-related marketing, 85–86
causumerism, 8
celanthropy, 5, 194. *See also* celebrity philanthropy
celebrity, 6–7, 45, 107–108
Celebrity Diplomacy (A. F. Cooper), 130
celebrity philanthropy
  history of, 21–22, 47–49, 87–88
  North American model of, 193–197, 214, 215
  praise and criticism of, 22–35, 43
  research on, 3–4, 108–109, 213–216
celebrity philanthropy documentaries
  dichotomous frameworks in, 118–121
  framing analysis and, 109–111
  The West Helps the Rest Save Itself through Western Organizations in, 118, 119–120
  The West Saves the Rest: Social Engineering in, 111–114, 118, 119–120
  The West Helps the Rest Save Itself through Western Organizations in, 114–115
  The West Helps the Rest Save Itself through Local Organizations, 115–117, 118, 119–120
  The (Diverse) Rest Will Save Itself from Problems Caused by the West, 117–118, 119, 120
  See also I Am Because We Are (dir. Rissman 2009); *The Lazarus Effect* (dir. Bangs 2010)
Cepeda, María Elena, 199
charity, 7, 21, 43–47, 154
charity of compulsion, 44, 49
Chávez-Silverman, Susana, 198
Cheung, Maggie, 175
Chikaonda, Mathews, 135–136
China
  fan-driven philanthropic initiatives in, 33–34
  Mutual Aid Societies in, 195
  politics of philanthropy in, 33, 179–184
  Sichuan earthquake and, 28–29, 174–178, 181–183
  Zhang Ziyi scandal in, 33, 173–178, 180
China Association of Social Workers, 183
China Daily (newspaper), 176–177
Chinese Red Cross Foundation, 34, 175–177
Chomsky, Noam, 156
Christian Dior, 28–29
Christianity, 45–46, 133–134, 155, 195–196
Clarke, Natalie, 131
Clemente, Carlos, 202
Clinton, Bill, 135, 136, 137
Clooney, George, 129
Coca-Cola, 181–182
Cold War, 21, 197
Cole, Joe, 91
Colombia, 197–198. *See also* Shakira (Shakira Isabel Mebarak Ripoll)
colorblind racism, 135
commodity feminism, 67

communalism, 162
community, 44
compassion, 32
compassion fatigue, 32, 45
Cooper, Anderson, 50–55, 56, 130, 136–137, 138–139, 140–141
Cooper, Andrew F., 29, 88, 89
Cordaid Memisa (Dutch Catholic NGO), 114–115
Corton, Eric, 110–111, 112
Cottle, Simon, 27, 29–30
creative capitalism, 21, 24–25
Crouching Tiger, Hidden Dragon (dir. Lee 2000), 173
culture heroes, 45
Cunina (Flemish NGO), 113
Curry, Adrianne, 69
CW Television Network, 65, 68

D
Daily Mail (newspaper), 213
Darnell, Simon, 89, 96
De la Rúa, Antonio, 202
Dell, 24
Demand Media, 72
demand obligation, 44, 49
Deng Xiaoping, 180
development
 aid celebrity and, 87–88
 sport and, 85–86, 88–90, 92–100
Development Challenges in Extremist Affected Areas (Government of India Planning Commission Report), 161
The Diary of Angelina Jolie and Dr. Jeffrey Sachs in Africa (dir. Huang 2005), 113–114, 118
Diary of Jay-Z: Water for Life (dir. Huang 2006), 113, 114, 118, 119
Dieter, Heribert, 87, 89
'Do They Know It's Christmas' (song), 87–88, 90, 213
Douglas, Susan, 140

Downtown Women's Center (Los Angeles), 75

E
Ebola epidemic (West Africa), 213–214
Economic and Political Weekly (journal), 159, 162
Edun, 131
8 Minutes in the DR Congo (dir. Serota 2009), 115, 116–117
Eikenberry, Angela, 108, 118
empathy, 44–45
Engels, Friedrich, 47
English, CariDee, 69, 71–72
Entertainment Weekly (magazine), 66
Eric Corton in de Centraal Afrikaanse Republiek (dir. Corton 2007), 110–111
Erik and Sascha in Afrika (dir. Zwart and Brussaard 2009), 114–115, 118
Escobar, Arturo, 97
Essence (magazine), 64
Esteva, Gustavo, 87
Evans, Danielle, 69

F
Facebook, 193
Fain, Sharon, 118
Fairclough, Norman, 86
Fall, Amadou Gallo, 98
Fans of Li Yuchun Charity Fund, 33
Federation International Basketball Association (FIBA), 86, 91–92
female empowerment
 America's Next Top Model and, 63, 64–65, 67–73, 75–76, 77–78
 Banks' career and, 63–66
 TZONE Foundation and, 63, 66, 72–78
The Feminine Mystique (Friedan), 67
feminist movement, 66–68. See also female empowerment
Forbes (magazine), 65–66, 173, 193
Foucault, Michel, 46, 214

Fox, Nicole, 69
Friedan, Betty, 67
Frontline (magazine), 157, 158
Fundación América Latina en Acción Solidaria (ALAS), 193, 201–202
Fundación Pies Descalzos, 13, 193, 198, 199, 203
Fundación Ricky Martin, 13, 193, 203–204
Fuse ODG (rapper), 213, 215

G
G8 summit, 26
Gap, 24
García Márquez, Gabriel, 201
Garrard, Virginia, 204
Gates, Bill, 21, 24–25, 26, 85, 193
Gates, Melinda, 21
Geldof, Bob
  Band Aid and, 87–88, 213–214
  documentaries and, 110–111, 117–118
  poverty in Africa and, 26, 29
Geldof in Africa: The Luminous Continent (dir. Maguire 2005), 117–118
Ghandy, Kobad, 163
Ghosh, Arunabha, 114
Gibbs, Nancy, 25–26, 203
gifts and gifting, 43–45
Gill, R., 77
girl power, 67. *See also* female empowerment
Girls in the Game (non-profit organization), 75
Girls Project, 75
GirlSpeak (project), 75, 76
Giving Back Fund, 182
The Giving Pledge, 25
The Global Fund to Fight AIDS, Tuberculosis and Malaria, 24, 131
The God of Small Things (Roy), 153, 156
Goldman, Robert, 67
González Abella, Carlos, 201
Gonzalez, Jaslene, 69, 71
Goodman, Mike, 157

Goodwill Ambassadors program, 27, 85, 127–128, 193
GQ (magazine), 64
Green, Michael, 203
Gretzky, Wayne, 91
The Guardian (newspaper), 153, 160, 164, 215
Guha, Ramachandra, 157, 158–160, 164

H
Haanstra, Anna, 99
Hallmark, 24
Hargitay, Mariska, 139
Harris, Daniel, 30, 32
help, 43–50, 55–56
Hero (dir. Zhang 2002), 173
Heroes in Ending Modern-Day Slavery, 193
Hewson, Ali, 131
Hill Collins, Patricia, 140
Hilton, Paris, 108
The Hindu (newspaper), 158
Hinduism, 155
Hoff, Erik van der, 111, 114–115, 118
Hollywood Reporter (magazine), 177
Hot Properties (sitcom), 69
House of Flying Daggers (dir. Zhang 2004), 173
House, Yoanna, 69, 71
Howard, Dwight, 92
Hu Jintao, 180–181
Huddart, Stephen, 108
Hung (television series), 69

I
I Am Because We Are (dir. Rissman 2009), 128, 133, 134–138, 141–143
Ifetayo Cultural Arts Academy, 75, 76
impersonal welfare, 44, 49
incoherence
  definition of, 43
  help and, 45–50, 55–56
  Jolie and, 50–55, 56

India, philanthropy in, 154–157. *See also* Roy, Arundhati
The Indian Express (newspaper), 160
Induwar, Francis, 163
Islam, 155
Italy, 195

J
Jackson, Steven, 89, 90
Japan, 195
Jay Z, 110–111, 113, 114, 118, 119
Jeffreys, Elaine, 47, 214–215
Ji Lingling, 176
Jiaduobao Group, 181–182
Jiang Zemin, 180
Jolie, Angelina
 credibility of, 130
 documentaries and, 110–111, 113–114, 118
 Facebook and, 193
 as Goodwill Ambassador, 85, 127–128
 incoherence and, 50–55, 56
 interview with Cooper, 50–55, 56, 136–137, 138–139, 140–141
 motherhood and, 138–139, 140–141, 142–143
 North American philanthropy and, 214, 215
 poverty in Africa and, 29
Joseph, Ralina L., 64, 72
JRAJ9, 63–64
Judaism, 134–136

K
Kabbalah Centre (Los Angeles), 134–136
Kapoor, Ilan, 8, 32
Kasab, Ajmal, 160
Kaye, Danny, 21
Keelan, Victoria, 134
Kevin Hill (television program), 69
KFC, 181–182
Khan, Aamir, 155
Khan, Shah Rukh, 155

kindness, 44
King, Larry, 129
King, Martin Luther, Jr., 154
King, Samantha, 85
Koss, Johann Olav, 91
Krizek, Robert, 128, 139
Kumar, Rajiv, 87, 89
Kutcher, Ashton, 65, 134
Kwong, Matt, 213

L
Lady Gaga, 193
Lara Croft: Tomb Raider (dir. West 2001), 127
Laskar-e-Taiba (Pakistani Islamist group), 160
Latinidad, 194, 198, 199, 200–201, 203, 204, 205
Latin(o) America, philanthropy in, 35, 195–197, 215. *See also* Martin, Ricky (Enrique Martín Morales); Shakira (Shakira Isabel Mebarak Ripoll)
Lawrence of Arabia (dir. Lean 1962), 127
The Lazarus Effect (dir. Bangs 2010), 128, 134, 136, 137
Le May Doan, Catriona, 94
Lee, Chris (Li Yuchun), 33–34
Leefwereld in Beweging: Roos Van Acker (dir. Neuskens 2009), 115, 118
Li Bingbing, 216
Li Yuchun (Chris Lee), 33–34
liberal feminism, 67
Liberation Tigers of Tamil Eelan (LTTE), 164–165
Liebowitz, Annie, 131
Liekens, Goedele, 111, 116, 118, 120
Life Moments (reality television series), 76
Lindsay Lohan's Indian Journey (dir. Sahota 2010), 115–116, 118, 119
Linkletter, Nicole, 69
Littler, Jo, 157
Liu Xiang, 182
Live Aid concert (1985), 87–88, 90, 117
Livingstone, David, 47

223

Lohan, Lindsay, 110–111, 115–116, 118, 119
Look to the Stars: The World of Celebrity Giving (website), 3, 22, 76
López Rivera, Oscar, 198
Louis Vuitton, 131
Lower Eastside Girls Club, 75, 76

M
MacPherson, Elle, 140
Madonna
  motherhood and, 139, 141–143
  Raising Malawi and, 127–128, 130–131, 133, 134–136, 137–138, 141–143
Magubane, Zine, 27, 30
Mahato, Chhatradhar, 163
Malcomson, Scott, 201
Maoism, 160–163, 164–165
Marshall, Jonathan Paul, 214
Martin, Ricky (Enrique Martín Morales)
  criticism of, 200–202
  effectiveness of, 203–204
  Latinidad and, 197–199, 205
  North American philanthropy and, 193–197
Mathare Youth Sport Organizations, 90
Mayhew, Henry, 47
Mazza, Valeria, 64
Mbembé, Achille, 100, 110
McDonald's, 92, 181–182
MDGB group, 182
Meisel, Steven, 76
Memoirs of a Geisha (dir. Marshall 2005), 173–174
meritorious charity, 44, 49
Messengers of Peace, 27
Michaels, Meredith, 140
Michavila, José María, 202
Microsoft, 24
Millennium Development Goals, 90
Miller, Sienna, 110–111, 115, 116–117
Ming, Yao, 91

missions and missionaries, 30, 47, 133–134
Moore, Demi, 134
Mora, Naima, 71
Morton, Andrew, 130
Mother India (dir. Khan 1957), 153
motherhood, 138–143
Motivating Our Students through Experience (mentoring program), 75
Mudenda, Constance, 137
Mumbai terrorist attacks (2008), 160, 164
Mutombo, Dikembe, 91
Mutual Aid Societies, 195
My Fair Brady (reality television show), 69

N
Nakayama, Thomas, 128, 139
Narmada Bachao Andolan (protest movement), 156, 158–160
Nash, Steve, 91
National Basketball Association (NBA), 85–86, 91–92
Negra, Diane, 67
Negrón-Muntaner, Frances, 200
Nehru, Jawaharlal, 158
NetEase.com (Chinese web portal), 183
new momism, 140
New York Times Magazine, 66
Newsweek (magazine), 64
Nickel, Patricia Mooney, 53–55, 108, 118
Niebuhr, Reinhold, 154
Nike, 85–86, 91
Nokia, 181–182
Nolan, David, 27, 29–30
Nowitzki, Dirk, 92

O
Obama, Barack, 193, 198
Ogundipe-Leslie, Molara, 132, 136, 140, 142
Olympic Aid, 91
Omvedt, Gail, 159
On Philanthropy (online resource), 195
Outlook (magazine), 158
Oxfam, 27

P

Parashar, Swati, 161
Patkar, Medha, 158, 159
Penrice, R.R., 63
People (magazine), 29
The People for Children (project), 193
People for the Ethical Treatment of Animals (PETA), 28
People's Daily (website), 176, 180
philanthrocapitalism, 21, 203
philanthropy
   definition of, 44
   history of, 46–49
   origins and use of word, 7, 154
   See also celebrity philanthropy
Philanthropy and Social Change in Latin America (Sanborn and Portocarrero), 195
Phiri, Mannesseh, 137
Pieterse, Jan Nederveen, 96, 109
Pigford, Eva, 69, 70
Piqué, Gerard, 202
Pitt, Brad, 130, 138–139, 214, 215
Playboy (magazine), 69
Playing for Good (charity), 108
Ponte, Stefano, 8, 85, 87, 88, 94–95
Portocarrero, Felipe, 195
post-racial politics, 135
postfeminism, 67, 71–72, 77–78
Poverty Reduction Strategy Papers (PRSPs), 90
Pratt, Mary Louise, 93–94
Preston, Angelea, 70
Product RED campaign
   Bono and, 89, 94–95, 127–129, 131–133, 140
   Gates on, 24
   motherhood and, 140
   role of products in, 88
   White Saviour and, 127–129, 131–133, 134
Puerto Rico, 197–198. *See also* Martin, Ricky (Enrique Martín Morales)

R

radical feminism, 67
Raiders of the Lost Ark (dir. Spielberg 1981), 127
Raising Malawi (charity), 127–128, 130–131, 134–136, 141–142
Razack, Narda, 93
Red Cross, 91. *See also* American Red Cross; Chinese Red Cross Foundation
Reebok, 92
Richards, Jeffrey, 129–130
Richey, Lisa Ann, 8, 85, 87, 88, 94–95
Ricky Martin Foundation (Fundación Ricky Martin), 13, 193, 203–204
Right to Play (non-governmental organization), 86, 89–90, 91, 93–99
The Road Home (dir. Zhang 1999), 173
Rojek, Chris, 5, 7, 107, 214
Rondot, Kahlen, 71
Rosaldo, Renato, 216
Roti Kapda aur Makaan (dir. Kumar 1974), 153
Roy, Arundhati, 153–154, 156–165
Rozario, Kevin, 30–31
Rugley, Naduah, 70

S

Sachs, Jeffrey, 25, 113, 118
Sachs, Wolfgang, 98
Sadie Nash Leadership Project, 75
Said, Edward, 136
Salvation Army, 47
Samsung, 181–182
Sanborn, Cynthia, 195
Sandoval-Sánchez, Alberto, 200–201
Sardar Sarovar dam, 156, 158–160
Scheeren, Ole, 175
Schweitzer, Albert, 47
Sengupta, Nirmal, 159
Serious Request (radio telethon), 111
Shakira (Shakira Isabel Mebarak Ripoll)
   criticism of, 200–202
   effectiveness of, 203–204

Latinidad and, 197–199, 205
North American philanthropy and, 193–197
Twitter and, 193, 216
Sharapova, Maria, 86
Sheen, Martin, 108
Shoket, Ann, 76
Sichuan earthquake (2008), 28–29, 174–178, 181–183
Simavi (Dutch NGO), 115
Simeon, Dilip, 162
Simons, Sylvana, 111, 115, 118, 120–121
Simpson, O.J., 134–135
Singh, Tavleen, 160
Slim Helú, Carlos, 202
Soccer Aid Appeal Video From Haiti (UNICEFUK 2010), 112
social control, 44
social media, 33
socialist feminism, 67
Sociedades de Beneficiencia Pública (Secular Societies of Social Benefit), 195
Spain, 195
Spice Girls (pop group), 67
The Spirit of the Red Cross (dir. Flagg 1918), 31
Spirituality For Kids (later Success for Kids) (SFK), 134–136
Spivak, Gayatri, 131, 138
sport
　BWB program and, 86, 91–92, 93–99
　cause-related marketing and, 85–86
　development and, 85–86, 88–90, 92–100
　Right to Play and, 86, 89–90, 91, 93–99
Sport for Development and Peace (SDP), 86
Sports Illustrated (magazine), 64
Sri Lanka, 164
Srivastava, Devyani, 161
Stone, Sharon, 28–29
Stowers, Saleisha, 77
Strength to Love (King), 154
Stylista (reality television series), 65

Sullivan, Shandi, 71
Sundar, Nandini, 164

T
't Hart, Paul, 22, 26, 32–33, 214
Tasker, Yvonne, 67
Telefacts Zomer: Met Luc Appermont naar Filipijnen (Vroom 2006), 113
Thornton, Billy Bob, 139
Tianya.cn (Chinese blogging forum), 175–176, 181
Time (magazine), 21, 25, 65
Tindall, Karen, 22, 26, 32–33, 214
Tipton, Analeigh, 69
Tirupathi Temple (Andhra Pradesh), 155
Transformers 4 (dir. Bay 2014), 216
True Beauty (television show), 65
Truman, Harry, 87
Turlington, Christie, 140
Turner, Graeme, 6–7, 25, 156
Twitter, 193, 216
Ty Girl Corporation, 64
typeF.com, 72
Tyra Banks Show (television show), 65, 75–76
TZONE Foundation, 63, 66, 72–78

U
ubuntu, 133–138
UN Millennium Project (Sauri, Kenya), 113–114
UN Office on SDP (UNOSDP), 90
United Nations (UN), 21, 22, 26–27, 90. *See also* Goodwill Ambassadors program
United Nations Children's Fund (UNICEF), 29, 91, 112, 113, 193
United Nations Development Programme (UNDP), 91, 114
United Nations, Educational, Scientific and Cultural Organization (UNESCO), 101n.2
United Nations High Commissioner for Refugees (UNHCR), 29, 85
United Paramount Network (UPN), 64–65

V

vagrancy, 46
Van Acker, Roos, 111, 115, 118
Victoria's Secret, 64
The Voice (TV music competition), 202
voluntarism, 195

W

Wanglaoji, 181–182
War on Drugs, 197
Watson, Tom, 195–196
WB Television Network, 65
'Wealth' (Carnegie), 23–24
Weber, Max, 48
Weibo (Chinese social network), 216
welfare state, 109
Wereldjournaal: Sylvana Simons in Tanzania (Naus and Siezenga 2005), 115, 118, 120–121
West, Darrell M., 27–28
White House Initiative on Educational Excellence for Hispanics, 193
White Saviour
  as brand of cultural authority, 127–133
  motherhood and, 138–143
  ubuntu and, 133–138
WildAid (wildlife conservation NGO), 155
Williams, Jerome, 97–98
Williams, Liz, 70
Williams, Robbie, 110–111, 112
Winfrey, Oprah, 66
Winter Olympic Games, Lillehammer (1994), 91

Y

Yao Ming, 173, 182
Young Chicago Authors, 75, 76
Young, Steve, 91

Z

Zhang Yimou, 173
Zhang Yiwu, 173
Zhang Ziyi, 33, 173–178, 180
Zidane, Zinedine, 91
Zinn, Howard, 153
Ziyi Zhang Foundation, 175–176
Žižek, Slavoj, 26
Zunz, Olivier, 49